The Hidden Jury

The Hidden Jury

And Other Secret Tactics

Lawyers Use to Win

by Paul M. Lisnek

Foreword by Johnnie Cochran

SOURCEBOOKS, INC.®
NAPERVILLE, ILLINOIS

Published by Sourcebooks, Inc.
P.O. Box 4410, Naperville, Illinois 60567-4410
(630) 961-3900
FAX: (630) 961-2168
www.sourcebooks.com

Library of Congress Cataloging-in-Publication Data

Lisnek, Paul Michael, 1958-
The hidden jury / by Paul M. Lisnek.
  p. cm.
ISBN 1-57071-948-9 (alk. paper)
1. Jury—United States. 2. Fair trial—United States. I. Title.
KF8972.Z9L57 2003
347.73'752—dc21

2003005520

Printed and bound in the United States of America
BG   10 9 8 7 6 5 4 3 2 1

For my family,
the only jury that truly matters to me.
For your support, strength, and love…

Table of Contents

Foreword
by Johnnie Cochran

In America, our Constitution guarantees that each of us, when charged with a crime, is innocent until proven guilty and entitled to a trial by a jury of our peers. The jury system is the anchor of our liberty and we should never allow ourselves to take it for granted. In my forty years of practicing law—as a prosecutor, a defense attorney, and now a practitioner of civil law—I have always had enormous respect for jurors, the men and women who take precious time away from their daily lives to fulfill their civic duty. In countless cases over the years, I have put tremendous faith in their wisdom and integrity.

In an ideal setting, jurors work diligently to carry out their responsibilities: attending the trial, listening carefully to witnesses, surveying and debating the evidence, and, finally, rendering a verdict of guilt or innocence.

While I respect our jury system wholeheartedly, the fact remains that the system works best when the jury is composed of men and women who will bring a clean and unbiased slate to the case at hand. Therefore, the most important facet of any trial is the jury selection. Having the right people occupying the jury box can be the difference between winning and losing a case.

Although, like every lawyer, I have a great deal of confidence in my ability to select jurors, I also recognize that there are times when a client is best served by the expertise of a jury or trial consultant. Such professionals perform a variety of services, such as aiding in jury selection, setting up a mock jury session, or creating a mirror jury that can provide invaluable feedback.

For the O.J. Simpson trial, we were fortunate to have leading jury consultant Jo-Ellan Dimitrius on our team. In addition to advising on jury selection, Dimitrius undertook opinion surveys, worked with focus groups in Santa Monica, and assisted with writing the lengthy questionnaire we presented to prospective jurors. I was confident after *voir dire* that we had a jury who would be up to the enormous task before them. Dimitrius worked closely with us during the duration of the Simpson trial, and her contribution was invaluable. By contrast, the prosecution team also had a top jury-consultant firm available to them, but they elected not to use its services.

In general, prosecutors have been slow to adopt the scientific, analytical principles that professional jury consultants offer. However, in the future, as we face more complex legal issues that present contradictory interpretations, jury or trial consultants will become even more commonplace. That's why Paul M. Lisnek's vital book, *The Hidden Jury*, couldn't be more timely or more urgently needed.

I first met Paul when he served as jury analyst for NBC's coverage of the Simpson trial. Later, when I hosted *Cochran and Company* on Court TV, Paul was often a guest expert and the two of us would discuss a wide range of trial-related issues in front of—and behind—the cameras. In those days, he often spoke of his desire to produce a work that would illuminate how the entire jury-selection process has evolved and would examine how important the role of jury or trial consultants has become.

Paul brings several key qualifications to this exploration. First, he is a seasoned trial lawyer who knows how lawyers think and how the courtroom really works. This experience gives him a unique insight from which to articulate his views and draw conclusions. Second, he's a trial consultant and has advised on hundreds of cases for both the defense and the prosecution. He's been at the forefront of this evolution of "the new legal team," so he's extremely qualified to explain the

ABCs of jury consulting. Paul breaks down the complex processes in a way that both professionals and laypersons will understand and appreciate. Finally, Paul is an educator and lecturer who is passionate about the law and the jury process. As a gifted teacher, Paul is also cognizant that there are many students of the law who understand the importance of examining the underpinnings and of knowing how trials develop behind the scenes in the real world, as opposed to the seductive law dramas that dot the prime-time television landscape.

In *The Hidden Jury*, Paul opens the door so that the reader sees what happens in the courtroom during each step of a trial by the jury of one's peers. What are the behind-the-scenes manipulations? Why are particular jurors chosen while others are excused? How can jurors be judged by the attire they wear to court on jury-selection day, by the novel in their backpack, or by the pin on their lapel?

Paul has woven fascinating examples from court cases for which he has consulted and offers fresh insights into such high-profile cases as those of Heidi Fleiss, the Menendez Brothers, Louise Woodward, and the Martha Moxley murder case. He also discusses the myriad cases and legal actions involving allegations of sexual abuse of minors by Catholic priests and offers interesting insights concerning the Whitewater litigation. He uses these examples to illustrate how the jury system works and, in some instances, ponders how a different verdict might have been produced.

The Hidden Jury explains why focus groups and mock trials are fast becoming key tools for trial lawyers, why community attitude surveys can occasionally turn the tide in a case, and why the venue where the trial will take place is of utmost importance. Moreover, this book details the essential work trial consultants do in preparing difficult lay witnesses and in reviewing cases following the verdict for clues as to why and how the jury reached their decision. Paul also predicts a future wherein consultants will play a larger role in mediating small-scale legal cases.

Thanks to Court TV, Americans have become much more aware of what goes on inside the courtroom. They sometimes feel like they are there, participating vicariously in the process. Yet, without a firm understanding of the jury system, one of the most important perspectives in courtroom trials remains in the shadows. Now, with Paul's book, courtroom enthusiasts and students of law can learn even more about the fascinating trial process, from the moment a case begins until a verdict is delivered. Paul takes the reader on a riveting ride, instructing as he goes along. Indeed, after reading this important book, all those interested in courtroom law will have a better understanding of why it's imperative that—despite the inevitable challenges that may occur—the American trial-by-jury system must continue to be defended. *The Hidden Jury* provides us with the tools for a better understanding of this remarkable system.

Should We *Really* Kill All the Lawyers?

Lawyers have a bad reputation. As a lawyer and a jury consultant, I live with jokes, insults, and questions. I have lost track of how many times I heard someone try to wow me with: "What do you call a hundred lawyers at the bottom of the ocean? A good start!" Or, someone might wander over to me at party and blurt, "How do you live with the fact that you represent guilty people?" Some people want to relive the O.J. trial and always start with, "But O.J. did it! Why is he free?" Even the relatively sophisticated crowd might ask, "Isn't the voodoo you do to help other lawyers pick juries unethical?"

The reality is that most people do not understand how the system works. Famous lawyers write books about the cases they have tried so they can talk about how great they are (and I am not saying they are wrong). However, you probably read those books with some hope of gaining insight about what happens behind the scenes; you might want to learn a little about how the system really works, but instead you get memoirs.

It is time to pull the curtain back on the process in order to help you understand what lawyers and trial consultants are really trying to accomplish behind the scenes and in the public courtroom. It also is time to get the age-old nagging questions about guilt and innocence, civil liability, and damages addressed and answered. That lawyers represent "guilty" people has always triggered distaste in the American experience. These questions have been around for a long time, and we see them tweaked every week on *The Practice* or Court TV.

The reality is that most people do not have their first encounter with a real lawyer (and "lawyerly" behavior) until they find themselves embroiled in an unfortunate divorce, an unexpected auto accident, or perhaps something as simple as the need to draft a will. It is no secret that lawyers are not highly rated on the scale of public trust, but oddly enough, surveys about lawyers and trust often note an important exception: people think their own lawyers are terrific. So, if you have not had a need for lawyers, then you probably do not think too highly of them. If you have worked with a lawyer, you probably like your own, but you think others are unethical. I want to dispel that myth.

It is true that lawyers can be intimidating; they speak a language all their own. In addition, it is difficult to overcome the perception that lawyers make money from other people's troubles. However, many lawyers and jury consultants make their living in whole or in part by serving the public interest and working to represent those without financial resources. In reality, most lawyers recognize the law as a *public* calling and act accordingly.

In recent decades, a group of professionals called trial consultants, jury consultants, and jury psychologists—all mean about the same thing—have added their expertise to the courtroom drama. While I am a lawyer, I am also a trial consultant. It is my job to help my trial-lawyer clients do the best possible job of representing, which means advocating for, *their* clients. We are a relatively new profession, but trying to choose jurors that reach a verdict that pleases one side or the other is as old as the jury system itself. The difference is that now we have *scientific* tools available to help guide our work with trial lawyers. This book is my attempt to explain where trial consultants fit into the big picture of criminal and civil trials, thereby providing a better overall understanding of the legal process itself.

On television dramas, you may see lawyers go head-to-head with their jury consultants, but for the most part, the jury consultant's work is hidden from public view. The invisible nature of our work is one reason this field of "jury science" arouses controversy in some quarters. However, hidden or not, you can be certain that in high-stakes or high-profile civil or criminal trials, the jury consultant's toolbox is in use and a team of individuals may be involved.

In some cases, no attempt is made to hide the work or use of a jury consultant. Some cases are so big and high-profile that it would make no sense to hide the fact that a consultant is being used. In other situations, the consultant is well enough known that it would be a waste of time to attempt to hide his or her presence. For example, Dr. Jo-Ellan Dimitrius often was in the courtroom during the O.J. Simpson trial. Because her participation was out in the open, the prosecution team tried to adopt the underdog position, a team with fewer resources and lacking in high-priced consultants. In reality, the prosecution had a very prominent trial consultant, Dr. Donald Vinson, although he mainly remained behind the scenes as he worked with the prosecution team. So, the playing field was equal in that case. (By the way, Vinson and Dimitrius ultimately joined together to form their own consulting firm.) And the media certainly focused on the work of these consultants through their own on-air experts, such as my work for NBC News.

Trial consultants work with lawyers in a variety of ways; jury selection is only one area. For example, I use my communication background to prepare witnesses to testify. Trial consultants have areas of specialization, and consulting firms are generally comprised of a team of individuals. Richard Gabriel, my partner and the cofounder of our company, Decision Analysis, specializes in communication skills, but he also leads the hard-core research team. Richard is also an author, and he spends much of his time in the trenches of the business. Dr. Sharon Gross, our director of research, digs into the data we gather. She sends the troops to the telephones to gather the data for community attitude surveys that take many long nights to complete. She searches for trends and the meaning inherent in the attitude scales filled out by mock jurors in survey after survey during a research project.

As you gain understanding of our work, you will see how each element fits into the grander scheme as we work on our cases. Our firm works on many different types of cases, both criminal and civil, the large and complex as well as the small and focused. Understand, too, that we have worked on all sides of cases. Some clients are plaintiffs in civil cases and some are defendants. Sometimes we assist the prosecution in a criminal matter and other times we work with the defense team.

Prior to forming Decision Analysis, Richard and I were part of Trial Logistics and worked with our colleague Jo-Ellan Dimitrius. Before that, I worked with other leading jury-consulting firms, including Tsongas Associates, led by Joyce Tsongas, and Trial Behavior Consulting, Inc., based in San Francisco and led (at that time) by Dr. David Island and now by Dr. David Graeven.

The issue of professionalism is very important to me and I have taught courses in this area at the law-school level and in seminars around the country. That interest led me to accept the position as an ethics commissioner in Illinois, and for many years I have served as chair of an inquiry panel on the Attorney Registration and Disciplinary Commission in Illinois. It is my responsibility to work with a panel of two others (one of whom is a lawyer and the other, by commission rule, is a layperson). Our job is to review investigations of lawyers and determine if formal charges shall be filed as a result of allegations made against them for a violation of the code of professional responsibility.

All in all, I have been blessed to work with the "best of 'em," and I share much that I have learned over the years. As an aside, I also served for many years on the board of the American Society of Trial Consultants and served two terms as the Society's president. My duties during these years kept me in touch with other "players" in what has been a rapidly growing field. While I served as president, we drafted and adopted the first CODE OF PROFESSIONAL STANDARDS (reproduced at the end of this book) for jury consultants, which remains a work in progress, in that our field continues to chart new waters.

The best way to share the secrets of the field is to get you involved in the day-to-day jury consultant's work. While I cannot always share real names and events because I am governed by agreements and codes of confidentiality, the important concept to understand is that the tools of research and analysis are consistent across cases, whether they are front-page news or not. So the cases I present may be composites or actual cases with the identities well disguised. When I mention recognizable cases, I discuss elements that are a matter of public record and add my personal observations. So, with that said, let's go behind the scenes for a realistic look at the world of jury consulting.

The first chapter describes the current state of the jury system. Chapter 2 starts with a macro view of the trial consultant's work. I take a look at the community in which a trial takes place and talk about how we study it to learn as much as we can about the environment in which we're working. In chapter 3, I discuss how lawyers test their case theory with the assistance of trial consultants in front of a mock jury in what is called a focus group. Next, I turn to juror profiles and address the issue of whether we can really identify with accuracy the person we want to sit on the jury. In chapter 5, I take you into the courtroom and look at the process of jury selection. Then, the show begins with chapter 6 as we look at the opening statements and closing arguments presented by trial lawyers. The role of witnesses, the way trial consultants prepare them to testify, and the structure and impact of direct and cross-examination are the focus of chapter 7. Next, I take you where no television show or newspaper has taken you before: we go into the jury deliberation room and understand what happens among the jurors. Finally, chapter 9 brings all of this together and asks you to revisit the questions I have raised in this chapter and throughout the book. You can then decide for yourself whether the concept of a fair and impartial jury is a reality, or, as I propose here, one of the greatest myths.

chapter 1

Fair and Impartial?
Not a Chance

"We, the jury, find the defendant *guilty* of the crime of murder in the first degree." With those words, and many less dramatic variations, juries first determine, and then publicly declare, who will walk away free and who will go to prison. While the role may seem less dramatic, every year juries hear arguments in many thousands of civil cases. They decide if a plaintiff should receive money and, if so, how much. Juries also send some plaintiffs home with nothing. The power of the jury is remarkable. Yet, even with all the media coverage of actual trials, including day-by-day and even hour-by-hour analysis, viewers are told little more than the ultimate verdict. The average citizen learns about the outcome of a case but rarely is privy to jury deliberations, the discussions and interaction that produce the verdicts, nor do most of us understand the activities and study that may go on prior to trial.

When a judge says, "Thank for you for service, ladies and gentlemen of the jury. Your work here is completed and you are free to leave the courtroom and return to your homes and families," he or she closes legal proceedings that may have drastically changed the lives of many people. Even if you have great interest in the case, you can only guess what the deliberations must have been like. Who influenced whom? Did some jurors "cave in"? How did one juror turn the opinions of all the others in what must have been a fascinating drama?

You probably remember the movie *Twelve Angry Men*, in which some well-known actors of the time portrayed jurors trying to agree on the guilt or innocence of an accused murderer. The entire movie took place in a hot, tense deliberation room. The movie begins with an initial vote among the jurors of eleven to one in favor of guilt. Only the juror played by Henry Fonda holds out because he believes that the others are too quick to make their judgment. The twelve jurors argue and then vote again, as Fonda urges the others to reconsider their opinions. One by one, he convinces the all-male, all-white jurors that reasonable doubt exists and they should not convict the defendant, who, incidentally, is never seen in the movie.

Twelve Angry Men often appears on television with continuing appeal because it showed long, agonizing debates between jurors and arguments that became personal. When these twelve men reached consensus, the viewers could see the great emotional toll taken by the deliberation process.

Many popular movies include trials integral to the plot. The power of the jury and of the courtroom is ever-present in most books, stage plays, movies, and television series that focus on the intrigue of legal cases. Rarely does a week go by on *The Practice* that we do not await at least one verdict to come in at the end of the program. But we never get to go inside the jury room. We hear the verdict rendered, but are not privy to the processes, dialogue, and arguments that produced those verdicts.

Murder trials as movie themes are always popular, but movies about civil trials have a following, too. Some, such as *Erin Brockovich* or *A Civil Action*, achieve great success probably because the lead characters attempt to outwit the mighty and powerful "Goliath" insurance company or corporation, leaving viewers to hope that the little guy ultimately prevails.

Some men and women idealistically pursue a career in medicine because they want to "make a difference," or "serve humanity." Likewise, I frequently run into law students who have been influenced by movies and legal dramas, particularly those where going up against a powerful "Goliath" and winning are common themes. The message comes to me most clearly as I travel the country lecturing to future would-be attorneys about the responsibilities of a lawyer and the challenges of law school that must be handled before they get into the profession.

One evening, a woman named Julie actually said that watching the *LA Law* reunion movie motivated her to go to law school. More than one young person has mentioned legal movies or even the prosecutors in *NYPD Blue*. They generally have focused in on criminal-law shows and become dedicated to either defending the innocents of the world as a public defender, or they have decided that "I could *never* represent a guilty person; I will be a prosecutor."

On those evenings, I have a bit of fun mocking the students who, when presented with a scenario from one of my cases, cannot see any possible defense and would not want to represent the "clearly guilty" defendant. By the end of the evening, they come to learn that trials are not about whether the defendant did the crime, but are about whether the prosecution can prove he did so beyond a reasonable doubt. Before law-school training, this is a concept that many people find difficult to accept. They want guilty people jailed and do not want the system to get in the way. Our Constitution promises us a trial by jury, and a significant part of criminal and civil trial preparation is focused on jury issues. Always remember, though, that lawyers attempt to avoid trials if they can. The practices of settling civil cases out of court and reaching plea agreements in criminal cases have greatly reduced the pressures on our justice system. But, when cases go all the way to trial, most are argued before a jury and cases are won and lost based on the strength of the evidence and how well the lawyers for each side present their case. Once a trial begins, the jury is the most important piece of the trial puzzle. This sounds simple, but of course it is not.

The Jury at Every Stage

In today's trials, jury preparation involves a combination of science and intuition. We use the latest "technology," drawing from research similar to that employed by marketing professionals, sociologists, and psychologists. Then, in order to fully use the research, we determine the best way to develop the *story* of our case. Next, we call on sophisticated communication skills as we present our case to the jury. Every day, lawyers make decisions about what information they will present and how they will present it. And finally, lawyers use all the tools at their disposal to predict what jurors will do with that information. While lawyers rely on developed courtroom skills, along with a good measure of gut instinct, today's trials are far different from the proceedings envisioned by those who drafted our Constitution and worked to guarantee the right to have a trial. Today, scientific methodology and sophisticated psychological theory play a role our forefathers could never have anticipated; and perhaps, neither could we.

Juries, Then and Now

Under our American system of justice, a "jury" simply means a group of people—referred to as our "peers"—who are selected randomly from the community. These men and women are expected to be fair and impartial in their determination of guilt or liability. Indeed, jurors must promise to maintain a mind-set in which they put aside their personal attitudes and biases. The experience of serving as a juror is different from many other situations. For example, when jurors render their decision, they are not required to offer any explanation about the reasons they used to reach a particular verdict. In other words, jurors are not held accountable for their decisions. They return to their lives and that's it. For the most part, all parties in the case must live with the verdict.

Certainly, lawyers may begin filing appeals and look for what's known as "reversible error" on the part of the judge. Ultimately, they may be successful in their efforts to gain a different outcome, but it is extremely rare for the conduct of the original jurors to be the cause, or be the source of, reversible error. Our office was involved in a case that did lead to a reversed verdict based on juror misconduct. That case was the famous Heidi Fleiss, or "Hollywood Madame" matter, in which four or five of the jurors met and discussed the case and deliberations outside the presence of the other jurors. While in most cases the court might never learn of such behavior, in the Fleiss matter, it was the work of our office that led to uncovering the serious error. I'll discuss that case in detail in a later chapter.

In the United States, the concept of a jury comprised of our peers represents a nearly magical idea, and we approach our system with an attitude that resembles reverence because it places great faith in neighbors and friends. We rely on the people within our communities to determine the resolution of a dispute when the parties involved are unable to reach a settlement on their own, or in criminal cases where a crime against one is said to be a crime against all.

On its face, the assumption that our peers can fairly evaluate and judge our cases makes sense. We generally presume that men and women living within the same community share a general set of beliefs and values. More than two hundred years ago, when our jury system first developed, our communities were small and generally rural, and the concept of shared values and beliefs required less analysis than it does today. Also, in the past our expectation of what constituted a peer was quite different. Today, our communities are diverse and large, and a community may include many millions of people. Logically, we can ask if a group of nonpartisan, unbiased jurors can be chosen randomly in our own backyard and produce a verdict that establishes what is right and just—or at least settled. Many people within the legal system, including lawyers, judges, and jury consultants, agree that most individuals bring their best intentions to their role as juror, and, in turn, those who serve on juries are afforded a measure of respect.

Our system has functioned uninterrupted for more than two centuries, and overall we believe our system works. The proof really is in the pudding, so to speak, and with the exception of the Civil War years, we have been a stable society and our system has survived the test of time. However, the system has survived because of its flexibility and adaptations to new technologies and, perhaps most important, evolving beliefs and values.

To look at the way our jury system functions today, we can view the system through the prism of actual cases, some of which you may have followed in recent years. Just the fact that you can actually follow cases closely, perhaps even viewing trials in real time on Court TV or other cable networks, represents a new development. In the United States, trials are supposed to be public, but the founders could not have predicted how the definition of "public" would expand and change over two centuries. The public's fascination with trials and legal issues could even be called a new phase in the evolution of our system. Viewers, some of whom refer to themselves as "trial junkies," now see the same warts and blemishes in our system that lawyers and judges experience.

Just as viewers can see or read about the failures of the system, the warts and blemishes of the "players" become part of public consciousness, too. For example, in a murder trial, we assume the focus will be on the accused, and if anyone's private life is probed, it will be the defendant's. This is not always the case. In a murder trial, the defendant usually is given great latitude when attempting to raise reasonable doubt, and if the defense strategy is to put the victim's unsavory private life on the table, then so be it. We can't pick up a newspaper article about the Robert Blake murder case and not read about the jaded past of his murdered wife, Bonny Lee Bakley. Blake may be the defendant, but Bakley's lifestyle grabs the lights.

Or, the parents of a murdered child may find that details about their lifestyle become part of the public trial. In one particular case, the parents of a kidnapped and murdered child found their sexual attitudes and activities widely discussed as part of the very public trial of the man accused of the crime. For several weeks, the discussions about the guilt or innocence of the defendant took a backseat to loud debates about whether the parents were fit to raise a child. Unfortunately, along with their horrible tragedy, these individuals will always be known by their "warts and blemishes." So, what a public trial meant even twenty years ago has changed.

Randomly Selected, Fair and Impartial Jurors…Myth or Reality?

The concepts of impartiality and random selection are key to understanding our democracy. Then we add in the reality that juries are not accountable for their verdicts, and we have a trio of concepts, the "big ideas" that differentiate our system from others throughout the world. These three concepts also represent the seeds from which have sprouted the increasingly important role of jury psychologists, also known as jury experts or trial consultants. By any name, jury psychologists have increasingly become the trial lawyer's secret tool or weapon. Lawyers use them to gather information, gain insight, and assist in shaping trial strategy, case theory, and ultimately the verdict. In order to understand how this trio of concepts functions in the real world of trials, we must examine their intricate workings, because in important ways they form the myths underlying our system, rather than its realities.

Fair and Impartial in the Light of Day

The concept of fair and impartial juries is a myth if there ever was one. In the purest sense, no such thing as a fair and impartial person exists. To be truly fair and impartial, the men and women sitting on every jury would need to leave all prior feelings, beliefs, knowledge, and personal leanings at the courthouse steps. However, jurors are human beings, and no one, not even the most well-intentioned individuals, can put aside existing core beliefs and attitudes. Although this has been true since the system was conceived, today we have ways to measure bias. That isn't a negative idea, although it may sound like it. Measuring bias is really nothing more than determining beliefs and values.

Virtually every juror believes he or she is capable of fulfilling the promise to be fair and impartial. No one truly intends to taint the way they process the evidence presented over the course of a trial with their own attitudes and values. Jurors sincerely believe that when they sit in the jury box, they put aside their biases and their basic outlook and simply listen to the lawyers and concentrate on the evidence. Then they sit down with their fair and impartial juror colleagues and, through supposedly frank and honest interaction, the right answer will somehow emerge. They believe that this process ensures that justice will be done. In a sense, jurors take their job seriously because they take citizenship seriously. In the end, however, jurors—and the public, too—are very naïve about what really goes on, not so much in the courtroom as outside the courtroom itself. Sometimes things are not as they seem.

If you saw the movie *The Sixth Sense*, then like most of us, you watched the entire film only to find out in the final moments that what we thought we had been watching isn't what we were actually seeing at all. We're surprised because we all want to trust what we experience.

In a courtroom, you want to trust what you see and hear as well, so you do not ordinarily think that your experiences are being guided or controlled. However, in a typical courtroom, that's exactly what is happening. The judges and lawyers meet to determine what evidence jurors will see and what is excluded. Lawyers decide on the order and manner of presentation and the jurors take it all in with trust in the process. This book is intended to provide you with a bit of the sixth sense, an opportunity to understand what goes into the decisions that lawyers make with the assistance of jury consultants.

Judges and lawyers are aware that the idea of fair and impartial jurors is an illusion. However, we do not have other language to substitute for the terms. For example, we cannot say "fair and impartial as far as it goes, taking into consideration all the factors that taint and bias your reality and view of the world." Built into our system, however, is recognition that common sense cannot be entirely put aside. As part of the jury instructions prior to deliberation, nearly every judge instructs the jurors *not* to leave common sense at the door. In reality, judges and lawyers expect jurors to bring their intelligence and everyday wisdom to the jury box as they form impressions of the evidence and events presented. However, common sense is a function of conditioning and influence. What is common sense in Saudi Arabia may not coincide with everyday assumptions or wisdom in a U.S. courtroom. So, even the concept of common sense is not one-dimensional or unchanging.

Common Sense and Candy Bars

Let's say your local convenience store—we'll call it a 7-Eleven—is robbed of $247 in cash, and on the way out, the thief grabbed a case of Milky Way candy bars. An hour later, police arrested the defendant two blocks down the street from the 7-Eleven. Our accused thief just happened to have $247 and just happened to be munching a Milky Way, with a full box of these candy bars in a bag. Wouldn't common sense lead a juror to conclude that the culprit was caught? Life experience says, "Sure, who else could have done it?"

But, after the prosecution has laid out the evidence—a by-now stale box of candy bars and the cash—the defense lawyer argues that her client was just a victim of circumstance. The defendant actually had $259 when the day started, but after buying a case of candy bars at Wal-Mart, by unlucky coincidence our defendant had exactly $247 left. Too bad no receipt is available, but does a reasonable person keep receipts for candy bars? Do you believe the defendant? It sounds like a bit of a stretch, but let's say a Wal-Mart employee testifies that the defendant is always in the store and often buys candy bars by the case. True, the employee cannot recall if the defendant was in the store on the day in question, but he has seen this individual many times before. Any doubts yet? What if the defendant's fingerprints are nowhere to be found in the 7-Eleven and the clerk can't make a positive identification?

Chances are, you have developed some doubts. Are they reasonable? Are your doubts sufficient to determine that the defendant is not guilty? When the judge instructs you as a juror in a criminal case that the burden of proof is solely on the prosecution to prove beyond a reasonable doubt that the defendant committed the crime, can you now vote with certainty that the burden has been met?

We could chew over every fact in the case and spend hours in the deliberation room, but the question is: on what information are you making your evaluation? If I presented this evidence to a group of randomly selected adults and then took a vote, I know from experience that some would convict our defendant with a sweet tooth and others would argue to their death that we have a case of mistaken identity. How you voted on our scenario isn't important; I do not know if the person is guilty either. But following along with the message of this book, what is relevant is your recognition that the process you used to evaluate bits of evidence most definitely relied on your life experience. The influence of your religious values, your attitudes about race, your impression of law enforcement, and even your opinion of discount stores may come into play. It is likely that you believe it is wrong to steal under nearly all circumstances, so a defendant on trial for theft may be in for a tough ride with you—and most people.

Who is this defendant anyway? And does the defendant's description matter to you in this fair and impartial world of jury service? I haven't mentioned much about our accused defendant, but does it make a difference if I tell you that the accused is black or white? Male or female? A teenager or a person in his forties? Chances are you create a picture in your mind about how a guilty defendant would look. What do people who are accused of stealing or robbing others look like in your mind? Your answers arise from the biases, predispositions, attitudes, and values developed over a lifetime. You form mental pictures based on what you expect or anticipate. I am confident that you filled in details as I laid out the story, and you probably formed an image of a person based on your experiences with or impressions of criminals.

You will notice that in the details of the case, I did not relate any descriptive specifics of the defendant. But let's say that the defendant in the candy case is an African-American teenager from the housing projects. With this information, how would you expect a jury member to react? If the juror was liberal, urban, and open minded, then would such a description offend him? ("How *dare* you contribute to a stereotype!") If the juror was a conservative, religious, middle-aged Caucasian, then might we expect that he is less offended by this description? And if she was an African-American, middle-aged female, would we expect the juror to think the system was persecuting this young man because of his race and age? Or, would we expect her to hold the defendant to a high level of proper conduct because, regardless of race, if this young man committed the crime, then he better do some time? Or, is race and age irrelevant for the person in this entire discussion?

These are the kinds of questions lawyers and, more specifically, jury consultants face in every case they handle. No magic answers exist, but there are trends and expectations. There are clients who look guilty (and may or may not be guilty) and there are clients who appear as innocent as the day is long but committed the acts for which they are accused. I worked with the U.S. Attorney in a case of financial fraud in which the "star" witness was the most clean-cut, blond-haired, blue-eyed, "John-Boy Walton" type you would ever expect to see. Yet, he had reached a plea agreement with the government because he was involved in the scheme and agreed to help out the prosecutors. He made a great impression and helped the jury understand that not all criminals look like criminals. His testimony was crucial to obtaining a conviction of the target defendant. Of course, I also recall that at the end of the case, before our John-Boy Walton went off to serve his own prison term, he turned to the prosecutor and said, "Hey, when I get out, maybe we can do a business deal together." Once a con man...

In another case a few years back, I had the opportunity to actually sit as a juror in a criminal case. The defendant was an African-American male in his late twenties, and he had been charged with possessing drugs with intent to sell and distribute. The evidence consisted of the many cell phones and pagers he owned and the testimony of arresting officers. During the opening statement, the defense lawyer alleged that according to its own objective eyewitness, a tall, slender police sergeant was on the scene and that the whole thing was a setup. The defense argued that this was an arrest made on the basis of race only. When the prosecution called to the stand the sergeant who was on the scene, a man resembling Danny DeVito took the stand. He was able to supply testimony that the eyewitness and the defendant were actually best friends, and that the eyewitness was nowhere near the scene on the evening in question.

In deliberation, the jurors looked to me because I am a lawyer and a jury psychologist. The judge and the lawyers had recognized me, and they allowed me to remain on the jury, which was quite surprising to me, to say the least. As I sat and listened, I learned that the jurors hardest on the defendant were the middle-aged and older African-American women who were angry that this young man had lied. They were offended that the white defense lawyer had played the race card. Their comments can be summarized as follows: "We don't believe him for one second! This fellow had all these cell phones and pagers, he was acting like a dealer and had no alibi except for one best friend whose testimony disintegrated before our eyes. The man's guilty."

I was the juror the lawyers (who talked with the jurors after the verdict) expected to lead the charge toward guilt. They thought that all my law training and middle-class lifestyle would lead me to give more weight to the possibility of guilt. They were wrong. I was prepared to go either way and didn't have terribly strong convictions until I heard from my fellow jurors. They had no doubt, reasonable or otherwise.

Jury consultants do not, indeed *cannot,* expect jurors to ignore what their experiences in life have taught them. After all, aren't life's experiences the best teachers of what should and should not be? Well, not necessarily, but most of us think it's so and that is all that matters. People tend to embrace their experience as a reflection of what is true, right, and defendable. They internalize their impressions of people, events, and even places as reality. These built-in biases form the heart of the jury-selection process and explain why jury experts use research tools in order to anticipate what they will find in the courtroom and what jurors will do. More often than not, the strong and defining life experiences of the jurors shape what they believe the proper outcome of a case should be.

Atmosphere, Illusion, Reality

If you believe stridently that the candy-bar defendant committed the crime, then you aren't likely to change your mind. Upstanding citizen or not, the middle-aged schoolteacher is guilty, according to you. When the trial is over, your friends and colleagues in the community may agree or disagree, and those who think your verdict was wrong may let you know how they feel. They followed the daily newspaper coverage or watched television talk/news shows and heard legal analysts debate the teacher's fate. But you end up defending your verdict. "You weren't at the trial," you say. "You didn't hear everything *we* heard. You didn't see the evidence and you didn't feel the atmosphere in the courtroom. What *you* read in the paper is biased, but what *we* experienced as jurors was the *real* story!" Another myth exposed.

I recall that in one case, the evidence of injury to the plaintiff seemed clear. A woman slipped and fell in the public bathroom inside a shopping center. She could point to a small patch of what appeared to be lipstick on the tile floor on which she slipped, severely spraining her ankle. The case might have been simple, but the woman was pregnant and lost the child after the fall. The case seemed fairly clear and there was evidence to support the plaintiff's claim. But the defendant had testimony of a doctor who reviewed the medical records and concluded that she would have lost the baby anyway; the loss was not, in his opinion, the result of the fall.

You might have expected the jury to negotiate its way on the amount of damages, but instead, the jury found in favor of the defendant and awarded nothing to the plaintiff. If you weren't in the courtroom, you didn't see the powerful defense testimony and, in addition, you didn't experience the relatively poor appearance made by the plaintiff. She became confused under cross-examination. Certainty became uncertainty. "Are you certain you stepped where this small mark of something is on the floor?" She responded, "I think so." That's all it takes for jurors to question the credibility of a witness. Coupled with conflicting medical testimony, including the fact that she had previously lost another baby, the jurors were led to a defense verdict. As you can see, the newspapers can report facts, but only the jurors experience the evidence.

The lawyers' job is to re-create reality in the trial. Specifically, they re-create the events of the past that led to an arrest and a trial. This sounds good, but jury consultants understand that nothing will actually be re-created in the courtroom. Rather, reality will be newly created. Past events will be presented the way lawyers choose to present them, all the while hoping the jury will interpret this reality in a way that conforms to their desired outcome. Reality includes not only the facts to be presented, but also the way in which the information is presented. The demeanor of witnesses and the parties can often be critical to the jury's evaluation.

A lawyer's skills can often influence the outcome of a case, including whether the matter will settle or see its day in court. In June 1999, following the pursuit of an automobile, Chicago police officers shot and killed an unarmed civilian sitting in the backseat of an automobile. The victim, LaTanya Haggerty, a young African-American female, had only her cell phone on her person when she was shot to death. Enter Johnnie Cochran. As trial neared, the case settled for $18 million. Most of us can't fathom any amount of money as acceptable compensation for the loss of a young and promising child. From that perspective, no settlement could be large enough to replace LaTanya Haggerty. But as settlements for this type of tragedy go, this was a huge amount for the plaintiffs, the surviving family members of Ms. Haggerty. These dollars are paid not by an insurance company or a large fund for these types of things, but come from taxpayers' dollars.

Clearly, individuals with the authority and responsibility for making the settlement decisions for the city likely considered what would happen when a jury heard the persuasive Johnnie Cochran argue the case. All things considered, $18 million started to seem quite reasonable in the case, at least when balanced with what may have been a much higher verdict if Cochran was able to enrage a victim-oriented jury. Settlement considerations would surely include consideration of the potential of aggravating race relations in the city, as well as tensions between citizens and the police.

Never mind that as a limitation, Illinois law would have structured the consideration of damages to consider primarily the projected lifetime income of the victim. This means that a verdict in the region of $18 million could most certainly have been reduced by the trial judge in the exercise of a power called "remittitur"; or, eventually an appellate court could have reversed the verdict and even required a retrial of the matter. I do not know if the city conducted extensive research in the case, but it seemed to me that settling the case instead of trying it indicates that the decision makers ignored the likelihood that jurors, for the most part, will do the right thing; that is, reach a verdict that is in accord with the evidence. The city attorneys did not trust a jury to hold on to their sense of reason and keep their feet on the ground, especially with the likelihood of Johnnie Cochran getting the jurors enraged over police conduct. Since the details recounted by witnesses in a trial are more a new telling of past events than they are an accurate recounting, effective lawyers can present their case with so much power and emotion that a jury becomes enraged and has no duty to account for or otherwise explain their verdict.

Where do witnesses fit in? Of course, witnesses are critical in a trial. The Wal-Mart employee and the 7-Eleven clerk will testify based on what they remember. However, as you know, each side's witnesses are expected to be "friendly" to the side for which they are testifying. This is why our system balances this advantage with cross-examination. Each side's lawyer attempts to uncover biases.

Our system is called "adversarial" because by oath, by law, and by custom, lawyers are advocates for their client's position in an adversarial system. This means that by definition, each side will be pitted against a lawyer who will argue just as vehemently for the other party's point of view and case. Through it all, lawyers are duty bound to do their job, which is to be their client's advocate. An advocate's role is to persuade the "trier of fact," the jury, that their reality is the true reality while the other side's version is distorted. What this means is that lawyers have to be concerned not only with the strengths of their case, but with the blemishes or weaknesses as well.

A witness who makes a poor appearance can kill a case. I recall a case in which the plaintiff, with whom I was working, was the president of a corporation in a case of sophisticated financial issues. He was a laissez-faire CEO who preferred being off on safari, letting his ponytail grow longer and longer, than being in the office running the business. He was not open to suggestions to modify his appearance so he would look like the CEO that jurors would expect him to be. He lost the case and I am confident his casual attitude toward his image contributed to the jury's decision.

Pre-trial work, presentation preparation, witness preparation, and the exact words we choose are all part of a carefully orchestrated attempt to shape and guide perceptions of the jurors and, ultimately, their interpretations of the evidence. Lawyers always know that jurors will process the information based on their preexisting attitudes and values, which are shaped by their life experiences. When it comes down to the realities of a trial, the concept of fairness and impartiality are relative indeed. The better the lawyers understand their jurors' attitudes, biases, and values, along with the life experiences the jurors bring to the specific trial, the more accurately they can shape the evidence and their arguments in a way that is favorably received by these triers of fact.

On one level, it may be hard to give lawyers too much credit for the ways they influence a jury because lawyer presentations and arguments do not constitute evidence. Every trial judge who instructs a jury tells the panel that they are to base their verdict only on the evidence presented during the trial. What the lawyers argue and say, the jurors are told, is not evidence, but is argument and should be regarded as such. Many of my lawyer colleagues will want to bite my head off for a statement like that because we are convinced that lawyers do have a major impact on the deliberation. The reality is, however, that poor presentations can lose a case, but strong presentations likely just help jurors to solidify the leaning that their underlying values and attitudes dictated to them in the first place.

For example, our newspapers have been filled with allegations of sexual abuse of minor boys and girls by Catholic priests in various dioceses. I have worked in these cases, and, while I have seen some very fine lawyering in the courtroom, the reality is that lawyers cannot overcome the preexisting religious values held by jurors and the existing filters in their heads through which every bit of testimony must flow. The abuse is typically alleged to have occurred over a period of many years, and the reports of the abuse by the victims appear to have been repressed for a decade or more. However, as various media force these issues to the top of the media agenda, more and more cases come to light, or are at least brought to public attention. In fact, while the topic of priest abuse is currently the focus of media banter, such cases have been around and litigated for many years.

I can summarize my experience in this area by noting that the Catholic Church, with all its power and influence over the values and belief systems of its members, appears powerless to present a defense and arguments that do little more than fall on deaf ears. This is especially true in areas of the country where the residents, and therefore the jurors, are serious about their religion and religious values. The national viewpoint on this issue may best be summarized in the words of a juror in one such case when, at the end of the trial, she approached the defense attorney in order to give him a big hug. "You were the best lawyer in this case!" she said. "We trusted you and we know you were sincere and honest…but you didn't have a chance." This is not much comfort when the verdict awarded very significant damages to the plaintiffs. It may be nice to hear a compliment from a juror, but the talent of the lawyer is no guarantee of success.

What is fascinating is the extent to which the public is convinced that the Church, as an entity, has engaged in a cover-up. The evidence is clear that when allegations of sexual abuse arose, the powers that be routinely reacted by transferring the priest to another parish. It is unclear whether the transfer was intended to remove the priest from temptation's way, based on a belief, sincere or otherwise, that such behavior wouldn't happen again. Perhaps they thought that the behavior was specific to a particular young boy or girl, and getting the priest "out of town" would end the behavior and also serve to quiet the building storm. Somehow, the Church's position shows a lack of awareness about the risk factors that could lead to new victims in new locations.

I have talked with many priests around the country about this issue, not necessarily tied to litigation, but certainly as part of self-education. I have concluded that the higher the priest is within the Church hierarchy, the more naïve he appears to be. On several occasions, I was startled when bishops and senior priests claimed that prior to accusations about a certain priest, they had no idea that any warning signs were present. It is as if they had blinders on about the day-to-day operations at the parish level. These individuals certainly have regrets, but at the same time, they continue to say that they just had no idea that anything was amiss.

Conversely, it has been interesting to speak with priests with whom some of the accused sex abusers lived and worked. In many cases, they harbor anger. Often, there are real personality conflicts between priests who live together, just as there can be with any housemates; familiarity can certainly breed contempt. So when one priest complains about another priest in the rectory, he may be told, in so many words, to fix the personality problems. This happens even amidst allegations of seemingly inappropriate behavior, which may not have risen to the level of sexual conduct (such as young people hanging around the rectory in the evening). In other words, potential serious conduct may have been put aside in "favor" of a more palatable explanation. Everyone can accept that conflicts naturally arise between priests who must live together day after day, year after year. A cover-up resulted, but that occurred in addition to the ordinary personality interplay that provided a veil with which to cover the real underlying behavioral problems going on. Church members, however, do not like to think about or recognize the negative side to a priest being a human being.

In one instance, a man who claimed to be abused by priests told me it all began when a group of young teens attended a weekend retreat. It was common, he told me, for priests to put their hands on a child's behind seemingly to lift them over a wall during games, or to encourage the teens to swim in the nude so they would be "free of restriction". For some, this behavior can be perceived as innocent, for others it was the beginning of the abuse of power and influence. You can see how important it is for the lawyers on both sides of the case to understand the attitudes, values, and experiences of jurors who will hear the case. Some people could never accept a pat on the behind as a sexual move, while others see it as abuse. Nothing a lawyer says in trial is going to change preexisting attitudes, but the lawyers need to understand the players, who make up the jury from the community, are in the game.

Jury Service Lotto

Jurors are said to be randomly selected, and in a certain sense that is true. You live in a particular locale, your name goes into a big anonymous "bowl," and you may or may not win in the game of chance called "jury duty." When you get your notice for jury duty in the mail, you confront a mystery, one that even the "Amazing Kreskin" cannot predict. When you show up in court, mathematical percentages determine what courtroom you are called into or whether you get called at all. Of course, this game of random selection has a rule: you must play to win. In this case, "play" means that our court system cannot reach you unless you are registered to vote, licensed to drive, registered for the draft, or are listed in some other public-registration mechanism. Being listed as part of a public record is what permits the hand of the legal system to reach out and pull you in. You may be required to serve for a day, a week, or even several weeks or months if the trial takes that long.

The concept of random selection refers to the way people are initially contacted. Once you are called into a specific courtroom for a particular trial, you are now part of what is called the "venire." Randomness ceases to exist, and lawyers spend considerable time avoiding anything close to random selection. They absolutely want to understand who is sitting in the box. The real work begins when they attempt to determine your attitudes and values, as evidenced through life experience and answers to the questions asked at the time of jury selection. So, in essence, lawyers want a jury of peers, but want to select those peers based on a set of criteria favorable to their client.

Going Home – Or Maybe a Pit-Stop on *Good Morning America*

No accountability then or ever—another of our key elements. In the "old days," jurors truly did render their verdict and go home. This is still the case for day-in, day-out trials, but in some situations, like a case that stirs up media frenzy, these men and women might sign book deals, tour the talk-show circuit, and give newspaper interviews. The power of the media has allowed trials into our homes, and that means that the public knows more and is therefore more curious about what was going on inside the heads of jurors.

In 1998, a Chicago teenager (legally a juvenile) was accused of shooting and killing a police officer, Michael Ceriale, during a middle-of-the-night drug operation. The jury hung at eleven to one in favor of conviction. A color photo of the lone holdout juror appeared on the front page of one of Chicago's daily newspapers. In the photo, he is standing on his front porch talking to reporters and attempting to justify his vote. Judges have the power to protect jurors from what has been called the "media circus." Clearly, though, the trend in our society seems pointed toward seeking the accountability that isn't actually required of jurors. Just as evident are the jurors, particularly in the so-called high-profile cases, who attempt to eke out, or perhaps get dragged out for, their proverbial "fifteen minutes of fame."

The real intrigue of uncovering the reasons for a particular verdict goes on behind the scenes. Trial lawyers and jury psychologists conduct post-trial interviews in order to gain insight into what happened at trial. The losing party may use the interview as a means of investigating the strength of a post-trial motion for relief from the court, such as a request that the judge reverse the jury's verdict. But mostly, it is about getting some feedback for future cases.

For example, in a product-liability case where my client, the plaintiff's lawyer, lost, he wanted some insight. At first, he called a juror and reported to me that the juror was a bit evasive, suggesting, "You didn't do anything wrong, or anything like that, it was just that we didn't think your client deserved any money." He asked me to follow up. I called and indicated to the juror that we were interested in her thoughts if she was willing to talk to me. As is my practice, I did not initially indicate which side I was calling for so as not to taint the feedback. "Well, that plaintiff lawyer was really arrogant. I mean, we didn't think the evidence was strong, but we really got a sense that his client was just lying because he acted so 'above us all.'" This is very telling information, and you can see how useful it is for the interview to be conducted by a seemingly neutral third party.

A post-trial interview may also help shape a post-trial motion or an appeal. In one case, we learned from speaking with jurors that they had seen and discussed some news coverage of the trial during deliberation, even though the judge had ordered them to avoid any media coverage. Those interviews became the basis for a motion for a retrial, which the judge granted. In addition, feedback from jurors helps lawyers prepare for future cases that involve the same or similar issues or parties. Most lawyers want to improve their effectiveness in the courtroom, and who better than jurors to help them accomplish that goal? Throughout this book, you will read about situations in which lawyers had much to learn from jurors.

Something Smells Fishy Here

As you read the theory and the stories here, I anticipate that you will have lingering questions running through your head: "Is this ethical? Can they really do this kind of research and strategizing in the legal process and an actual trial? Isn't it wrong to study communities and craft arguments so they potentially manipulate verdicts, and actually test them with mock jurors before the real trial?"

The work that jury consultants undertake is completely ethical as long as it is conducted in an appropriate way. For example, witnesses are generally prepared before they testify, which sometimes bothers non-lawyers because it seems like manipulation. A lawyer can never ask a witness to lie, so we will assume that the witness intends to testify truthfully. Yes, we prepare these individuals, and in doing so, we help them to face a stressful experience. Witnesses face the cross-examination skills of a presumably talented lawyer who, through the art of questioning, may lead the witness to say things and take positions that are not really true. That's probably a witness's biggest fear. Given the adversarial advocacy nature of our system, a lawyer who did not prepare witnesses would be considered remiss and could be accused of not zealously representing the client.

Our system works in such a way that lawyers are obligated to use all the tools at their disposal. No human being can approach a trial in a completely impartial way, unaffected by emotion or bias or life experiences, so it is part of the lawyer's job to uncover those biases and craft a case theme that best relates to the chosen jurors. Just as jurors will always rely on their common sense in combination with underlying values and attitudes, effective lawyers will learn how to avoid offending jurors' sensibilities. Therefore, I believe that failing to learn about the community in which a trial is going to take place, or to consider the types of themes and analogies that will assist jurors to understand and better comprehend a party's position in a lawsuit, may constitute malpractice. You would not hire a lawyer who said, "Hey, I have tried these kinds of cases in New York and Los Angeles, so fear not, the jurors here in Corinth, Mississippi, will love me too." That's a nightmare waiting to happen.

Of course, our best lessons come from life experiences, and I learned this point early in my practice. I was the lawyer in a commercial case where the trial was to be held in a rural community a couple of hours outside of Chicago. I gained my experience in the city and I showed up in court wearing a three-piece suit and a nice ring on my finger. Not having much experience as a lawyer at the time, I was nevertheless tuned in enough to recognize that everyone else in the courtroom was dressed in jeans and overalls. My opposing counsel wore a tattered sport coat, and here I was in a "sharp" suit. I was not going to fit in well. Before the trial began, I hurried into the restroom and removed my vest and slipped my ring into my jacket pocket. It was the best I could do to change my initial appearance and the image that this city boy was about to present to the rural jury. My client appeared wearing a salmon-colored leisure suit. I had failed to discuss dress and appearance with him ahead of time. I urged him to remove his tie, and trusted that his out-of-style outfit would actually play better than my suit. We lost that case. I even recall during the jury selection that there was camaraderie between many people in the courtroom. I asked one of the jurors whether he was familiar with the other lawyer in the case, and the judge responded, "Trust me, counsel, everyone here knows everyone except *you*, so just go on…." I never had a chance because, early in my career, I did not recognize the importance of studying and understanding the community in which I was about to try a case.

What's New? What's the Same?

Some observers and critics of the legal system decry the advances in jury science, and will claim that finding truly unbiased and impartial jurors is no longer possible because of the way we attempt to screen jurors and select or *de*-select individuals for a jury panel. Unfortunately, galloping advances in jury research has led to the proposition that the random nature of jury selection can no longer be preserved. Those who doubt the continued efficacy of the jury system claim that the average citizen is not well informed and is likely to be incapable of sifting through complex information. Other arguments are posed as well, but most come down to the notion that at one time a jury could be considered fair and impartial, but modern life has made this impossible. In fact, our understanding of people has taught us that there never has been such thing as an impartial juror.

It sounds strange, but these issues are debated in the same legal circles that are well aware that no lawyer wants a fair or impartial jury. Lawyers have always wanted a jury with people likely to see issues their way. Why would anyone think it could be any other way?

We often hear that in the past, good trial lawyers relied on gut instinct to choose a jury. Yet those who look to the decades prior to 1960 as an idealized past apparently forget that many biases were built into the system. For example, for most of our country's history, jurors were chosen from a pool of white men. End of story. Given that circumstance, one could reasonably say that those jury pools of the past were overflowing with bias. Today's critics say that jury research, or the study of the psychology of juries, is actually a means of rigging a jury. However, what could be more rigged than strictly limiting the categories of individuals who can even be considered for jury service? And what could be less fair to a client than failing to make every reasonable effort to uncover the most effective way to present his or her case to the jurors who will ultimately decide whether that client wins or loses the case?

Jury Research: The Science Is Born

The formal profession of studying juries has certainly been around for decades, dating back to the 1960s. In its practical form, jury consulting emerged in the early 1970s. In their book *Stack and Sway,* authors Neil and Dorit Kressel describe a well-known case that brought legal and social-science professionals together. Perhaps you are old enough to remember a conspiracy trial in which one of the defendants was Father Philip Berrigan. The case took place in 1972 and involved a range of activities, including breaking into draft-board offices and allegations of conspiring to harm public officials. These activities were carried out or planned as part of an ongoing agenda to protest U.S. involvement in the war in Vietnam. Father Berrigan was the most well known among a group of defendants who became known as the Harrisburg Seven.

Our society was undergoing rapid social change during the 1960s and 1970s. The Civil Rights movement had been increasingly successful and racial equality was a goal within reach; meanwhile, the women's movement was making progress toward legal and social equality. Perhaps most important, the polarizing influence of the Vietnam conflict brought out the vast diversity of opinions and values in our society, and people were constantly challenged by the First Amendment right to express views contrary to government policy.

Just as the defense team on the Berrigan case had feared, the government chose to try the case in the conservative community of Harrisburg, Pennsylvania. The defense team believed this was an attempt to "stack" the jury with individuals holding traditional and conservative values who, therefore, would be easily "swayed" by the prosecution's case. By using a group of non-lawyer social scientists, the defense conducted surveys and polling to determine the extent to which the community did not like their position. Using what are essentially market-research and public-opinion tools, the defense was able to come up with profiles of jurors that would be favorable to their side—something considered quite a feat at the time, especially in such a conservative community.

The community attitude survey used to understand the community and identify favorable jurors uncovered the hierarchy of values within the conservative community. The survey asked the respondents for their reactions to and attitudes about the Vietnam War, other situations that involved public protest, and situations in which citizens' rights to express opinions publicly outweighs the political pressures to enforce a law.

The defense team's efforts were successful, and Father Berrigan and his codefendants were convicted of only one minor charge. The jury hung on all the major federal conspiracy charges that could have resulted in long prison sentences. Post-trial interviews confirmed that the surveys had paid off; the pre-trial work had successfully identified the type of juror more likely to lean toward acquittal. Based on the trial result, it became clear that the jurors the defense chose likely understood the fundamental protections of our federal Constitution, which respects a person's right to have and express their strong beliefs and convictions. These jurors respected activities that involved exercising Constitutional protections, even placing them above the "law and order" mentality that the (and most) jurors typically had under ordinary circumstances. The individual jurors would have assigned a high degree of moral authority to priests and others with a religious vocation. Rather than using a one-size-fits-all application of the law, which is what a prosecutor wants, these men and women subordinated the anticipated "follow the law" conservatism with a "protect our fundamental rights" point of view. They were the same conservative people, but with different prevailing values and attitudes necessary for the defense to uncover in the Berrigan case.

In the early years, jury-selection consultants, as they were called, typically came from the academic world, and their cases had social/political overtones. This makes sense because as more people in our society are given a voice and a chance to participate in the legal system, it stands to reason that lawyers would want more information about the increasingly diverse populations from which they would select jurors. It logically follows that the legal system will not stay stagnate in the midst of a great change.

For example, the events of September 11, 2001 ushered in a new period in which attitudes and values may need to be questioned, reevaluated, and ultimately challenged. However, the essential principles of the legal system are always challenged when we face a crisis, and this one event initiated another debate about privacy versus security and civil liberties versus holding potential terrorist conspirators without filing a formal charge against them. Attitudes about patriotism, race relations, and racial profiling produced an impact that required new study and evaluation.

Jury psychology may have started with the idea of identifying favorable jurors, but it has evolved into a profession that works in every phase of trial. Put another way, my role, and the role of any trial consultant today in preparing witnesses or developing a case theme, is every bit as important to a successful outcome as our surveys and juror profiles.

Is It All Smoke and Mirrors?

As you can see, we have a legal system that claims to be fair and impartial, yet we know it is not. But that doesn't mean we should tear it down and begin again. Although the realities do not conform to the myths, I believe it is better to expose the myths, while we accept that our system chooses jurors whose ability to be fair and impartial is inevitably, indeed naturally, tainted by life experiences. It was always so and shall ever be so. What has changed over the years is our improved and refined ways of understanding, identifying, and choosing jurors and our decisions regarding the way we can, and should, present our cases.

In addition, media have the power to transport jurors from relative obscurity to sources of commentary and even education. If this is the way it is, then it is in everyone's best interests if we understand the playing field of today's courtrooms. Jury consultants and jury (or courtroom) psychologists are firmly in place, here to stay. In addition, you will understand cases, trials, and outcomes far better if you have a look inside the role we play before, during, and even after a trial.

chapter 2

My World and Welcome to It

Many lawyers approach trial preparation knowing that they need a trial or jury consultant, but they don't necessarily know what services will best serve them. Trial-consulting firms generally offer a menu of services and attempt to match the types of projects they can do with the most important needs of their clients. Clients dictate the scope of the projects because, without question, today's trials can be costly events, even without the added costs of trial experts. Lawyers use trial consultants to help them gain a competitive edge, so if their clients can afford them, they are hired.

A number of jury consultants (like lawyers) take on many cases *pro bono publico*, meaning that they offer their services free because the accused defendant is unable to afford basic legal services, let alone a jury psychologist. In addition, jury consultants may take a case because the matter or cause is deemed important for the good of the public and its interests. For example, I worked with a plaintiff in a civil-rights case against a federal agency. The plaintiff was a black man who charged the agency with what he alleged were racially based employment termination decisions. I worked for him because he had no resources in a case that appeared to have a strong foundation and because he was up against an entity, the government, that had comparatively unlimited resources. He was representing himself, and I advised him on case strategy and crafting arguments. It was a tough road, but there are times those of us who work in the system see the need to be sure the underrepresented have needed resources to use in their trials. It is part of a long-standing tradition within the law to "give back" for what is, in a sense, a greater good. For the most part, however, our clients must be highly motivated, because under certain circumstances our suggestions and resulting projects, whether performed free or for money, can add up to well over $100,000 in fees and expenses.

As a profession, trial consulting is criticized, even attacked to a degree, with critics usually claiming that our services encourage clients to pursue cases that may be deemed to lack merit. These are the so-called "frivolous" cases people like to discuss, because with the assistance of a jury consultant, an otherwise losing case becomes a winnable one. This particular criticism misses one of the most important features of this work. Working with a consultant may actually *prevent* a case from going to trial. By using one or more of our tools, we end up assisting our lawyer clients to understand that they would be better off settling their case out of court. So, in many situations, jury consultants help lawyers to "unclog" our courts and facilitate case settlement, rather than adding to the proverbial long delays in resolving legal matters. In fact, in many cases it is the very research conducted by jury consultants that leads the lawyers to reach a settlement of the case. In one matter, a plaintiff saw that the evidence for his allegations of medical malpractice was not strong enough to convince mock jurors, and he ultimately dropped his case rather than to continue to accrue additional expense.

What Do *You* Think?: A Primary Tool

The community attitude survey is one of the most basic jury-consulting tools, but by no means does every case require a study of the prevailing attitudes in the community about a specific issue or concern. Still, considering the early history of jury consulting, (for example, the Harrisburg Seven case, referred to in the previous chapter), one could say that the jury-consulting field was built on the foundation of the community attitude survey.

Not every client we work with needs such a survey because some lawyers have significant experience in their communities. When they must make financial trade-offs, they may forgo the expense and time involved because they have a strong sense of the prevailing attitudes and values in the community in which the trial takes place. In addition, lawyers may not need a survey if the issues raised in the case are typical—mainstream—and therefore not expected to trigger any unusual reaction.

Likewise, where the potential damages in a civil case are not likely to be significant, it is unlikely for a community attitude survey to be conducted. In essence, a community attitude survey is an expensive project that is not economically feasible in small-budget cases. Unless an important legal or social principle is involved, you would not spend $25,000 to learn what your chances are of either collecting or paying $5,000. In addition, for the common accident cases and smaller medical malpractice cases, lawyers often look at verdict reports to get a good idea of how juries in a community have responded to similar cases. Typically, unless the case has reached the nightly news reports, it is rare to use such a survey in common, low-verdict situations.

Of course, typical doesn't mean universal. Exceptions to this rule exist. I was called into a criminal case where the defendant was charged with driving while intoxicated. Since it was a first offense, it probably could have been handled with a plea. But the defendant was a socialite in this small town. Everyone knew her and she did not want the incident or a conviction to become part of her public persona, as that would surely destroy her image. She was willing to spend whatever it took to avoid a conviction. If she was going to face a trial, then she had to win; there was no alternative.

For most individuals, a survey would be cost prohibitive, but the socialite wanted one conducted because it was important to measure her image in the community and, therefore, how its citizens would react to the charges against her. She also ran a series of focus groups (with jurors from surrounding communities who did not know her). This woman spent freely only to learn that most jurors were convinced she was guilty. For her, the research revealed that the road ahead was a difficult one; however, she had enough money to investigate the plausibility of various options. Additional research proved the point that trial consultants can uncover prevailing attitudes and values, but we cannot change them. The research showed that her status in society worked against her because the individuals who would be sitting on the jury of her peers believed that people like her would at least try to buy their way out of a legal problem. In a way, our client served as living proof of the research.

Ultimately, this woman was convicted, but the reason involved her unwillingness to deal with the reality that her behavior on the videotape taken by the police at the time of the arrest made her condition clear. She could have adopted a strategy that would have made her appear more like "common folk," but she seemed unwilling or unable to even try. She was not the most pleasant person to work with when the results did not go her way, which as you can see, was the story of her case. During one conference, I ended up resorting to an old line, "Hey, don't shoot the messenger. We don't create the attitudes, we just measure them." She probably still believes that we just did not find the right angle, one that would end up getting her off.

The world of celebrity cases provide numerous examples of people who will spend significant money in a case where the financial damage might be low, but the preservation of reputation is critical. Consider when Carol Burnett sued the *National Enquirer* for falsely reporting in March 1976 that Burnett was boisterous and loud in a Washington restaurant, argued with Henry Kissinger, knocked a glass of wine onto a diner, and giggled rather than apologized for it. She won $2 million. In many of those cases, the monies are donated to charity, but the plaintiff celebrity has made his or her point. Rumors can destroy careers, and the legal system is often the only means of challenging those who will stop at nothing to make money at a celebrity's expense.

A Brand New Day and a Brave New World

Community attitude surveys may be most useful in situations that represent new types of cases and even new law. For example, when the Harrisburg Seven case was tried, civil disobedience still seemed novel.

However, when you think back on the era of the 1960s and early seventies, acts of civil disobedience involved breaking laws that increasing numbers of people thought were unjust in the first place. In the Harrisburg Seven case, the civil disobedience involved sabotaging federal property, including conscription records, as a protest against the Vietnam War, but not as a protest against any particular law. No one could say for sure how a jury might respond to the defendants in the Harrisburg case, especially because the defendants included a priest. In general, members of the clergy are afforded a degree of respect in our society, but the prosecution logically believed that even a priest would not be excused for egregious crimes that could appear to involve national security. The defense conducted the survey, however, and saw that attitudes were more flexible than anyone had known.

Not long ago, our firm was hired in a medical-malpractice case that involved biotechnology and, by extension, bioethics, which is one of the newer areas of the law. In this situation, our client requested a community attitude survey, because the legal team didn't have sufficient information to predict how potential jurors would feel about a medical-malpractice issue when a component of the case concerned a surrogate mother. Attitudes in this very tricky, but fast-growing legal area end up all over the map.

On the surface, the allegations addressed medical procedures and techniques. Some preexisting conditions of the surrogate mother seemingly went unrecognized, or perhaps ignored by the plaintiff parents, and the case became a matter of who knew what, who told what to whom, and who hid information. However, there was little question in my lawyer-client's mind that the arguably tangential issue of surrogate parenting could likely influence the way jurors perceived the evidence related to the defendant's behavior.

In this case, the physician was approached by a married woman, who asked him about the possibility of hiring a surrogate to carry a child for her and her husband. He found the surrogate and served as her doctor for the pregnancy and birth. Unfortunately, medical complications during the birth and delivery led to lifelong injuries to the child. Underlying the medical issues was an ugly battle of allegations between the infertile couple and the biological, or surrogate, mother. The lawyers wondered if jurors' existing attitudes and values regarding surrogate parenting could affect their interpretation of the evidence they heard as a whole, and if so, then how would the attitudes color their interpretation.

We learned that in the urban community in which the trial would have taken place, prospective jurors were able to focus on the physician's work and not get caught up in their attitudes about surrogate parenting, which varied widely. In certain communities, such as venues where citizens tend to be religious and the range of religions is narrow, attitudes about surrogate parenting were more likely to affect the case in a way detrimental for the defendant physician. In this case, the venue for the trial was not only urban, but upscale as well. One of our researchers joked that those who were not considering surrogate parenting were thinking about their next plastic surgery. Prevailing attitudes allowed the lawyers to focus their case on the underlying facts of the case and the specific issue of malpractice. This was another situation in which research tipped the scale and allowed the plaintiff party to save face, accept a settlement offer, and avoid a trial.

Thirty years ago, this kind of case was still in the realm of science-fiction writers and futurists, the men and women who had predicted that biotechnology would catapult us into a "brave new world." And so it did. Today, community attitude surveys may attempt to discover attitudes about such things as artificial insemination, in vitro fertilization, cloning, and, as odd as it may sound, the custody of fertilized eggs. In fact, there have been several lawsuits involving divorced couples that have opposing ideas about the disposition of fertilized eggs. One party may want them destroyed, while the other party seeks to keep them, and in fact "own" them, which raises a new kind of property issue the judges of the past would not have anticipated. These issues also stir the passions of third parties, that is, individuals with a political/philosophical agenda who come to the court as an interested party.

Biotechnology issues also include end-of-life issues. A community attitude survey may try to determine attitudes about the "right to die" or a family's preferences about life support. Again, these issues exist today because they *can* exist today. Only a few decades ago, the medical community did not have extensive tools to prolong life, so the clash between opposing philosophies was debated in classrooms or living rooms, but not in courtrooms. Today, community attitudes about end-of-life issues may be of critical importance in certain kinds of trials. The criminal trial of Dr. Jack Kevorkian may represent the most obvious example, but numerous medical-malpractice cases involve issues of life and death. Juries are asked to determine if individuals, such as physicians, or institutions, like hospitals, are responsible for premature death. When designing a community attitude survey, a jury consultant may need to probe ideas and inclinations about even *defining* death, along with the old question about when life begins.

While some of the biotechnology issues remain in the realm of family court or are determined by judges, not juries, scientific issues eventually find their way to criminal and civil cases. DNA evidence is a classic example of scientific advances that have significantly influenced the way cases are tried, including, of course, accurately establishing paternity.

In criminal cases, attitude surveys may well probe community attitudes in terms of trusting DNA evidence. After the O.J. Simpson trial, it became clear to most lawyers that it is not enough for potential jurors to believe in and support DNA evidence. In addition, these individuals had to trust the integrity of the evidence, which means having confidence in the way this kind of evidence is handled. The whole country, indeed the world, learned about the potential for contamination of DNA evidence. Since that has entered the public consciousness, community attitude surveys now must measure the issues that qualify, perhaps even diminish, public acceptance of DNA evidence.

It is easy to see, by the way, how these research efforts in court cases can be extended to inform legislators about prevailing public opinion about issues that fall into certain kinds of categories. For example, when community attitudes are assessed, the issue of surrogate birth may be related to opinions about same-sex adoptions, for example, or the rights of a volunteer sperm donor. Perhaps a man has agreed to father a child for a lesbian couple. Later, he decides to exercise what he believes are parental rights. Does the surrogate father have rights? Well, we do not know. He may have rights in some states, but not others. It is a relatively new area of law.

In nearly all cases, the research is conducted for specific clients in a specific case and these parties do not want to share the results with anyone, certainly not the other side, much less the public. Eventually, though, it is possible that a legislative body, for example, may seek to have this type of research done in order to inform their work on certain issues.

Your Attitudes Have Many Uses

When jury consultants conduct a community attitude survey, they are thinking about the kinds of jurors that might be predisposed to their client's case. But they also use the information to help develop a case theme. Since I have a background in communication, I often become involved when we need a viable theme for a case. Developing a theme then helps the lawyers establish direction when they craft their opening statements and closing arguments. The notion of a case theme does not call for voodoo or for creating nonexistent facts, but it does involve searching for just the right analogy or metaphor to help jurors relate to what would otherwise be complicated concepts. In other words, the jury consultant has to work with the client to translate the message into terms that make sense to the layperson.

One of my clients represented a school district in a legal malpractice claim against a law firm for mishandling a municipal bond issue. We came to learn that members of the community were loyal to the school district but had a difficult time comprehending the case. Jurors who had the experience of applying for a home mortgage were better able to understand the problem because issuing municipal bonds parallels a layperson's experiences with getting a home mortgage loan. We crafted an opening statement, complete with charts, that illustrated the parallels. The plaintiff's lawyer didn't believe he could ever find a way to get a jury to understand the complexities of the case. Our research showed us the way, and ultimately the verdict in the case was in excess of $50 million.

Given that many cases involve complex technology, including medical data, lawyers are concerned that jurors may ignore important evidence because they do not understand it. The half-life of a drug or the science of DNA testing may be critical elements in a case, however, which means it is even more important to find a way to communicate the information clearly. Sometimes this means illustrating and clarifying by using analogies and metaphors. The community attitude survey helps find the life experiences among potential jurors that will help them understand the complicated nature of a specific legal matter.

Sorting Out the Questions

A community attitude survey is not an inexpensive proposition. Even a limited reach into the community to obtain a relevant pulse on the issues of the case will cost in excess of $10,000. More typically, this type of project costs $25,000–$50,000. So, two things are important: first, the client must have issues that warrant conducting a community attitude survey, and second, the client must have the resources to fund the research project or have a good reason one should be done *pro bono*.

Before we design the survey, the client-lawyer begins raising a range of concerns. In a case involving toxic waste or damage, how does the community feel about large corporations? From the company's perspective, can they overcome an image of environmental destroyer and be deemed "innocent" of (legally, "not responsible for") the claimed injuries?

For example, tobacco manufacturers wonder in every case whether they can overcome the generally negative attitudes about cigarettes or cigars. They process and sell what is known to be a cancer-causing product, and yet they attempt to find a panel of jurors that will find them not responsible for the illnesses and often subsequent death of a plaintiff who wants to hold them responsible. In general, will juries hold smokers responsible for their own conduct and vices and not transfer the blame? These are common cases in which community attitude surveys are most useful to help parties determine whether they want to proceed with a trial or settle out of court.

I worked in a tobacco case in which the community attitude survey suggested that the plaintiff (for whose side I was employed) could fare well in the community. As we settled in at the counsel's table, ready to get jury selection underway, a last-minute settlement offer came to our side. We stepped out for the lawyer to present the offer to his client. I will never forget the interaction.

"They have offered us $250,000—what do you think?" the lawyer asked.

The trusting client said, "What do *you* think? Should we take it?"

Ultimately, accepting or rejecting a settlement offer is the client's decision and the lawyer threw the question back. "It's up to you. You have to decide what's in your best interests."

The client's next question is every plaintiff lawyer's dream. "Will you get enough of a fee if we settle? Settling is okay with me, but I want to be sure you will get enough for all your work."

The lawyer just smiled and said, "Don't worry about me."

I admired the way my client handled that interaction. It was certainly in his interests in this uncertain case to accept the offer and avoid the trial, but he kept his inclination out of the exchange. The client ultimately decided to accept the offer. She made the decision without feeling pressure, and everyone involved walked away pleased, even the defendant, who also wanted to avoid a trial.

Attitudes and Place

The location of the trial may be of paramount importance. This is true in both civil and criminal matters. We need only flash back to the O.J. Simpson trial to see the point. In *People v. O.J. Simpson,* prosecutor Gil Garcetti faced the location dilemma. Should he try the case in Santa Monica, the location of the courthouse closest to the site where the murders of Nicole Brown and Ron Goldman took place, or should he move the trial to downtown Los Angeles? Keep in mind that in the Simpson matter, allegations of a racial bias emerged early in the case. To most observers, it seemed clear that given the weight of the evidence the prosecution expected to accumulate against Simpson, a mostly if not all white jury in Santa Monica would quickly and easily convict him. In addition, Simpson actually lived in that area of the county, so weren't those residents his peers?

But what would a downtown L.A. jury do? It was far more likely that the jurors called for the case would be African-American and other minority individuals, as opposed to more well-to-do white people. Were these Simpson's peers? After all, Simpson is black and has community and family ties to the black community. But his second wife, one of the victims, was white, and beyond that, Simpson enjoyed significant wealth and fame and ties to the white community, too. So, who were Mr. Simpson's peers? Both sides of the issue had supporters and detractors, and arguments flew freely.

I speculate that Gil Garcetti probably believed it didn't matter much where the case was tried. Just before the trial began, I ran into him one evening at a theater in New York City. We talked briefly about the circus atmosphere surrounding the case and his belief that the prosecution team would win the case regardless of where the trial took place. He was well aware of the ordeal ahead. I remember asking what he thought of the Broadway show we were watching. I don't remember what he said, but I do recall that we agreed that the "real show" was about to get underway on the other side of the country. He probably believed that with the overwhelming evidence they expected to present, any twelve individuals, regardless of their race, background, and life experiences, would simply have to convict on the evidence of the case. From the looks of things, this case represented a sure win for the prosecution if there ever was one.

Community attitudes may be multi-layered, so a superficial look won't always suffice. For example, Gil Garcetti was concerned with the appearances and repercussions of the chosen venue because the community itself was still coping with the Rodney King/LAPD scandal and its aftermath. These events were still fresh in the minds of everyone in the community. His decision to move the case downtown most certainly involved his attempt to avoid nightly news broadcasts that would again feature L.A.'s ugly race problems. These problems reflected badly on law enforcement and the courts. Gil Garcetti no doubt considered everything and made his decision, and then he and others received the shock of his career when O.J. Simpson walked out of the courtroom a free man.

Was Garcetti's decision made in a vacuum? Surely not. Before Garcetti made his decision, the prosecution team would have gathered a great deal of information that analyzed data about the L.A. and Santa Monica communities. This data would provide profiles of both desirable and undesirable potential jurors. For reasons that are not completely clear, prosecution lawyers apparently chose to ignore the proverbial handwriting on the wall. Instead, they forged ahead based on instinct, assumptions, and their commitment to the case; these are all strong reasons, but just not the right ones for such a situation.

I have strong reactions to the Simpson case because I served as NBC News jury expert for the criminal trial and other later cases. Part of my preparation for the *Today Show*, *Nightly News*, and other interview programs was to watch the strategic steps taken by the players. NBC based me in Los Angeles for critical parts of the case, and I was in and out of the courtroom throughout the proceedings. I believed at the time that the case should have been tried in Santa Monica. It was the more sensible place given the site of the crime, and the peers for O.J. were clearly more likely to reside in Santa Monica than they were in the greater downtown L.A. arena. That is not Monday morning quarterbacking; it is what any jury consultant for the prosecution would have urged them to do. But the ultimate decisions belong to the lawyer-client and not to the consultant.

In the Simpson civil trial, the plaintiffs received a verdict in excess of $30 million. I doubt that any member of the Goldman or Brown family holds much hope that they will actually receive that sum of money. But the Simpson civil case was a rare event, because it was never about money for the plaintiffs. The civil case was always about the peace of mind that resulted when a jury held Simpson responsible for the killings of Nicole Brown and Ron Goldman.

During that time, I lectured quite a bit in various parts of the country, and I was fascinated with the range of responses from lawyers about the civil case against Simpson. Many lawyers said that they expected the plaintiffs to settle that case before trial. They believed that Simpson would offer some sum of money to avoid this next spectacle. And for lawyers, that makes sense. Most cases *are* about money, and settling a case is a positive thing because it means we managed to bring many minds together to reach agreement. But I knew that the Simpson civil case would never settle. One evening I was in "the green room" along with Fred Goldman (Ron Goldman's father) as we both waited to go on the air for a television program in Chicago. While we chatted I told him what I was hearing from other lawyers. He just shook his head and said, "They just don't get it. I don't give a crap about the money. But some people will never understand this." He was right.

Changing Venues

Changing the venue of a civil trial may have important implications, just as it often does in criminal trials. When you hear that a lawyer has filed a motion with the court in an attempt to move a case to a different locale, it may be because the party being sued in a community is concerned about how they will be viewed. Therefore, they would rather have the issues heard elsewhere. For example, I am involved in a case regarding issues of breach of contract and allegations of misuse of corporate information and trade secrets. The plaintiff, an Illinois corporation with officers who resided in Florida, chose to sue a group of defendants, most of whom also resided in Illinois. Yet the lawsuit was filed in Florida. The decision about where to file a lawsuit is often a strategic one that must be done in accordance with legal rules. For example, one can only sue someone else in the place the defendant resides or where the events that led to the lawsuit took place. Without getting into the complicated issues involved, these plaintiffs likely figured they would get a more sympathetic hearing in a Florida court; or perhaps it was just more convenient for them since they live in Florida and hoped they could keep the case in the court system there.

You can be sure that the defendants would want to have the case transferred from Florida to Illinois; one or both parties might be interested in studying the community attitudes in both Florida and Illinois. They would want to find out if something specific in the prevailing attitudes in Florida was behind the decision to file there. Of course, it is possible that the original filing in Florida was simply an act of incompetence or party arrogance, but the trial itself will expose any errors in reasoning. This type of case illustrates that sometimes lawyers do not know if they are up against a clever strategist or an idiot. Ultimately, it was decided not to conduct a community attitude survey because the defendants did not believe that prevailing attitudes relative to the case would make much difference.

In another case, a lawyer needed more time to prepare his case. He decided to file an "eleventh hour" change-of-venue motion on the basis that he could not get a fair trial. He had a decent argument to make, and we conducted a community attitude survey to find support of the position. This was an expensive road to take for the purpose of getting more time, but it was successful in that situation because it actually led to a settlement of the case as the other side decided the delays and costs that would be incurred were not worth it.

The Wake-Up Call

Occasionally, our firm receives a call from a frantic lawyer who tells us about a client who wants a jury consultant to show up in court that day. As odd as it may seem, more than once we have dropped other work and rushed off to the court. In one instance, a lawyer asked me to appear in court to help him with jury selection for his client, a woman accused of shoplifting. Her case was going to trial, and while it may seem odd that the lawyer suddenly wanted a consultant, as it turned out the defendant came from a wealthy family. Her relatives had not considered retaining the services of a jury consultant until the day before the trial was scheduled to begin. In other words, the woman's parents wrote a big check to cover expenses at the last minute and the lawyer called me at 7:00 A.M. He had never hired a consultant before, but I showed up to assist with *voir dire,* or the jury selection.

In this case, I helped him ask questions and advised him about the jurors he could challenge and remove. However, our early morning exchange was not so promising. "Paul, I need you here, buddy," my desperate client said. "It just occurred to my client that she should have a jury consultant here at the table with me and I knew you were the guy to call."

I paused a moment and said in my most supportive tone, "You know, not having read anything about this case, I can show up with a shield but without a sword." What I meant was that I could sit in court and pay close attention to the nonverbal cues of potential jurors, the manner in which they spoke and carried themselves. I had more experience with interpreting nonverbal communication than my desperate lawyer-client. But without any preparation, I was not sure I offered much more than another set of lawyer's eyes and ears. As it turned out, the woman was acquitted, so everyone ended up happy.

In another case, my "spontaneous" consulting happened in a strange manner. I met my client in court as we were going to go off to lunch to discuss the trial strategy. The case was on the trial call, and the parties assumed the judge would assign them a date in the coming few weeks. Everyone present was surprised to see the judge order the trial to begin the following morning. The judge's next case had settled and he wanted to leave for vacation. In addition, the lawyers in our case had confirmed that their case would likely take only two or three days to try. All these factors created the "you're ready…let's do it" court decision. After a very long night spent drafting opening statements and planning the case presentation strategy, we were ready to go.

This "seat of the pants" consulting is exactly the opposite of the kind of scenario trial consultants prefer. We like to plan, brainstorm, and research. When cases are just dropped in our laps at the last minute, we have no choice but to fall back on instinct and experience. We cannot forget luck because it seems to have a role in every trial, no matter how little or how much preparation we do.

Virtually every trial consultant prefers to start trial preparations at least six months prior to the trial. We need that much time to evaluate, design, and execute a research plan. One of the reasons jury consulting is controversial, by the way, is that we do so much research. For some reason, using intuition and some experience with past cases does not trigger the same kind of suspicion.

The key to a successful community attitude survey is defining the scope and asking the right questions. Scope is important because like consumer-market research, respondents will give up only a few minutes of their time to answer questions during a telephone interview. The more issues we add, the more time it takes, and we then risk more refusals from people who simply will not cooperate longer than a few minutes, especially since they are not compensated for taking part in these surveys. In other words, we need a large number of people to hang in with us on the phone long enough to complete the survey. Like many people, you may have experienced hanging up on anyone who calls you in the evening, so you can understand why we need many people making calls.

Even a limited survey effort requires about fifty completed interviews, and it takes hundreds of calls to achieve even this small number. In most community attitude surveys, we use 150 to 300 completed interviews, so the shorter we can make them, the easier it is to complete the work. Ordinarily, we like to keep the interview to about five minutes; only rarely will the calls go beyond fifteen minutes.

We need to gather demographic data (age, race, gender, income, etc.) about everyone who answers the survey because this provides the framework from which our profiles will emerge for desirable and undesirable jurors. In a criminal case in which the defendant is well known, the lawyers are concerned about community impressions and, hence, the location of the trial. For example, in a case involving allegations of fraud in a relatively complex scheme of financial issues including stock sales, we wanted to learn the extent of the defendant's bad reputation. We knew the defendant, we'll call him Tony, was not an admired man, but our client (his lawyer) wanted to learn if the specific bad impressions of Tony could outweigh the fact that the matter involved was extremely complex. We set out to learn:

- What are the prevailing attitudes in the community about Tony?
- Do people remember him from his early days in business? (Tony was a bit of a braggart in his younger days—he announced he was going to put a company out of business and had succeeded.)
- Are they familiar with his investments in sports teams?
- What do they know about buyouts and mergers and financial disclosure?

- What is their current impression of his family life? (We knew his nasty divorce would come up in one way or another, not to mention the unexplained death of his first wife.)
- What have they read and heard about this case?

In some situations, accepting the prosecution's plea offer may be the best outcome. This case happened to be one of them. The prosecution's case was quite strong, and they had more than a dozen charges against Tony. Tony's lawyer was a client with whom I had worked in several previous matters; he knew the case was definitely an uphill battle. The community attitude survey, while not exactly a pleasant experience for Tony or the lawyer, convinced both of them that they stood very little chance of impressing a jury. Tony had accepted that many people did not like him, but for years he could chalk that up to his perceived power. "People don't like power, but they respect it," characterized his attitude going in. "He's a legend in his own mind," better describes the prevailing community attitude toward him. He hadn't appreciated how quickly respect evaporates when people believe you are guilty of a serious crime.

Because this was a white-collar crime, Tony was a free man for the nearly twenty months it took to go to trial. He sported a confident attitude until the research began accumulating. In essence, we could not come up with a community attitude survey that offered positive information. He was too well known for his own good. In a way, Tony was much like the socialite in that negative attitudes toward an individual are very hard to overcome. Of course, this dislike becomes even more important if the evidence against them is quite strong.

In addition, in Tony's case, no strong, supportive theme emerged. In some cases, you can offer up your defendant, so to speak. A lawyer can say (in various ways): "Look, my client is not a nice person. Just ask his ex-wife. But that doesn't make him a criminal." James Woods did a Hollywood job of that approach in the opening scene of the movie *True Believer*. In that story, he defended drug dealers and called them scum in court, but he won cases on constitutional issues involving search and seizure. (That happens in fiction more than in everyday trials.) We had no such possibility with Tony. Ultimately, three years in prison sounded better than fifteen to twenty, so he took the offer.

In one case, I worked with a criminal defendant who, while he may or may not have been guilty of the fraud alleged, refused to accept a plea offer made by the prosecution. His wife was very ill and he was focused more on caring for his wife than on his own freedom. He was prepared to roll the dice and wanted the trial delayed as long as possible. He may have made the right decision, for while he was ultimately convicted, he was at home with his wife until her death.

No One Ever Calls Me

During election season, we hear the daily poll update, which tells us what voters are thinking and how they are leaning on key issues and candidates. Yet, many voters complain about never being asked to participate in a political poll. The same is undoubtedly true with community attitude surveys. The science of both polling and attitude surveys is quite reliable, and a relatively small sample can yield quite accurate results. So, your community may have a population of tens of thousands, but researchers can talk at length to only a few (maybe 50 to 150) to get a statistically significant sense of what is going on within the group as a whole. Of course, as a researcher, I have a different view. Given the number of people who hang up, say nasty things, and otherwise won't participate in a survey, it is hard to imagine we have *not* yet reached you.

Who are these callers? Often they are college students or others who want some extra income. We train them to be sure they have excellent telephone manners and demeanor, but since they are scripted from beginning to end, it is not essential that they have a background in marketing or interviewing skills. We reserve the right to listen in on the interviews to ensure that they are being handled properly. I recall one instance where an interviewer was "fudging" the demographic information to get someone to qualify for the survey who did not qualify (they were underage) just because it was a cooperative respondent. In jury research, you cannot play games; the responses must be legitimate and proper.

In order to participate in a community attitude survey, respondents must be qualified, which is a process not unlike a salesperson "qualifying" a buyer. Participants are qualified through an initial series of questions, once they agree to stay on the phone at all. We ask the questions because we must be certain that these individuals are eligible to sit on a jury, and in addition, that they don't have particular experiences in their background that may automatically disqualify them from being selected for a jury. We also screen for issues that prevent the participant from being fair in the particular case for which the survey is conducted.

Perhaps most important, we need to be sure that the respondent is not connected with any media organization, since our clients usually like to keep a low profile when conducting this kind of research. Having a member of the media involved, even inadvertently, would not bode well for maintaining confidentiality. I can attest to the experience of granting an interview "off the record" to a reporter who (after assuring me he would protect my identity as his anonymous source) went on to publish everything I had said, along with disclosing my identity. I read my words in the Sunday paper and then called the reporter and asked him why he did not honor his confidentiality agreement. "Hey," he said, "I can't do that. That was the risk you took, man." After that and other experiences, I'm wary of reporters and have learned that there's no such thing as "off the record."

If your telephone rings and one of my researchers is on the other end of the line; this is what you are likely to hear:

> Hi, I'm Tim Lawson of the Research Group, a national research firm. We're conducting a public opinion poll on people's attitudes toward celebrities involved in legal cases. These questions take about ten minutes to answer and all responses are completely anonymous. Your number was randomly selected. We do not know your name and will not ask for it. I don't wish to sell you anything, I just want your opinions. You don't have to answer any questions you don't wish to answer. Do you have the time now? [If so, we proceed.]

1. Are you at least eighteen years old?
   a. If not, is there someone in your household who is at least eighteen and a U.S. citizen who might be interested in helping out? (If not, we thank the person and terminate the interview.)
   b. If yes, we ask for the *first* name, and if the current time is not convenient for the respondent, we arrange a future time to call.
2. You are: ____male ____female.
3. Are you a United States citizen?
4. Are you a registered voter?
5. It is important that you be fluent in English. Do you consider yourself fluent in English?
6. Do you or does anyone in your household personally know any celebrity?
7. Are you or is anyone in your household a lawyer?
8. Are you, or is anyone in your household, employed in the fields of journalism or media news?

Assuming you are eligible to complete the survey (questions 1–5), the balance of the questions assure us that you are not fundamentally biased, which would prevent you from proceeding. Questions about celebrity are modified to fit our case. If political figures were involved in our case, we would ask if you had any close ties to a politician. If the case involves priests, we would want to be sure you do not work for one of the offices or agencies of the Catholic Church. The survey is an attempt to get a read of the existing attitudes in the community, but it is important that the survey reach those who would be qualified to sit on the jury.

Safely out of the realms of law and media, we would now be interested to know something about your lifestyle and demographics:

1. What was your last year at school?
2. What was your primary area of study?

3. What best describes your employment situation?
____Employed full-time ____Employed part-time, or ____Unemployed
4. What type of work do you currently do or have you done in the past?
5. What is your marital status?
6. Do you have any children?
7. What is your ethnic background?
8. What age group are you in?
9. What is your political affiliation?
10. What best describes your political leanings? ____Conservative ____Middle-of-the-Road ____Liberal
11. What is your household's annual income?
12. Have you ever served on a jury?
13. Do you rent or own your home?
14. Have you ever served in the U.S. Armed Forces?
15. Do you read the newspaper daily?

This information helps shape an impression of whom we're talking to, and helps us define profiles for the types of jurors who likely would be favorable to our client, and equally important, those who are likely to be adversarial to our client's position. These demographic questions ultimately assist in creating the juror profile of both desirable and undesirable jurors. Lawyers want to know, as a guideline, whether their desired jurors tend to be of a certain race, sex, age group, and such.

So, I Qualify....What Do You Want to Know?

Once the respondent passes the screening questions and has provided the additional lifestyle information (we might ask the lifestyle questions near the end of the survey), we are ready to take the participant into the case. Often, we begin the inquiry by reciting a brief summary of facts from the case, facts that frame the questions that will emerge. This is not as easy as it may appear. For example, if the client does not want it known that he or she is conducting a community attitude survey, then the facts and names may be changed to preserve confidentiality. We did not hide much when it came to Tony's financial-fraud case because he was not concerned about being identified. When a defendant is well known, we usually do not want to hide too much.

We never indicate who is sponsoring the research, so the respondent does not know which side is asking the questions, although they will speculate. Our office worked in Whitewater-related matters. Normally, this would not be public information, but the *Washington Post* and other newspapers around the country reported the identities of all the consultants who had been hired. If people knew who sponsored the research, we would have tainted the results of a survey that asked people for their opinions about President Clinton's activities, the activities of other politicians, and other related matters. A known call from the arm of Ken Starr would produce results very different from a known call from the Clinton (or other defense) camps.

We often say we are conducting a research project, making every effort to remove the expectation that the work is actually being done for the trial by a specific party. This is a step away from complete disclosure, but protecting the rights of the party likely outweighs the failure to disclose the case-specific nature of the project. Many people are quite willing to assist scientists who are engaged in research, and independent opinion research is considered scientific.

If you get a call asking you to participate in a research project, you will not know if it is a truly objective exercise designed to lead to publishing a scholarly paper, or whether you are aiding the work of a litigant. It may or may not matter.

Next, we ask a series of questions to find out the respondent's basic attitudes. The questions depend on whether we want to get a read about prevailing general attitudes in order to see how they might influence a verdict in a case, or whether we are after case-specific reactions. For example, in the Whitewater matter, we were interested in issues involving politics and the social demographics of the people involved. In Tony's financial-fraud case, we asked about attitudes toward business and lifestyle.

After completing the attitude questions, we recite a brief summary of the facts of the case, and then ask questions related to the specific scenario. For Tony's case, we might have asked:

1. Based on what you have heard, what verdict would you tend to give? ___Definitely not guilty _____Probably not guilty _____Not sure ____Probably guilty ____Definitely guilty
2. With 1 meaning Extremely Weak and 9 meaning Extremely Strong, how weak or strong do you feel about your verdict choice?

Extremely Weak: 1 2 3 4 5 6 7 8 9 Extremely Strong

We may present several fact scenarios and ask these same questions, but we have to choose carefully because most people will go along with a phone interview for just so long.

What Do You Do with All That Data?

When we have stacks of surveys, it is time to bring in those who crunch the numbers and develop the theories. Every response to both close-ended or scale-type questions asked are analyzed by computer and by an actual person. We analyze the data for trends and findings. Aside from all the technical statistical terms researchers can throw around, all lawyers really want to know is if the results are statistically significant. That is, is the possibility that the results are due to chance less than 5 percent? Are we at least 95 percent certain that the results do not result from statistical chance? That's the standard for statistical significance.

During the 2000 election, the polls of likely voters showed results well within the margin of error, which made predictions virtually impossible. If less than 1 percent separated the two candidates and the margin of error was four percent, we stayed in a tie for the last days prior to the election. On Election Day, we still had a virtual tie.

In one of our firm's cases, the lawsuit at hand was between two very large corporations who were competitors, and each "owned" its town. That is to say, they were each the centerpiece of what we might call a company town; most everyone in the community worked for the company or had a relative who did. Company A sued Company B for patent-infringement violations in Company B's hometown. This astounded Company B. Why wouldn't Company A sue at home, which they could have done? Company B hired us because they wanted to know whether something was up in the local attitude of Company A's town. Perhaps there were labor issues or other factors that led Company A to file this litigation away from home.

It turns out that the community-attitude research showed no evident problems in Company A's town. In other words, no reason existed for Company A to sue outside of its own hometown. This told Company B that there would also be no reason to try to move the trial back to Company A's town. The case remained in Company B's own backyard, which on many levels gave them comfort once the research was completed. The case ultimately settled out of court, so we will never find out what was behind the original decision of Company A to sue outside its own backyard. But you can see why our client needed to know what it faced in the venue where the case could be heard.

During all the Whitewater-related litigation, we were retained to do research in one facet or matter. The community attitude survey in that case was designed to gauge the general attitudes of the population in the Little Rock area toward the political issues raised in that case as well as the high-profile figures involved in one of the several cases being heard there. Whereas in most cases, jurors know nothing about the parties involved, this case was unusual because of familiarity (both personal and public) with the individuals involved. In general, the participants perceived President Clinton and the First Lady as powerful people. Kenneth Starr, the Whitewater Special Counsel, was seen neither as powerful nor powerless. James and Susan McDougal and ex-governor Jim Guy Tucker were all seen as relatively powerless.

Of special interest was the community's view of Kenneth Starr as neutral to "bad" on a scale of "goodness." The McDougals, Tucker, and Newt Gingrich (who was not a respondent in the case, but was still a powerful figure in national politics) also were seen as "bad." In addition to personal power, parties perceived as most abusive were the Internal Revenue Service, the White House, and "Big Business." People split on their opinion of whether Kenneth Starr's Office of Independent Counsel and Congress tended to abuse its power.

It became clear that pro-prosecution jurors in that area tended to be Republicans and Independents, not Democrats. They tended to be men in the age ranges of thirty-five to forty-four and fifty-five to sixty-four and were more likely to be married or living with another person. They tended to have military experience in their background and were more likely to be employed in the fields of technical services, clerical jobs, or the arts, but they also had financial savvy. This is the kind of profile that prosecutors and defense lawyers would have available to them, because we can expect that both sides are conducting such research in a high-profile case. We can assume that the research design is similar for both sides because they are looking for the same type of information. Each side would use this research and the profiles as they sit through jury selection and try to find the jurors that best match (or don't match) the composite or suggested profile. Demographic profiles are just a starting point. Just because you are a Republican male, forty-two years old, and a former army sergeant with a wife and family does not guarantee the verdict vote. It just means that the research suggests that in this particular case, you are more likely to be a prosecutor's juror. We still need to ask questions during the jury selection to find out whether that juror is, in fact, likely to lean toward the prosecution side, or is an exception to the general trend.

For example, in a case involving complex allegations of patent infringement, our research indicated that people with higher levels of education tended to be more likely to see the infringement. Yet, in the actual case, it was a juror with the least amount of formal education (just short of a high-school degree) who said in deliberation, "Hey, you don't need to be brilliant to see that these guys [referring to the defendants] tried to steal that company's idea. I don't understand all the technicalities of this stuff, but it's just so obvious!" He didn't fit the profile, but he did fit the plaintiff's desired juror. We will discuss that process more in chapter 5, which concerns jury selection.

These are the kinds of conclusions and directions that can be gained from community attitude surveys. Cases involving allegations of sexual abuse of minors by Catholic priests, along with subsequent actions by bishops and officials in various dioceses, continue to proceed across the country. Both sides consider it critical to gain an understanding of community attitudes about all related issues.

Our firm has worked on a variety of cases involving religious issues and matters of public expectation and trust regarding Catholic Church conduct. Not all issues have the public profile as the sexual-abuse cases. For example, we have researched things such as land acquisition (or sale), and both sides in this type of litigation wanted to know what the community was thinking.

Having worked on both sides of many cases involving the Church, we know from our community research that individuals do not easily falter in their faith and trust in the Church. However, when the factor of sexual abuse is introduced, regardless of any other matters at hand, people who were once likely to side with the Catholic Church tend to distrust its evaluations. This lack of trust can extend to psychiatric evaluations about sexual misconduct. Individuals likely to side with those who accuse the Church of wrongdoing tend to think such information is quite informative and reliable. In addition, when the conduct of priests is involved in any kind of litigation, certain people believe the Catholic Church should investigate a priest's past before placing him in a position of trust and influence. These individuals believe the investigation should be as thorough as what the government might do before it issues security clearances. Others hold less stringent expectations for allowing a man into the seminary and ultimately put in charge of a congregation.

You can clearly see how the results of this research can be used to craft the strategy for case themes and arguments. Clearly, as the number of cases filed against the Catholic Church mount, community attitude surveys will be critical in the outcome of the cases, whether they are settled in or out of court.

Big Civil Actions Mean Big Surveys

It is clear that the prevailing attitudes in a community are critical to the way a case is perceived in that community, which is why lawyers often carefully consider where they will file a lawsuit, given options in filing. For example, a plaintiff has the option of suing for damages in a civil case either where an event, such as an accident, happens, or wherever the defendant resides. That makes sense. But consider just how powerful such a decision can be. In the world of airline-crash litigation, Cook County, Illinois, where Chicago is located, is a magical place for plaintiffs because history has shown that Cook County juries will award very large sums of money when the case warrants a verdict for the plaintiff. Some lawyers will say with a tone of ironic humor, "If that case is worth $1,000 somewhere, it's worth $100,000 in Cook County."

A plane crash is most certainly followed by lawsuits filed on behalf of the relatives of the deceased victims. The plaintiff lawyers who sue the manufacturer of the airplane have the option to sue in the jurisdiction where the plane went down. Now consider the Chicago-area headlines in 2001 that proclaimed: "Boeing Moves to Chicago." You may remember the very public courtship of Boeing by Chicago, Dallas, and Denver started the moment Boeing decided to move its corporate offices out of its long-time home base in Seattle. This news made headlines all over the world (although I never really understood why), but for aviation trial lawyers, and for our purposes here, the selection was potentially monumental, and there may well be a flurry of litigation filed in Chicago.

Even prior to Boeing's decision, lawyers from all parts of the country tried to find a way to file their airline-accident cases in Chicago. Past cases tried in Chicago led to verdicts of $25 million or more for the families of crash victims. Seattle was Boeing's "company town," but the move of corporate headquarters to Chicago brought both the company and legal jurisdiction to the city. By the way, the presence of United and American Airlines in Chicago was already a means of keeping cases involving those airlines in Chicago, but the presence of Boeing solidifies the matter.

It is probable that a new community attitude survey is needed. With Boeing in Chicago, and all of the positive (though waning) press that came from that event, it is possible that Boeing has shifted attitudes toward the positive among local juries. We will soon find out if Chicago has, in effect, become a company town for Boeing.

You can see the power of community attitude surveys. They give us the pulse of the community at a particular time about the parties and issues involved in a case. But the pulse of the community can change in an instant. The world's communities witnessed such drama on September 11, 2001.

Will We Ever Be the Same Again?

You might wonder if juror attitudes and beliefs were significantly altered after the events of September 11, 2001. On that day, a group of deranged terrorists caught America off-guard.

Naturally, we need to question how American jurors may have been changed—or not changed—as a result of, first, the terrorist events, and second, the profound fear that seemed so prevalent in the aftermath of that day. It is difficult to predict future trends in this situation using past experience as a guide because America has no history with this kind of attack. Pearl Harbor comes closest, but there were no jury studies at that time. Even if there were, it was a different time and a very different kind of technology responsible for the events that led to a prolonged but traditional war. In addition, in 1941, average citizens knew only what they could glean from gathering around the radio and reading the newspapers. There were no amateur videographers recording every moment from every angle for constant television replay (and analyzed and discussed over the World Wide Web). And this is a distinction with a real difference. Today, we miss nothing. If we happen to miss an event when it happens, we will catch it on the tenth or fiftieth replay that day. And we can see it on any one of nearly a dozen networks and cable channels, such as CNN, MSNBC, Fox News Channel, and so forth.

In the immediate aftermath of September 11, our emotions were intense and raw, and fear continued for some time with every airplane we boarded and every elevator ride to the top of a skyscraper. Although the source remains unknown, we may feel a touch of apprehension as we open our mail or even if we come across something that could be a mound of white powder. The fear of anthrax goes on, although it fluctuates because other issues may seem more immediately important. All these fears and uncertainties influence future behavior of jurors, at least in subtle ways, and jury consultants were immediately at work to explore the impact, both short-term and lasting.

What does seem certain is that Americans' new feelings of vulnerability must be juxtaposed with the strength of mind that comes from patriotism and a desire to avenge the deeds. It is too early to predict with certainty the long-term changes in jurors, but we have been hard at work to measure and assess the short-term impact.

The immediate impact was clear. Trials were postponed in the days immediately following the attack, and many lawyers sought continuances for the weeks that followed. In fact, the email list that connects many members of the American Society of Trial Consultants was filled with debates and questions, and we looked for insight in terms of experiences and research. How could we expect jurors to concentrate on any case? For weeks, few Americans could think about or discuss anything except the events of September 11. In our Internet discussions, consultants asked what civil dispute could possibly warrant serious attention from jurors who seemed to be preoccupied with news and updates and even fears about the next attack. And what criminal defendant wants his or her future determined by a group of shaken, unfocused, and emotional jurors? For all practical purposes, rational decision-making in the courtroom came to a temporary and necessary halt in many locales. Clearly, anyone representing an Arab-American or Muslim was well advised in the immediate aftermath to postpone the case indefinitely, or at least until rational thinking returned.

Research has long taught us that Americans have short memories in many ways. It is not that we have or ever will forget the September events, but we know that we return to our routines and our way of life and that we tend to move forward without necessarily taking the time to let the "dust settle." For all our focused intensity when something first happens, the next big story tends to overtake the last event.

We do know that in the days just after September 11, many jurors who were asked during jury selection whether they felt they could concentrate on the case at hand admitted that their emotions were too raw. In some trials, potential jurors acknowledged that they had ties to the victims and asked to be excused. But within a few weeks of the events, consultants began to report that jurors had returned to rational thinking. This contrasts with some of the irrational thinking that was part of the initial response. For example, throughout the fall we heard reports of fear among people boarding flights in which passengers who appeared to be from the Middle East were also boarding. This fear became so intense in some situations that these innocent individuals were pulled off their flights. Near the end of 2001, an American Airlines pilot refused boarding to a member of the Secret Service whose credentials, the pilots said, were questionable. The agent was also of Middle Eastern descent, so what effect this fact had on the pilot's decision was clearly a factor for investigation in the months that followed. Likewise, in courtrooms, for weeks after September, any person with a Middle Eastern appearance probably triggered discomfort in some jurors. Still, life eventually returned to a sense of normalcy.

In one post-9/11 case, I worked with a lawyer and his plaintiff client, Ali Famed, a young man of Middle Eastern descent. Famed went out to a nightclub one evening and upon arriving saw a friend having an argument with some other people. Because his friend was also of Middle Eastern descent, Famed decided to step in and help. Specifically, Famed was concerned that his friend was having difficulty expressing himself because English is his second language.

As soon as Famed stepped into the fray, a bystander spontaneously slapped his face, and before he fully absorbed what had happened, another slap came, this one from a woman. Acting from instinct, Famed threw a punch, which hit the woman in the face. Famed stepped back and began to walk out of the club. By this time, he wanted to extricate himself from the situation.

While he was standing outside, the bar's bouncer walked up to Famed and asked him to come with him. Then they walked up to the woman and the bouncer asked, "Is this the guy who hit you?" When she said yes, several bouncers proceeded to beat the plaintiff very badly, ultimately leaving him with permanent head and face injuries, including an inability to smell or to distinguish taste.

Famed filed a civil lawsuit against the club and its bouncers. The problems we, as his trial team, faced included a concern over the way the jury would receive the case from a person of Middle Eastern descent, given the post-9/11 climate. In addition, we had to deal with the reality that during the initial incident, Famed had punched a woman in the face.

Jury selection was fascinating. As you would expect, some jurors indicated that the fact that the plaintiff hit a woman was not something they could easily put out of their mind. But the judge said he would not excuse these jurors for cause only for that reason. However, in the end, the jury ended up to be quite diverse, racially and ethnically.

Since Famed has a Ph.D., I advised his lawyer to refer to and address his client as Dr. Famed, and we advised Famed to shave his beard and to appear as "American" as possible at trial. Actually, while Famed had an accent, he'd been living in the United States for more than a decade and had married an American woman. He was about as Americanized as most people, which is a difficult "state" to define precisely, but is about perception and overall impressions. We still couldn't be sure that jurors would look beyond his status as a Middle Easterner at a time when tensions were running high.

As for the fact that the plaintiff had hit a woman, I advised my client to deal with it up front. He questioned the jurors about it during jury selection and put it out front in his opening statement. "My client hit a woman. It was wrong; he knew it was wrong; he knows it is wrong, and he has regretted taking that step from the moment it happened."

Most trial consultants advise their clients not to hide the bad facts. Put them out front and deal with them. Desensitize the jury to the potentially harmful point, or when the fact eventually comes up the jury will inevitably question your intentions. We knew there was no way that the fact that the plaintiff had earlier hit the woman was *not* going to come into evidence.

In the end, the jury got angry with the defendant. To send a message, they awarded $500,000 to Famed as punitive damages in addition to the compensatory damages. In essence, they said, "Employees have to follow rules; they can't take the law into their own hands." It was encouraging to see that the jury was neither blinded by the background or nationality of a party nor were they unable to dissect bad facts and separate them from the facts that were most closely tied to the claims. It was a victory that had seemed unachievable to the client and his lawyer, but thorough and strategic preparation led to ultimate success.

As jury consultants, we study a variety of potential questions. For example, is it likely that criminal defendants accused of involvement in a violent crime will have tough going and for how long will this effect be a part of decision-making? The reasoning goes something like this: we were helpless to stop the terrorists who attacked the World Trade Center, but we are anything but helpless to ensure that violence-prone individuals are convicted. The phenomenon of "benefit of the doubt" may have been weakened, at least for a period of time. However, police testimony and other governmental investigations, areas once thought to trigger a skeptical response, might now be met with greater trust and acceptance. Apparently some people renewed their respect for a variety of "public servants" whose actions were viewed as heroic during the days that followed the attack. Our jaded attitude toward the Federal Bureau of Investigation (FBI) has been replaced with an increased desire to empower the FBI and CIA, even though compromises to civil liberties may result. The question is how long and to what intensity the feelings will last. It already appears that Americans may have a heightened sense of awareness and concern, but that sense of cynicism has returned.

What would the effect of these attitudes have in a civil dispute? Consider a medical-malpractice case. Prior to September 11, many people may have distrusted certain medical professionals, like an emergency-ambulance technician or a doctor whom they did not personally know. Does it not make sense that jurors may be more likely to support—or want to support—physicians and others in the health-care profession? Some consultants may argue limited impact in this area because in reality there was little work for physicians to do, as few survivors were found. But, research teaches us that attitudes about one group (such as emergency personnel) can extend or spill over to other groups, such as doctors and nurses through what is known as the "halo effect." The extent to which the depth of positive attitude toward emergency personnel extends to other professions or situations is the focus for future community-attitude research.

The Church finds itself in a contradictory situation. Clergy of all descriptions have been essential to the spiritual recovery of survivors. The heroic efforts of Father Mychal Judge, the priest killed by the collapse of the World Trade Center while in the act of administering last rites to others, moved many people on a national level. However, the deep-seated reactions to growing abuse allegations overshadow the positive work of clergy during and after September 11. This national issue provides a perfect illustration of why jury consultants and lawyers can never take certain attitudes or prevailing views for granted. They can change in a moment and can be overshadowed by other events, which take center stage in a trial.

If the halo of September 11 continues to exist in the coming months and years, the anticipated result will be lower damage awards. This result can most likely be expected in what are called soft-tissue injury cases where the plaintiff's complaints are primarily subjective and unsubstantiated by objective medical records.

I have worked in many cases as a jury consultant and arbitrator where the plaintiff complains of constant neck pain or back pain (often considered soft-tissue injuries involving muscles and nerves). However, the medical records cannot verify the existence of the pain because these injuries cannot be detected through X-ray testing. In many of these cases, the plaintiffs even stop getting medical treatment because their doctors tell them, "There is nothing I can do for you; you'll have to live with the pain." Now a jury or arbitrator must decide whether to believe the claims of pain. Is it real, entitling the plaintiff to more money, or are the claims of pain inflated just to trigger sympathy and higher awards?

In the current world where doctors are highly regarded and can testify that the claimed pain is most certainly real, jurors may be persuaded. On the other hand, as the halo fades, and jurors once again feel a bit of skepticism toward certain testifying physicians, then they may —fairly or unfairly—come to resent those plaintiffs and determine that they should just deal with the pain.

Understand that as new events unfold, attitudes and values will continue to be reshaped. Research has taught us that members of each generation share some common values. For example, it is fair to describe the veterans of World War II as conservative, and the Baby Boomers as having a stronger tendency toward liberal attitudes. It appears that recent generations have illustrated a return to at least some conservative values and attitudes; in fact, teenagers and young adults in their twenties as a group have taken us back to a conservatism not seen since the World War II veterans. For example, these young people have grown up in a more open society. They take for granted attitudes about equal treatment of all citizens and they may hold broader views about sexuality issues, but they also tend to be very strong advocates of personal responsibility. In that way, they resemble their grandparents more than their parents.

Since September, early research, coupled with historical research that has evaluated the behavioral shifts in people in response to crisis events, suggests that for the months and years to come, most people will experience a lingering sense of vulnerability and desire to protect the safety of themselves and their families. We may be quick to become angry and rise against others we believe pose a threat to our way of life and freedom to be and do as we wish. In fact, an AOL survey conducted a week after the attacks showed that 75 percent of the people believe certain changes such as a heightened sense of security in airports and other public places would be permanent; 25 percent said we would return to normalcy eventually. Most research suggests that our values and belief systems will remain much as they were before September 11. Rest assured, however, that case-specific research will be conducted by trial consultants to measure lingering effects of the terrorist attack, but only as they are relevant to the case at hand.

Moving Ahead

With each community attitude survey conducted, the jury consultant presents the results of the survey report that includes analyses and conclusions. Usually, the lawyer is most concerned with the section called "juror profile." Lawyers actually want to know the types of people who are more likely to be favorable to their side, and some lawyers probably rely on this information more than they should. "Yeah, yeah, I see what the community thinks…but who am I after to sit in that jury box?" is the typical question on the mind of the trial lawyer. In reality, no one can predict what one particular human being will do even though it is based on a profile of similar people. This can only suggest what any individual might do. Yet, the juror profile is the piece that lawyers find most intriguing.

With the analysis of the community attitude survey data in hand, the lawyers are ready to craft their case theme and theories to fit the types of jurors they hope to reach. This raises the next question: "Will anybody buy our version of what happened in this case?" Answering that question involves using the next tool in the box, the focus group, the setting where the case truly is tested and put together and where argument and evidence meet. In many cases, this is the first time the evidence and arguments are subjected to the most powerful test there is: the reaction of a group of non-lawyer laypeople. These individuals will never actually sit on the jury for the case, yet they will have a powerful impact on the way the case is shaped and presented to the real jury.

chapter 3

If It Doesn't Fit, You'd Best Quit

In a lawsuit, jury consultants get one chance, one shot, to evaluate the attitudes of potential jurors and then to monitor and read their reactions as the case is presented. Therefore, to present the strongest and most complete and coherent case possible, jury consultants use focus groups and mock jury trials to help craft the stories.

In a mock trial, jurors hear lawyers argue their case and listen to witnesses testify in what constitutes a fairly complete picture of what will unfold at trial. Logically, in a focus group we narrow our focus and address key issues or concerns the lawyers have about the case. In a focus group, we usually forego the witness presentations and rely on the arguments of the lawyers. The lawyers argue their case as though evidence has been presented, and we tell the jurors to assume they have heard what we tell them they have heard. In other words, we provide the kind of information key witnesses would present in a trial and then ask jurors to start from that point. It is the trial without the trial. Lawyers love this tool because it allows them to present as strong a case as they think they can offer without having to face any of the mishaps that may occur in the real trial setting.

Lawyers rely primarily on focus groups more than they do on mock trials because a focus group is easier and less expensive to put together. In addition, a focus group provides detailed information on the specific issues or case theme that the lawyer is concerned about. In addition, a focus group can be used to measure the best direction in which the case should move in terms of its story or theme. Lawyers who have never done a focus group are often skeptical because they can't believe there is anything any non-lawyer could teach them. As one lawyer client said to me, "I don't do focus groups. I have been trying cases for thirty years and there is nothing I have to learn about how to try my own cases."

At one point, that lawyer's client, an insurance company, insisted he conduct a focus group. Since the client was paying the bills, he reluctantly did so. The experience amounted to a "conversion," and he swore he would never try another case without conducting a focus group.

While a community attitude survey can provide powerful information about the pulse of community attitudes and values, there is nothing quite like the immediate reactions and responses elicited from the mock jurors who hear both sides of the case in the focus group. These test jurors are asked to tell the lawyers what they think about what they've heard, and, equally important, provide impressions about the lawyers who have presented the information. The lawyers get to perform (as they love to do) and present key documents, about which they may want feedback. They put forth their story in the strongest way they can, but always within the boundaries that the evidence permits.

The lawyers who will actually try the case most often make the focus-group presentations, although sometimes someone else, such as a trial consultant, steps in to present the argument for the opposing side. I sometimes serve in this capacity, playing one side of the case or the other, and sometimes presenting both sides' arguments to our jury. There is practical value in that method. Rather than reducing the impact of the information, having one lawyer or trial consultant present both sides of the case may actually reduce the effect individual personalities have on the jurors' leanings and, therefore, their verdict.

I recently worked for the defense in a case in which the plaintiff, we'll call her Betty, was hit by a city bus as she crossed a busy street, but not in the intersection. She sued the city, the bus system, and the driver. The defense lawyers with whom I worked wondered the extent to which jurors would hold Betty responsible for crossing a heavily traf-ficked street at night, which meant she had to dodge between cars and, in general, take a few chances. Taking the other side, would they believe that a public transit company was responsible because it was their job to avoid injuring anyone at any time?

The arguments as drafted were emotional and powerful. This was one of those cases where I got to step in and present the arguments for both sides. It was strange for the focus-group jurors to watch me enter, leave, and then reenter the room to present both sides of the case, but it was also fun. First, I took the role of the plaintiff's lawyer to plead with the jury to award money to poor injured Betty:

> Why are we here? What is this case really about? We can't bring Betty back to how she was before the accident. All of Betty's doctors and therapists believe that she will not make any more improvements. Betty will experience these permanent impairments and disabilities for the rest of her life. She has a per-manent and irreversible spinal-cord injury. She has brain damage to the frontal area, subcortical left hemisphere, and areas affect-ing her speech, memory, learning, emotions, and motor skills. She also has left-sided paralysis and stuttering speech. Betty has reached maximum medical improvement. They all agree that she is permanently impaired and totally disabled as a result of this brain damage and spinal-cord injury. She has chronic neck, chest, and low back pain; she has a loss of range of motion in the cervical spine because of the cervical fusion. She has a herniated disc in her low back, nerve damage, and a constant tingling sen-sation across her neck and shoulders and into her arms as a result of the cervical injury to the spine. She has an irreversible impair-ment to the her left side, which has limited her ability to grip with her left hand, and a devastating limp that causes her to drag her left foot and occasionally lose her balance. She has a constant ringing in both of her ears. She is severely depressed. She is required to take medication daily to control her seizures, as well as antidepressants. She takes medication to help control the

chronic pains that she feels day in and day out. So I ask you again, why are we here? Our judicial system provides that the only way to try to make a person whole again is to compensate them with money. How much money would fairly and reasonably compensate Betty? There is no amount of money that will bring her back to the way she was. We can all agree to that. What we don't agree on is what is reasonable.

Then I left for a few minutes and came back "in character" as the righteous defense lawyer who demanded that no money be awarded to foolish Betty in whose presence no bus driver, no matter how qualified and careful he or she was behind the wheel, stood a chance. But, the lawyers wanted to address the damages issue in case the jurors did feel that their client was responsible for what happened. So, in part, I began to address that issue:

We are very sorry for what happened to Betty Smith. We are here today willing to compensate Betty for her injuries, if you find that we are even responsible for causing them, which we believe the evidence will make clear…we are not. But if you find us responsible for her injuries, we are willing to do what is right. Willing to provide her with enough money so that she can live comfortably for the rest of her life. But like all good stories, this case has a twist. Betty's injuries are not as severe as her lawyers would have you believe….

By the time I returned to deliver the plaintiff's rebuttal, the jurors chuckled at my Dr. Jekyll and Mr. Hyde performance, but they also understood the job I had to do. In their deliberations, jurors were able to focus on the arguments and even referred to me as the "plaintiff's lawyer" or the "defendant's lawyer," thereby reflecting their understanding that I was standing in for real people. They kept their discussion to the arguments, and the phenomenon of "lawyer personality" stayed out of it, although in the drama of a real courtroom, theatrical skills do influence people. (As it turned out, the focus group found for

Betty, the plaintiff. The reasons for their verdict illustrate another issue, including what ultimately happened in that case, and are discussed later in the chapter.)

What's the Point?

The reason we have focus groups in the first place goes to the heart of the nature of storytelling and perceptions about truth. At some point in almost every trial, one witness or another will hedge when answering a question. When pushed for a clear answer, especially a yes or no answer, the witness will balk. "The accident happened *two years* ago," he will say, "I don't remember if the oil stain was on the sidewalk at the time I saw that guy over there smash into the back of Mrs. Green's Cadillac." Or, when preparing a witness, a lawyer drops an entire line of questioning because the witness cannot recall mundane details about streetlights or barking dogs or the color of a dress.

An issue in itself, the nature of human memory is always a presence because a trial is always about events in the past. We have a trial for the purpose of traveling back to an event or series of events that happened at a particular time in the past. By necessity, we are left with the reality that *there is no reality*. The issue at hand (e.g., the accident, the murder, the armed robbery, the oil spill, or medical incident), did occur, but all we are left with are participants' biased and tainted memories of the event or of all the steps that led up to the event.

In my experience, no one ever steps forward at the scene of a car accident and says, "It was all my fault!" More likely, we usually see individuals gathered around their vehicles pointing fingers at others and talking about the wrongs committed by just about everyone except themselves. After they have committed a crime, criminals take the time to craft an alibi to use just in case they are questioned by law enforcement.

As we all know, some alibis stand up under scrutiny and some do not. I vividly recall a young man who said he could not possibly have committed a robbery because he was at home taking a shower at the time of the crime. It turns out that he did not have a shower in his bathroom, which is an easy item to check. His alibi did not hold up and he served time, in essence because he forgot the difference between a shower and a bath. Neither side needed a focus group for that case.

Where There's Smoke…
Well, There's Smoke

By their nature, trials juggle various versions of the truth. All lawyers agree that it is rare to go into any trial with witnesses and jurors who demonstrate true neutrality. When men and women in jury pools insist they have no biases at all, it usually does not take long to poke holes in that myth. Most of us admit we have to put aside our biases, and in some cases, neutrality isn't a realistic concept. I recall Ruth, an elderly woman who had been screened for participation in a focus group I was conducting for a complex tax-fraud and extortion case. Ruth's favorite expression was, "Where there's smoke…" She nodded sagely, but she always trailed off and never finished the sentence. The expression "Where there's smoke, there's fire," is very common, and actually, it about sums up the challenge every defense attorney faces. Many people harbor a natural bias against a person who has been arrested, especially when police and forensics teams appear to have accumulated enough evidence to justify a trial.

In this case, the defendant was a lawyer who was accused of paying off a judge to attain verdicts in his clients' favor. His defense was that the judge actually forced him and other lawyers to provide the judge with "loans" that he would eventually pay back. The judge's trial was scheduled for a later date, and his defenses included an ill family member and full intentions of paying off the debt. But, for the lawyers accused of the payoffs, it was unclear whether jurors would see them as crooked in and of themselves, or honest players caught between a rock and a hard place.

Ruth probably seemed like a biased juror, because she focused on all this smoke and nearly drove everyone crazy repeating the expression so many times. Our team found out later that a few other mock jurors thought she was likely to be trouble and in the end, unbending. Ruth surprised us, though, because, based on the evidence she heard, she concluded the whole case was all smoke and no fire. She ended up believing the defendant had been framed and it was the judge who was the real "bad guy" in this matter. Not only that, she saw the "fire" surrounding one of the prosecution's witnesses. She ended up being influential during mock jury deliberations, and "acquitted" our client. The feedback we received from her helped the lawyer modify and draft the very questions he would want to ask the witnesses in the case. These questions would not only be favorable to our client, they would shore up the case against the judge, who Ruth was convinced was the guilty party, anyway.

Our client was acquitted in the actual trial, and the judge was later convicted in his criminal trial. The next time my client had a white-collar crime case, he asked if we'd find some of those "where there's smoke there's fire folks." Actually, there are probably many criminal defense lawyers who would prefer to find some "where there's smoke, then someone else may have started the fire" kinds of jurors!

Creating Doubt until the Smoke Clears

The lawyer's primary role involves creating doubt in competing accounts of an event. The lawyer's ability to challenge contrary accounts creates the battle between a witness who tries to withstand the challenge of cross-examination and a lawyer who tests every nook and cranny in that witness's account. This show of skill in the adversarial battle can mean the difference between a win and a loss. Unfortunately, the very skills that a trial lawyer must develop in order to be successful are the same ones that create the distrust of lawyers in our society. That situation also leads to the perpetual question, "But what about the *truth*?" The truth is, when it comes to accidents and many other kinds of cases, many versions of the truth exist.

Lawyers can shift the story they tell the jury in order to increase the power or desired impact of the message. Lawyers must stay within a reality the evidence can support, but they can—indeed, must—craft an account as complete, consistent, and coherent as the evidence supports. Research suggests that jurors will look for the holes in the "story," but the stronger the account, the more likely jurors will work to defend and support it.

When they find a particular fact that serves as the "driving force," jurors sign on to that side. For example, during the focus group (discussed earlier in this chapter) for the case in which Betty sued the transportation company, I presented evidence (in my role as plaintiff's lawyer) that the bus driver was not wearing his glasses. When I read the defense argument to the jury, it clarified that he rarely wore his glasses and did not have much need for them. But as I read the plaintiff's rebuttal arguments, I continually pointed to the restriction on the bus driver's commercial operator's license, and this became a fact that transformed into the driving force. It became the piece of evidence that made Betty's foolhardy traffic dodging irrelevant.

We recommended that the defense consider settling the case if it could because the research was strongly suggesting that jurors were going to hold the driver and the city bus company primarily responsible for the injuries sustained by Betty. The case ultimately did settle, and in this case, going through the trouble of having a focus group probably ended up saving money. In that situation, not wearing glasses was the smoke that led to the conclusion that fire was indeed present.

The Anatomy of a Focus Group

Assembling a focus group is not a small undertaking, nor, as you recall, is it inexpensive at $10,000–$35,000. The first question the jury consultant asks the client is a simple one: "What do you want to know?" We ask this question when forming a community attitude survey, too, but we are asking for different kinds of information when we design the focus group. Here, the intention is directed to specific issues, themes, and arguments of concern to the lawyers. In many situations, the lawyers have a good sense of typical profiles of jurors in the community in which the case would be heard. For example, we knew that the jurisdiction was a strongly plaintiff-oriented city and county in the city bus case, and our focus group confirmed that point and led to a settlement.

Some lawyer clients find ways to cut the costs to a bare minimum by using their own conference room, or getting friends of friends to come in and listen, or by limiting the scope of the data analysis and report. However, these cost-trimming measures may make the whole project a waste of time. The mock jurors sense the lack of reality and are influenced by the informal nature of the focus group. Perhaps most important, they may know too much about which side is directing the "production."

A formal mock trial would include the components that jurors see at trial (namely, opening statements), then testimony presented by key witnesses (live or on videotape) for each side of the case, and then closing arguments for both sides. This project obviously yields much valuable information. A focus group is usually conducted for a certain purpose, such as understanding juror reactions to case themes, and is generally limited to the presentation of lawyers' arguments, with references made to testimony but without the actual presentation. Where the primary concern in a case is the evaluation of a specific witness, then a focus group could be conducted where the jury watches that person testify and then deliberates about the witness's effectiveness. Obviously, the cost of a mock trial increases from $10,000 to $25,000 beyond a focus group because of the additional analysis of the actual testimony, not to mention possible travel expenses. When many millions of dollars are at stake, or a client's life is on the line, the lawyers may decide to hold a series of focus groups, each concentrating on a particular case issue or witness analysis, or even run a series of focus groups followed by a full-blown mock trial for the most complete analysis and understanding that, oftentimes, money can buy.

I tell my clients that I would never go to trial without first testing my case in front of average people. It is too easy to live with a case for months and years and to lose all objective insight about how the case will resonate with non-lawyers. There is no such thing as a sure thing, or in this case, sure verdict. Lawyers will tell you that they fear most losing the cases they believed could *not* be lost. We need only pose that question to Marcia Clark and Chris Darden, the prosecutors in the Simpson case.

In the more recent Martha Moxley murder case, defendant Michael Skakel (whose family is related to the Kennedys by marriage) was accused of committing the murder of Martha Moxley decades ago. To be sure, this was a tough case for the prosecution to prove beyond a reasonable doubt. I had a few discussions with defense lawyer Mickey Sherman, whom I greatly admire. I would have complete faith in him as my own lawyer. However, when we discussed the possibility of conducting focus-group research, Mickey, relying on his years of experience, said, "I know this case is getting a lot of media attention, but you know, it's just an old-fashioned murder case. It's a whodunnit…and my guy didn't do it."

As you know, Skakel was convicted. I am not saying that a focus group would have produced a different verdict, but it makes the point that no case is a certain matter; there may always be something to learn in the test and research. Even if done with all corners cut and as inexpensively as possible, I believe trial lawyers must experience some version of this layperson reaction through the focus-group project before risking it all at trial.

Mock jurors are paid for their time. How much they receive depends on geographical location, how far they had to come to participate, and how much time they spend. In general, jurors in large cities will receive somewhere in the neighborhood of $125–$150 for a full day's participation. The fee tends to be somewhat less in smaller towns and perhaps a bit more on the East Coast (where everything seems to be more expensive anyway). The whole process is both serious and in a way exhilarating. After all, we are trying out approaches to the case, and the brainpower in the room is considerable. There is a natural adrenaline rush involved in "performing" for a mock jury. Depending on the results, lawyers may either know they are on the right track or they go back to the drawing board and look for new themes and arguments.

Actually, some of the individuals we recruit for our focus groups have a similar excitement about participating in the project. I have seen men and women become absorbed in the intellectual challenge of a trial, while others are visibly affected by the emotional content of the presentations. For example, in a case involving the death of a newborn infant, the plaintiff parents alleged medical malpractice. Our client was the law firm representing the physician, who maintained that he did everything medically possible to prevent the death. We presented both sides at the mock trial, and we knew that the basic fact of the case, that is, the death of an infant, was so powerful that testimony and arguments were likely to arouse strong emotional responses.

Sure enough, we ended up with a jury with some men and women able—and willing—to set aside emotional content and focus on the intellectual challenge of examining scientific evidence, while others were focused on the emotional reality of grieving parents. The gravity of the case affected our mock jurors. Oddly, Harold, one of the five men present, behaved in such a tough, emotionally detached way that if he were on an actual jury, he might have exerted a negative influence, even on other jurors who were able to set their emotions aside.

While it is true that legal issues are supposed to be decided on facts and law, it is naïve to think, as some lawyers do, that emotional issues will not work their way in. In this case, Harold waved away all discussion of the grieving parents as "totally irrelevant." More than that, he acted obnoxious during mock jury deliberations and accused one of the other "jurors" of being a whiner when she spoke sympathetically about the parents. Harold was correct in one sense; these issues were irrelevant in a legal sense, but even the lawyer arguing for the physician knew that having such an insensitive man on the jury could mean trouble.

We learned about Harold after the fact, so to speak. As logical and scientifically complete as our arguments were, our mock jury found for the plaintiffs. We were quite surprised because our screening process had attempted to find individuals who could be fair when presented with scientific evidence in an emotionally charged case. When we talked with the mock jurors, we found out we had come close to finding the mix of people we were looking for. But we had not detected Harold, who not only dominated the group who favored the physician, but whose negative personality caused them to migrate away and join the group that tended to believe that something more could have been done during the birth to save the baby.

In this case, the physician's lawyer asked us to do another focus group, which probably would have been a very sound idea had the case gone to trial. However, a settlement was reached before we could move ahead. Although I cannot say for sure, it is possible that a plaintiff-side mock trial also showed that striking a balance between a situation that arouses strong emotions and the scientific evidence was so difficult that in the end, the parents agreed to settle, too. They could have ended up with too many individuals who leaned toward Harold, but without his morale-busting personality.

In movies in which legal issues and trials are central, you sometimes hear a lawyer say to another, "What will it take to make this go away?" This is a Hollywood way to say, "Give me an opening number." Focus groups can be extremely helpful when lawyers grapple with the pros and cons of offering a monetary settlement that will, in fact, make the case go away. I have heard many people, including hospital administrators and doctors, squawk loudly about settlements because they are sure they can convince a jury that they did nothing wrong. But medical injuries fall into a category filled with emotional hazards. This is true if the injuries were allegedly caused by medical personnel or by serious accidents.

Consider the world of workman's compensation cases. A person loses his fingers or an arm or a leg while on the job and he anticipates large sums of money to carry on his life. When there is a valid claim of product liability against a manufacturer of machinery, for example, there may be a large settlement. But Josh lost three fingers while performing his duties, which involved the coupling or attaching of railroad cars. It turns out that a fellow employee did not perform his job correctly, thereby causing Josh's injuries. Josh called me to explore his options against his employer. He was frustrated because a workman's compensation lawyer had told him that his fingers had a set value, and represented the maximum he could collect.

Statutes and books exist that establish the value of a finger, an arm, a leg. Under the law, that figure will be the limit an employee can collect, at least without a claim against someone other than the employer. So, the loss of a finger may be deemed to be worth $7,500 and the loss of a leg may have a value of $20,000. Odd as this may seem, the law considers these provisions necessary if we maintain a society in which companies can continue to function without being wiped out by a single event. At the same time, the law provides some degree of rational compensation (rational to everyone, perhaps, except the injured person).

Many public-policy issues exist that provide a rationale for such laws. For example, these laws maintain some stability of production and manufacturing. Without them, employers would be at constant risk of losing everything as a result of an on-the-job accident. In these cases, the law removes the highly emotional issues and an employer's risk. However, in cases falling outside of workman's compensation, the range of possible settlements is wide open.

I recall one case in which a van exploded on impact with another vehicle and killed the parents and orphaned the children who were also in the van. It was at the actual trial during the jury selection that the defense lawyer had a good sense that the jurors were not open to accepting a defense. He looked at one juror in the front row and said, "Ma'am, we have a defense to this case. You have to listen to that defense. Do you understand that?" The potential juror looked back at him and said, "All I know is that I see a bunch of kids over there without their parents and someone's going to pay for that." She was excused, but he lost the case anyway. If he had done the research that we on the plaintiff's side had done, I wonder if he would have settled the case before trial, or at least have had a better sense of the type of the reaction he was in for with particular types of jurors.

How Did You Find Harold?

Just as we do when we create a community attitude survey, the jury consultants create a "screener" to use in recruiting the mock jurors for the project. Jury-eligible residents of the community are called, and if interested in the project, we screen them to make sure they are not biased and also to ensure that they would be qualified to actually sit on a jury in the case. As I mentioned in the previous chapter, you won't have priests sitting on a priest abuse case, or a police officer sitting on a police abuse case.

Typical screening tools ask standard demographic questions, including age, income levels, education, etc. In long trials, lawyers know they will most likely have retired individuals on their jury, and often some public employees, from postal workers to IRS auditors to schoolteachers. Public employees are available jurors because public policy accommodates jury service. In a medical-malpractice case, our screening tool would ask questions about medical knowledge, but also about ties to individuals in health-care professions.

When one of my clients was involved in a criminal case in which the death penalty was possible for the defendant, we asked different types of questions. The case was expected to take a long time, so to be realistic, in the juror-recruiting phase we had to recruit the kinds of people who were most likely able to sit on a case for several weeks. In other words, we needed to look for recruits among government employees and retired people, with a desired balance between blue-collar and white-collar workers. In an extended trial, those men and women who are self-employed would typically number no more than one or two.

As I have said before, in a death-penalty case, we must exclude men and women who do not believe in the death penalty because they would be excused from a jury in such a case. So, even if we are representing the defendant, when it is time to choose the actual jury, we can only look for individuals capable of looking at the death penalty on a case-by-case basis. We would be unlikely to include individuals who had lost relatives or close friends to violent crime, although if we were on the prosecution team, these would be desirable jurors.

We determine political leanings by asking participants which party or philosophy most reflects their beliefs. However, if I find out that you vote a particular way, that does not tell me how you will find in my case, death penalty or otherwise. We can make broad generalizations about the link between your television-watching habits and your religion, but this does not tell us if you will send a defendant to death row. On the other hand, if I find out that you will send a thirty-year-old to death row but not a sixteen-year-old, I have a bit more information about your beliefs. I may or may not want you on my jury, depending on the case and other factors.

Do We Want to Win or Lose?

Most people assume that jury consultants want to look for jurors likely to be friendly or favorable to their case. That may be true at the time of trial, but in a research focus group or mock trial, we prefer to recruit men and women who are the most adversarial to our client's position. If the focus group proceeds as it should, our client will lose in the focus-group jury deliberation. The underlying reasoning here is that the greatest learning takes place in an adversarial atmosphere. I may want some hard-nose death-penalty advocates for my focus group, so we can see how these jurors respond to our evidence and arguments. This is a research project designed to teach the weaknesses and pitfalls of our case, and who better to teach us this information than jurors who are predisposed to finding against our position?

I recall in one case I worked with a lawyer who got very frustrated that the jurors recruited to hear the case gave him a hard time in deliberation. "Gee, I'm dead at trial if this is what happens." But this was not the trial. "Listen up," I said, "these folks are trying to tell you what doesn't persuade them; they are showing you your weaknesses. We'll talk about the evidence we have that combats their concerns." The coming days were filled with document and deposition review, and we made major modifications to our approach, which proved to be valuable because this lawyer won at trial.

I look at the mock trial and the focus group as educational endeavors. Lawyers might wince when we end up listing all the weaknesses in their cases, but we want to learn about the problems we have from jurors in our mock trial, not from an actual jury who returns with a losing verdict. I have experience with lawyers who end up frustrated and angry at the focus-group jurors who do not deliver the verdict the lawyer had worked so hard to get. A lawyer in a death-penalty case responded to the mock jurors sentencing his client to death with a thirty-minute lecture on the evils of capital punishment. This research can be a frustrating or painful experience. It is not easy to have a jury tell you that all your hard work and passionate arguments nevertheless led them to find against your client.

In general, lawyers and jury consultants want to know answers to these kinds of questions:

• Is there one fact or another that will likely weigh on a juror's mind?

- Is a timeline that seems strong to the lawyers likely to be met with disbelief by the jurors?
- Can a large corporation really convince a jury that it cares about the community, thereby triggering sympathy that can lead to victory over an individual who claims to be a victim of the corporation's evil ways?
- How will the jury react to the key witnesses, who may come from all strata of society and may invite an initial level of distrust?

There is nothing like losing a mock jury trial to answer those questions.

Where Is the "Hole" in This Case?

We never know what part of our account will have an impact on a particular juror. One well-publicized case, in which I worked with the defense, involved a fifteen-year-old boy who lived in a housing project. Early one evening, this young teenager was riding up to his apartment in an elevator. The elevator stopped at a particular floor. A madman entered, pressed the "Stop" button, and began to stab the young boy relentlessly, leaving him for dead. Later, the boy was found and had somehow survived the vicious attack. Sadly, however, he was left in a state known as near-locked-in syndrome. The boy could not move any part of his body, except his right thumb. He could make no sound and was unable to communicate in any other way. However, he was not in a vegetative state—far from it. This boy's mind functioned perfectly. He understood his surroundings and everything going on. Some would consider this a fate worse than death, because he would never be able to communicate, yet he had fully working mental capacities. This was an extremely sad situation.

But whom do you sue? With truly astounding medical bills, there was no way the boy's family, already living in public housing, could handle the cost of his lifelong care. But who should be responsible? The madman who committed the act was nowhere to be found, but in a civil case, would it matter if he were caught? What resources would you expect him to have? None. Therefore, thinking strategically, it would be a waste of time to consider suing him. Lawyers make an ethical attempt to find a viable defendant who can pay a substantial verdict; it's the only way to make a difference in an injured plaintiff's life. Although there are notable exceptions, in most personal injury cases the goal is a money verdict that can be paid, not mere vindication and principle.

In this case, the young boy's lawyers decided to sue the elevator company who held a service contract on the elevators in the housing project and were obligated to fix them whenever a breakdown occurred. The alarm should have gone off when the madman hit the "Stop" button, but no such alarm activated. In addition, the lawyers sued the security firm charged with the responsibility of protecting the complex. One could certainly argue that they failed in their duties and responsibilities in this case.

Of course, the defense lawyers chose not to roll over. In fact, they felt very much in the right. The elevator company defended themselves by citing reasons the alarm did not work. Apparently the tenants of the building had a habit of disconnecting the alarm bell so they could stop the elevator and carry their groceries off and into their apartment without setting off an emergency response. The elevator repair personnel repeatedly came out to reconnect the bell, only to find the same situation occurring again and again. In addition, while the elevator company acknowledged their duty to repair the elevators, they also noted the very dangerous environment in which they had to work, thereby making it difficult to find serviceman willing to return on a daily basis. The security firm defended themselves by pointing out that it is impossible to be everywhere at all times. Their bottom line was that if a madman wants to commit a crime, he or she is probably going to find a way to do it. Bad things just happen, and a terrible tragedy had occurred with no one to blame but the madman himself.

If you were a juror, what would you do? Everyone, including the defendants, felt sorry for the young boy. The medical testimony presented by the plaintiff suggested that the youngster could live a normal life span, while the defense testimony suggested that he could survive only a few years. What evidence would you believe? And knowing that you only get one chance to award a verdict, that is, the boy can't come back in the future to ask for more, what is the right thing to do? The defense believed that community sympathy and concern, although undoubtedly present, were not enough to hold them responsible. Their point was that if anyone was responsible for the damages, it was the madman, wherever he was.

So, you see the conflict. The defense presented a very reasonable position, but it was presented in the worst possible context. Could the defendants overcome the sympathy factor? We conducted focus groups and an interesting point emerged. Part of the presentation included showing of a "day in the life" videotape, which informed the jury about the boy's current life. For example, the tape portrayed the indisputable fact that he could only sit in a chair while others tried to figure out what he needed. He could press a button with his right thumb, his only means of communication. This was his life. When the mock juries came back with their verdict, they awarded amounts in $50–60 million-dollar range.

The defense became extremely frustrated with the outcome of our mock trial. One lawyer did not even want to meet with the jurors after their deliberation. "I have been practicing law for over thirty years and there is nothing that these people can teach me about trying a case," he said. "They're wrong and that's it." Once again facing the trial lawyer's ego, I asked him to indulge me, meet with the jury, and put his frustration behind. After all, the defense paid a great deal of money for the event, so they might as well see it though.

What I really wanted to tell him was that there are lawyers who have thirty years of experience, and lawyers who have *one* experience for thirty years. Maybe it was time to open his mind to a changing world. But I wanted to continue working for the client, so I kept quiet on this point.

The lawyer ultimately relented and agreed to meet with the mock jury. This is how it went.

"We're mad at you," one juror said as soon as the lawyer walked in the room.

"Hey, what did I do?" he asked.

"When you showed us the 'day in the life' videotape," the juror continued, "you were telling us how much you cared for the boy and how bad you felt bad about what happened to him, but you didn't even watch the tape. You just sat there and talked with your colleagues and paid no attention. And that's not right. That's not the behavior of someone who cares."

This really provoked the lawyer's ire. "How dare you say that? I have seen that videotape more than one hundred times and I know every inch of that tape. I didn't have to watch it to know it."

But the juror, this layperson who supposedly had nothing to teach the lawyer, knocked the lawyer over with his response. "You are supposed to be a performer and an advocate. Don't tell us you care and then act like you don't. We held you accountable for your rude behavior."

The lawyer left that interaction and demanded to do another focus group, which took place a few weeks later. This time around, he introduced the tape and sat and watched it. His eyes filled with tears as he demonstrated powerfully just how much the scene touched him. And this time, the jurors believed he was sincere. What verdict do you give now? Now that you like the defense lawyer, can you still hold the defendants responsible for the conduct of a clearly mentally deranged man who stabbed this poor boy and took off? The juries deliberated and this time came back with an award of $25 million. So, the bottom line: a strong defense cut the verdict in half. But half was not enough to risk trial.

So, was this verdict fair? It was less money, but did it address the issue? It appeared there was no way a jury was going to let the defense walk. The jurors offered an explanation, summed up by the statement: "This boy needs to be taken care of and you are the only people to do it. You just have to take care of him."

The case settled, so it never went to trial. Interestingly enough, the case settled for about seven million dollars, a sum large enough to take care of this young boy for the rest of his life, but obviously nowhere near the sum the defendants may have faced had the case been submitted to a real jury. By the way, the research conducted for this case cannot definitively conclude that an actual jury would *never* have accepted the defendants' position and, therefore, find for the defendant and award nothing for the boy. So even the plaintiff's lawyers must consider the risks of not winning at trial. Ultimately, the decision belonged to the boy and his family. They believed the settlement would ensure proper care for life, and this was their ultimate concern. Might they have gotten more money at trial? Sure. Might they have lost, and be left to fend for themselves? Sure.

Determining the meaning of the research and what role it plays in the "odds" is part of the decision-making process of teams involved in every case. Whether any party "rolls the dice" on what a jury will do should be decided only after considering carefully conducted research designed to guide the participants.

Measuring Opinions

Focus-group jurors may see some exhibits or even hear from a key witness or party if lawyers want feedback about a particular individual. The central testing ground is found in the arguments presented by the lawyers. This testing ground represents the best way to find out if a specific theme is effective or whether certain facts trigger desired or undesirable reactions. During this process, jurors respond both quantitatively (that is, by circling numbers along a scale from 1 to 5, which represent points along an agreement scale from strongly disagree, 1, to strongly agree, 5, or some such spread of options) on surveys they complete throughout the course of the project, and also qualitatively (free-form answers) through open-ended questions on the surveys. These surveys provide participants with anonymity, so their personal reactions can be offered freely. Jurors also hold open deliberation after the presentation of evidence in the case, including discussions facilitated by the jury consultant. It is important to monitor both group discussions and individual reactions because some mock jurors sit quietly during discussion or can be intimidated by a powerful personality on the jury. Yet when given the opportunity to respond on a survey, they almost always give truthful reactions.

I recall Franklin, a man in his mid-thirties. Coincidentally, he was recruited to two different focus-group juries I have handled during the past few years. He stands out in my mind because he is a contemplative man; he sat quietly through the presentations and in jury deliberations. He would try to speak but it was always tough for him to get the floor. At times, the foreperson of the jury would say, "Let's hear from Franklin," who would slowly rise from his chair and seemed able to speak only by pacing the floor and gathering his thoughts. That generally frustrated a few other jurors. Within minutes, they would interrupt and cut him off in order to resume the discussion at a pace that suited them. Franklin would just sit back down.

However, on written surveys, Franklin spoke volumes. Usually at the extreme of an issue, he would want to award the top dollar in a personal-injury suit, and in a drug case, he was prepared to convict with the maximum sentence if asked. He brought an interesting background to the table. While Franklin lacked a college degree, he was always taking courses at a community college or a Learning Annex. He worked a myriad of administrative temporary jobs, but never seemed to be out of work. He always seemed to be in touch with a variety of people, but not because of any work-related duties, just because he was out and about. Yet, because of his communication style, no one let him express his worldly views in the deliberations. In the real world, his positions might never be aired. In the world of jury research, we captured his leanings, opinions, and analysis through surveys, with the need to fight for the floor eliminated.

When we examine the totality of juror reactions, we then determine if we need to restructure the case theme or the way we present the arguments in order to better fit with the advice of mock jurors. Obviously, we hope to have the most powerful impact possible on the actual jury, should the case ultimately go to trial. In one case, the plaintiff's lawyer in an automobile accident case centered his arguments on a defective door handle. The results of the focus group made clear to him that the jurors did not believe the door handle was defective, or at least was not the primary cause of the plaintiff's accident. They were most bothered by the uncertainty of the plaintiff that he was not wearing his seat belt. As a result, the plaintiffs reworked their case theme to address specifically why wearing the seat belt should not be seen as critical to the evaluation. In other words, they chose to address the issue head on instead of waiting for the jurors to uncover it themselves in deliberation.

In another case, the plaintiff had a difficult time getting mock jurors to see the defendant corporation as an evil entity because the corporation employed much of the town and was very well known for its philanthropic efforts and constant assistance to the community. The strategy shifted from "the evil corporation" to the "corporation that, in this instance, had a reckless disregard for the plaintiff." The lawyer then offered the argument that the generous company should be willing to step up to the plate and fix what it had broken, so to speak. This was much more palatable for jurors. Always focused on the truth, there is nevertheless significant impact in how an argument is couched and ultimately presented.

Whose Interests Come First?

Jury consultants seek to recruit enough jurors to create two or three juries because they do not want to trust or rely on the deliberation and decisions of just one jury. With one jury, it is possible that we recruited an aberration or a particular group that comes up with an off-base and wacky result for whatever reason. While that also happens in the real world, this is the time for controlled research. With two or three juries, we have a stronger basis for comparison, which gives us a more realistic sense of the likely result.

Matt, one of our clients, insisted on saving money by not recruiting jurors from the community, and instead bringing in people he knew. I spent hours trying to talk him out of proceeding with his plan, but nothing I said had any effect. He wanted the candor, but in a predictable way and from people he knew and trusted. As he presented his arguments, I watched the group. They were indeed his "fans," hesitant to be critical in their analysis.

This case involved the allegations of several homeowners, all of whom had custom-built houses in a large development. Matt represented the developer. The plaintiffs were alleging poor building foundations and constant leaks in roofs and walls, among other improper construction methods. The owners also alleged that the houses were built on land known to be inappropriate for such buildings. The developer's lawyer knew it would be tough to convince jurors that this situation was not the fault of the developer, who, after all, made a significant profit on the project.

During the mock trial, even Matt's friends seemed quite willing to tell him that they did not think he could overcome the strong evidence against his client. Matt's friends turned out to be exactly right. This defense lawyer ultimately faced a verdict against his client for several million dollars. However, one thing remained consistent: the mock jurors and the real jurors at trial liked and admired Matt. That did not help his client, and he walked away unwilling to see that his own need for fans undermined his client.

The Honored Guests

You may have noticed that jurors are always treated with a degree of respect not necessarily afforded others in the courtroom—specifically lawyers. Jurors are viewed as individuals who are giving up their time to carry out a civic duty. When jury consultants hold focus groups and mock trials, we also make every effort to make jurors comfortable and keep them engaged in the process. Our jurors are paid for their participation, but they can easily lose their interest if we do not provide the right environment. For example, food is important in these situations. We offer icebreakers like coffee and pastries before we begin, and goodies, like candy and peanuts, are available all day. Participants may be a bit nervous when they arrive, perhaps because they are uncertain about what to expect. Food tends to help everyone relax and begin chatting with each other in a familiar atmosphere.

Before we begin the actual work, the jurors complete and sign a confidentiality agreement that tells them that the work they are involved in is about a real case and it is important that they agree not to disclose their participation until after the actual case concludes. Obviously, this is meant to protect the sanctity and quality of the research and protect the clients as much as we can.

We also tell the jurors that they will be observed all day long during proceedings, as well as audio- and video-recorded for further study. The consent form reflects these conditions. The jury consultant functions like a "master of ceremonies," and has a variety of jobs. For example, once we are underway, we read a fact scenario to the jurors and find out if anyone is familiar with or involved in the case. We introduce the lawyer who will deliver the plaintiff's case (in a civil matter) or the prosecutor's case (in a criminal case).

In many situations, jury consultants retreat to a room behind the one-way mirror so they can observe the presentation and make notes about the lawyers' arguments and skills. In a civil case, the plaintiff's case is presented first because at trial, the jurors will hear from the plaintiff first. The way we frame lawyers' arguments is discussed in another chapter, but for now, it is important to know that we want to gather the mock jurors' reactions to the plaintiff's case upon completion of the arguments.

Some consultants gather information only after the completion of all arguments, but our firm likes to know how the jurors are being affected every step along the way. So, first, the plaintiff's lawyer presents the case. If the lawyers want to test reactions to particular witnesses, then their presentations may include videotaped testimony taken from a deposition. We may present visual aids, such as charts, and other demonstrative evidence that jurors can react to. Once the presentation is completed, the jurors are guided by the jury consultant to complete a survey, which measures their reaction to what they have just heard and seen. We are looking for feedback about the clarity of the arguments and how the lawyer is influencing jurors up to that point.

An example that most frequently exemplifies the value of visual assistance to complex points is the visual timeline. A timeline can pull together seemingly disconnected events by tying them together in one place. Color, dotted lines, and symbols are effective ways to show jurors how a series of events transpired. In effect, it forces the other side to respond to a reality being presented not only in words but also in consistent solidifying graphics. In many of my cases, the lawyers like to keep certain key events or consequences covered. As they walk through the timeline, they unveil the key point, permitting the jurors to "follow the bouncing ball" and in many cases, reach the desired conclusion before the lawyer unveils it. In one case, a "smoking gun" document was made part of a timeline as the lawyers illustrated how the impact of the document created a chain reaction throughout the company, which led to significant losses. When the jurors actually got to see and read the document, it served to confirm what the visual graphic was illustrating.

Another lawyer then presents the defense case, including any demonstrative evidence and videotaped testimony they may wish to test. Remember, whether it is the plaintiff or defense that is sponsoring the research, all presenters come from the same firm. The lawyer pretends to be from the other side of the case in order to foster the greatest degree of realism for the jurors. Once again, the mock jurors complete a written reaction to what they have heard.

Because the plaintiff has the burden of proof, he or she is given the opportunity to present a rebuttal argument. This argument must be responsive only to what the defense has presented and cannot open any new doors or present anything that has not been discussed up to that point. Not every focus group provides further argument, but if the defense is conducting the research, for example, we want the plaintiff's case to get an additional opportunity to win the jurors over so we can be more certain of the strength of the defense case we are trying to build. If the plaintiffs were conducting the research, this final phase may be skipped. Following the rebuttal argument, we again measure the reaction.

Sometimes the attorneys want to know exactly which points, or sentences, produce the most intense reactions in the jurors. To gather such data, the jurors are given real-time reaction-measuring dials. This device consists of a little dial that jurors hold in their hand. When we begin, the dial is set in the neutral position; then, as each lawyer presents the argument, the jurors adjust the dial: upward for positive reaction and downward for negative reaction. The dial readings are matched to the specific words spoken at that particular time, which allows us to gauge exactly how jurors react moment by moment. The report we read resembles the readings on a heart monitor attached to hospital patients. We can see the line as it moves up with positive reaction, down with negative reaction, or just maintaining a flat-line position illustrating neutrality.

In most cases, the dials remain at or in a neutral zone. Then there is something said that has a "whammy" impact. In one case, the lawyer described the injuries of his client and when he said, "she will tell you ladies and gentlemen, that the pain felt like going through open-heart surgery without anesthetic...." we watched on the monitor as every dial raced for the highest levels of emotional impact. In one case that included political issues and elements, it was fascinating to watch as those with a liberal bent shifted their dials in agreement with the arguments being made on behalf of the plaintiff, while simultaneously, the more conservative mock jurors shifted their dials in the opposite direction. The same occurred during the defense's presentation. You can see the value of understanding people's preexisting attitudes because this "dial behavior" illustrates that one argument can trigger significant response in many people; the dials show that the responses may be equal in impact, but on opposite ends of the spectrum.

Because they are expensive research tools, reaction-measurement dials can add a few thousand dollars to the cost of the research process and analysis. However, the additional data are often fascinating to lawyers and can prove helpful in drafting the opening statements and closing arguments. You may have seen similar devices used during political debates or speeches. The networks assemble focus groups comprised of typical voters, and as the candidate speaks, these men and women provide positive and negative responses moment to moment. These focus groups are designed to add interest for viewers, but campaign operatives pay close attention, too.

Researchers must be careful not to place too much emphasis on the reactions to individual statements in terms of trial runs. Where a politician is giving a stump speech and there is a consistency in the research in the reactions, the value is clear. But for a one-time presentation, the measured responses are responding not only to the words, but the manner in which those words are spoken and the presentation component may or may not be the same when the actual presentation is made.

Remember that decades-old research has taught us that words are less than 10 percent of the impact of our messages; 90 percent is in the use of voice and body in relating those words. A difference in the manner of presentation, or even the delivery of the same words by a different person, can produce very different responses in people, and therefore on the meters. We often see this difference when different lawyers present opening and closing arguments during mock trials.

Once the presentations are complete, we want the jurors to have a chance to discuss amongst themselves what they have seen and heard. This is the deliberation and it is exactly what the real jury will do. However, in a mock trial, the lawyers, the clients, and the consultants get to watch and listen through a one-way mirror to what the jurors have to say. This is the most fascinating part of the case for the lawyers and their clients because they never get to do this in the real world.

Just as in actual cases, the mock jurors need to be instructed about the law that will guide the deliberative process. Jurors must conduct their deliberations within the framework of the law that the court has determined must be used to reach a verdict. So, in the focus group, the jury consultant takes on the role of judge and reads a set of selected jury instructions, which are based on those that may actually be given to the real jury at trial. Then, the jurors are divided into two or three groups and sent off into separate rooms to deliberate. Following the deliberation, the jury consultant enters the room to explore the dynamics observed during the deliberation. Finally, everyone who wishes to joins the jurors at the end of the day to pull together the events of the mock trial together and answer any remaining questions.

We'll Be Watching

As I mentioned, we usually hold a focus group at a facility that has one-way mirrors that allow consultants and client observers to view the jury deliberations without being seen by the jurors. When such a facility is not available, a camera is put in the room and the consultant and lawyers view the deliberation in a nearby room through a video feed. All this is designed to provide the most realistic setting possible.

From time to time, jurors will remark during their deliberations about the one-way mirror and the fact that their words are being listened to and analyzed by the facilitators who sit on the other side. Sometimes they do it for humor, but sometimes because they need clarification and request help. I recall a situation in Hawaii when the jurors did not react favorably to a lawyer who had flown over from the mainland. They enjoyed making comments about his bad fashion sense. They knew I was listening, but may not have realized that he heard too. He sat quietly and blushed as his colleagues got a good chuckle.

We also watch for the impact of the deliberative process. Is life really like the movie *Twelve Angry Men*, when one juror stands up against the other eleven and one by one turns each of them around to his way of thinking? Realistically, that is probably not going to happen. There will be a different split, and if we have an eleven to one split, it is difficult for that lone juror to hang on to his or her position. It does happen occasionally, though.

An interesting twist is a case in which an individual goes up against "the system" in the hope of tapping into victim sympathy. In the last chapter, I discussed the case that involved a defendant who had been arrested for driving while intoxicated (after she drove into a tree). Her defenses included that her failure to submit to the Breathalyzer test, together with other questionable blood results taken later, did not equate with guilt. You will recall that this woman was willing to pay whatever it took to keep a clear record. Unfortunately, the videotape evidence taken at the time of her arrest made it clear that she had difficulty walking straight, as the officer had instructed her to do, and she also slurred her words.

The community attitude survey provided insight on prevailing attitudes about drinking. No one seemed to care if someone was a drinker or how much he or she drank. In other words, the survey did not illustrate any moral or religious issues associated with drinking alcohol. But in this specific case, mock jurors were clear about their leaning: "She was drunk—*please!*" one juror said. "Just look at that tape. Hey, she's a nice person, but it's so clear. If you did the crime, ya gotta do the time. Sorry."

All in all, we found that a mock jury did not care about the fact that the defendant drank, but they did think she had to pay the price for breaking the law. Sounds like common sense, and it is. This case suggested that even bright lawyers and carefully crafted arguments would have a tough time going up against everyday logic.

In another case, a large corporation claimed that it had been duped by one of its lower-level employees, thereby committing the corporation to a bad deal. The lawyers anticipated that jurors would accept the image of a naïve corporation. They did not. Sometimes, it is useful to confirm through research the immediate reaction that even the researcher has, which is, "Oh please, no one is going to buy this." We don't know until we test it out. In another case, the mock jurors chastised a lawyer for arguing how right his client was when it was clear (at least in this research stage of the case) that he was less than prepared for the case. I recall a juror saying in deliberation, "Oh please, if he wants us to believe him, maybe he should know his own case." That is not the kind of reaction a lawyer wants his own client to hear.

Circumstances do matter to juries. I recall a case in which the defendant, who, with a previous conviction on his record, possessed a firearm in violation of a state law prohibiting convicted felons from knowingly possessing a firearm. The defendant was mentally challenged, having the mental ability of a seven-year-old, and he was not even able to write his name, except with an X. He had the gun because he saw an ad about becoming a detective and he knew that detectives owned guns, so therefore he needed one. He was a harmless individual, but he was in violation of the law. The defense acknowledged at trial that if they were simply going to follow the law, the defendant would have to be convicted. Still, the lawyer asked the jury to look beyond the law and to do what was reasonable and sensible in the situation.

Ultimately, the jurors found the defendant not guilty because during their deliberations they questioned the defendant's capacity to appreciate what he was doing with respect to his gun. Since the law required a mental state of "knowing," the jurors believed they were following the law by finding the defendant not guilty. This case was both interesting and instructive, in that it explored the difference between the letter of the law, so to speak, and the spirit of the law. The case became the subject of a PBS special some years back. The point is that both circumstances and special conditions influence jurors.

Typically, jurors do not refuse to follow the law given to them by the court, but rather will find a way to read and interpret the law in a manner that leads them to their desired verdict. The recent Arthur Andersen trial is a good example. You will recall that the first trial to arise from the Enron fraud matter was the government's case against Andersen. In effect, the jurors were asked to decide whether an entity called Arthur Andersen, through the people who made up its partnership, committed wrongdoing. The charges included improper accounting procedures and fraudulent handling of financial records.

Once the matter went to the jury, the jurors hit a stumbling block in their deliberations. Understanding the need to apply the law given to them by the judge, the jurors in the Arthur Andersen trial asked the court to guide them on the issue of whether they, as a jury, had to find that one person did all the wrongful acts. Or, was it sufficient for them to find that several people who worked for the firm could have played a role in what was ultimately the fraudulent conduct? After all, in a sense, the jury was deciding whether this corporate entity was to be held responsible for wrongdoing through the actions of its human members. Once the judge told them they could read the law to say that they did not have to find one person responsible, the jurors found their way to a guilty verdict. If they had been of one mind at the onset, they may have read and interpreted the law in the same way without coming back to ask for the court's guidance.

The Research Can Be Fallible

As systematic as our research appears, it is not without risk. I once worked on a case where it became clear that the other side had conducted a focus group. We learned about the situation because one of the mock jurors knew the lawyer for our side. She called him after the research project to tell him that she had participated in a focus group. As if that were not bad enough for the party that conducted the research, she asked my client if he wanted her notes and other information about what had happened, what the arguments had been, plus the verdicts. As the lawyer looked at me, he saw my face shift from jury consultant to my other role of ethics commissioner with the Illinois Attorney Disciplinary Commission. He knew exactly what he was going to do. "Thanks, but no thanks," he said. "It's not right. They are entitled to do their research and we will do our own. But thanks for the call."

This lawyer did not want to win in an underhanded way—or even play the game in such a manner. We ask jurors to pledge confidentiality and even sign an agreement that they will keep the procedures confidential, but the human factor always exists, either the "traitor" or "loyalist" factor that we must guard against.

Evaluating the Next Steps

Once the research results are in, we can decide how we want to handle the case. We might choose to go to trial with a case we would otherwise have expected to settle, or vice versa. In order to determine the next step, we need our client to craft the arguments for the other side and present them to the jury. Writing the adversarial arguments is probably the easier task when compared to writing your own argument. Lawyers know the weaknesses of their own cases better than anyone else. They may know of a smoking gun the other side is not yet aware of. Or, they may recognize a weakness that the other side has not yet perceived. This knowledge allows the lawyer to draft a stronger opposing argument than the actual opposing side is capable of at that time. In one case, my clients in a product-liability case were concerned that the defendants would focus their defense on particular instructions in the manual that accompanied a piece of machinery. While the instructions were certainly part of the case, it was not the center of the defense's arguments. Instead, the defendants kept pointing their fingers at improper training, which the plaintiffs were prepared to address.

We want the strongest possible adversarial arguments presented because the best way to learn about our case is to put all the weaknesses in front of the jury. These mock jurors represent the best tool to help us learn ways we can fix our weak points and strengthen our overall case.

This is why losing the focus group is the best result because it gives us the best information about improving our case. Lawyers do not really want to learn nothing more than how wonderful they or their case is.

What the Mock Jurors Think

As part of the process, our recruited jurors complete a lengthy survey, which gathers their existing (or more realistically, preexisting) attitudes and values about all relevant issues in the case. This information might include knowledge of certain medical information if the case involves alleged malpractice. Or, if the case involves pedestrians and accidents, then perhaps consultants will gather information about traffic signage or public-transportation companies.

These surveys gather a significant amount of information, but this is necessary for a thorough analysis once the project is complete. Survey data will be evaluated along with the information gathered from the case presentations. At the time participants complete a lengthy survey, they don't know what lies ahead of them for the day, so we can expect that their answers are not biased by the information presented later about the case itself.

A Closer Look at Jury Instructions

Within our system, a behavior isn't anything until we give it a definition under the law. This definition guides the deliberation and often determines the verdict. In a criminal scenario, jurors would be instructed to consider all of the evidence presented in the case and also remember that the burden of proof rests solely on the prosecution. The instructions would make it clear that the defendant has nothing to prove and that he has no responsibility to testify or offer anything in his defense. In that regard, the jury would be instructed that if the prosecution does not prove every element of the case beyond a reasonable doubt, then the defendant is entitled to walk free.

When people watch trials on television, they typically decide on a gut level, based on media coverage, whether they believe a defendant is guilty of the crime he is accused of. They wonder how a subsequent verdict seems to go against common sense, at least common sense as they see it. When they are watching a trial—or selected pieces of a trial—they may put aside the idea of the state's burden of proof in a criminal case. Since they are disinterested viewers, they are allowed to do that. They may become caught up in the drama of the trial and declare guilt or innocence based on what *should* make sense in light of what they view as either overwhelming or "underwhelming" evidence. In many situations, trial observers find the concept of the state's burden of proof just too difficult to accept, so since they have no stake in the case, they can easily dismiss it.

If you recall, two brothers, Eric and Lyle Menendez, admitted to killing their parents. I suppose they could have defended the case by claiming an intruder got into the house, but the evidence was clear (including a confession by Eric) that such a claim would not prove convincing. So they talked about the emotional, physical, and even sexual abuse they endured for years. In their first trial, the prosecution did not address that defense very well, and instead focused on the horrendous nature of the crime. It seemed any reasonable juror would see how guilty they were. But the jurors in the first case hung. Those men and women could not reconcile the crime with the alleged abuse because of the burden-of-proof issue. In other words, in the first trial the prosecution failed because they did not address all the issues. Decisions about what issues to emphasize and address become important when crafting theories and defenses. This is where strategy, the game-like approach lawyers must take, comes in.

I worked in another case where an important part of the alleged crime consisted of the conviction that the defendant acted "knowingly." What does that mean? It means that he must have recognized what he was doing. If he was intoxicated at the time, could he act knowingly? You can see how laypeople get frustrated when verdicts do not reflect public sentiment. However, lawyers, judges, and juries have a very specific job to do, which is to determine if the defendant's behavior is proven beyond a reasonable doubt to reach the requirements set forth by the laws selected as those that were breached.

Think of the public disgust directed toward Judge James Warren, the judge in the San Francisco dog-mauling case. Two dogs killed the victim, Diane Whipple; the jury found the defendant, Marjorie Knoller, guilty of second-degree murder. Knoller's husband, Robert Noel, was found guilty of manslaughter. The public loved those verdicts, but expressed shock when Judge Warren reversed the second-degree murder conviction. He found that the evidence did not prove beyond a reasonable doubt that Knoller knew her dogs would fatally attack Diane Whipple. The proof did not rise to the level required by the statute involved in the case.

When the judge announced his decision to set aside the verdict, he said (as reported in the court record), "This does not in any way excuse or change the horror of what happened....I don't believe there is anybody in San Francisco who would rather not see Ms. Knoller go to prison for second-degree murder...." But, in his opinion, the state did not meet its burden and he saw no other options. Judge Warren's actions represent both the painful reality and the safety of our legal system, whose built-in checks and balances allow for the judge's discretion.

Strategy is equally important in civil cases, even though the burden of proof is different. In such a case, the jury decides which position is more likely. In a criminal case, "likely" does not carry much weight. But in a civil case, whichever position triggers the better than 50 percent position or leaning wins.

Common Sense and the Law

Research in legal cases is critical because what appears to be common sense may not necessarily produce an expected or hoped-for result. Based on experience, we know that legal instructions directly influence jury deliberation and verdict.

It is fascinating to watch the jurors deliberate because, to coin a phrase, "Jurors say the darndest things." Earlier I mentioned a case that took place in Hawaii. It involved a conflict between the property owners and the insurance company that held the policy on an old building. All the lawyers involved in that case were local counsels except for one, and he had traveled from the mainland to represent a defendant. In actuality, he was a member of the plaintiff's team, and in the focus group he was designated to play the role of the other side.

As I mentioned earlier, all legal arguments and evidence aside, the jurors could not get beyond their dislike for his clothing. "Where *did* he get that *jacket?*" and "Wasn't it pitiful?" were actual phrases that were repeated during early deliberations. I mention this case again, because eventually, the jury did address the evidence. They had to decide the intent of the insurance company when it made certain payments but refused to make others. They had to determine if the insurance company's acts were proper within the scope of the law presented to them. Some jurors believed that the insurance company (represented by the adjusters and other claims folks who appeared before them in the focus group) was interested in preserving the property and the heritage. Others thought this was about simple economics and there was little concern for preservation.

The lawyers and party involved learned a great deal about how they were perceived by these men and women, who were a good match for the type of individuals who would ultimately hear this case. Yes, jurors can be ruthless, even though they do know they are being observed. There is safety beyond that one-way mirror. Put differently, maybe that is a one-way mirror to true feelings, but that is what the clients are paying to learn. As odd as it sounds, the lawyer's jacket still kept coming up. Superficial details may influence a case in ways we cannot know unless we do research.

By the way, these types of reactions and findings regarding personality and clothing are not unusual. In the O.J. Simpson criminal case, the prosecution conducted focus groups in Arizona where jurors similar in life values and attitudes to those anticipated in Los Angeles would likely be found. These focus-group jurors had real distaste for prosecutor Marcia Clark's hairstyle and clothing. This kind of information is often insulting and hard to take, but you may remember that by trial time, Clark showed up with a new wardrobe and hairstyle.

Taken together, these superficial concerns may lead some clients to ask the jury consultant to present both sides of a case. They do not want to hear about the influence of that day's clothing or hairstyle. Their concern is a well-crafted theory and argument, and if that means using a consultant to present both sides, then at least they have equalized the negatives.

Testing the Tools

The best focus-group experiences teach lawyers something about the case at hand, but also provide insights about thought processes and the way jurors evaluate information. In the van-explosion case I mentioned earlier, I was working with the lawyers who represented the orphaned children. The action against the vehicle designer and manufacturer was quite emotional, but to award money, the jury would ultimately need to look beyond the emotion. Could the jurors find a causal connection between the explosion and problems in the design and manufacture? During the focus groups, the plaintiff's lawyers wondered about the impact of an animation videotape they had hired some engineering experts to create. Was it persuasive, or would jurors react negatively to what at that time could be seen as an expensive trial tool? Would this video suggest that the plaintiffs were already well-off and did not need money? The results surprised everyone.

During the deliberations, which followed the presentation of all the evidence, one of the jurors spoke up. He was an elderly man named Lee who sat rather quietly, until he said, "You know, I am not an educated person. I am certainly not an engineer. But for almost fifty years I have been a car mechanic, and I can tell you that the animation tape was just wrong. Metal doesn't bend up like they showed in that tape. It wouldn't have happened that way. While I think the defendant is still responsible, that tape doesn't help the plaintiff's case in terms of who did it."

Lee was right, and all the highly paid experts ate crow. They had to quickly revise the animation to better reflect, maybe not what they thought was the case, but what this old-time mechanic knew from his experiences in life. The case went to trial, and the defendants knew they had an uphill battle. You will recall that during the jury selection, the jurors in this pro-plaintiff community gave the defense counsel a tough time. While the defense counsel pleaded with prospective jurors to listen to "our side of the story," those jurors were not going to let orphans go home empty handed.

What actually happened was that prior to the real jury returning with its verdict, the defendant offered five million dollars to settle the case. The plaintiffs accepted the offer as the jury deliberated. Curiosity usually gets the best of lawyers, so the jurors (who indicated they were close to reaching a verdict) were allowed to complete their deliberation. Their verdict meant nothing because the case had settled, but the jury award was eleven million dollars. For the plaintiffs, this was not good news, although they still enjoyed the satisfaction that they had agreed to a healthy settlement. For the defense, the reaction was, "Whew, close call."

No one knows what a jury will actually do, and in this case both sides were satisfied that they were acting in the best interests of their clients. From our perspective, we learned that nothing is a more powerful guide for jurors than their common sense and life experiences, and attorneys better not ignore juror comments during focus-group research. It also shows the importance of trial tools such as videotapes and charts.

What's with the Youth of Today?

We always learn something from focus-group jurors. Sometimes, like the auto mechanic, a juror teaches us something specific. Other times, we learn we cannot teach or reach a specific kind of juror. This is important information to have when the actual jury-selection process gets underway. For example, I once worked with the plaintiffs in another automobile-accident case in which the plaintiff was an elderly man who was struck while in his small pickup truck. He was thrown from the vehicle because, as the lawsuit contended, of a faulty locking mechanism in the driver-side door. The evidence also included the possibility that the driver was not wearing his seat belt; he just didn't recall. He knew he did not like the seat belt, finding it too restrictive, but had no exact memory of whether he wore it that day or not.

The focus-group jury included two Generation Y jurors, meaning these jurors were in their twenties. They were convinced that the plaintiff was not wearing his seat belt, and as a result, was solely responsible for his injuries. Research has taught us that this newest generation of eligible jurors tends to bring very conservative views to the jury box.

Far less liberal than their parents, these younger men and women bring a skeptical life value with them, as a general rule. Our research concern was whether there was any way to convince them to overlook or otherwise set aside the seat belt concern.

As it turned out, there was no way they would do so. When I facilitated the discussion after the deliberation, I offered a set of scenarios including: What if this was your mother who was thrown from the car? How about your best friend with you in the driver seat? Nothing pulled them from the position: "You don't follow the law, you pay the consequences. We are all responsible for our own actions." The case settled because a trial was deemed too risky.

In a criminal case involving the sale of marijuana, it was interesting to see the lack of interest in some younger mock jurors. They had a tough time seeing anything particularly wrong in the conduct. At the same time, they were among the first to recognize that they were to follow the letter of the law, so they ended up being tough on the defendant. Liberal social attitudes do not always overcome the more conservative attitudes about personal responsibility that younger jurors tend to bring to the process.

Evaluating the Verdict

It is irrelevant whether or not the focus-group jury reaches a verdict, except that everyone is always curious to know whether they have "won or lost" the focus group. Participants' comments and measurements of the mock jurors' leanings are really all that matter. Again, the most useful focus groups are the ones my clients lose, because that scenario has the most to teach us. However, after several negative focus-group responses, we may learn that the client is not likely to see victory in the case. This is equally important and may drive attempts to settle. After all, we do not need to disclose the results of our research, and we use whatever bargaining position we have available to us.

In other situations, a focus-group experience may clarify what arguments were going to win the day. I once worked on a case in which the government had condemned some property for the purpose of legally taking over the land for a particular use. The owners of the land ran a boat-storage facility near the old entrance to a marina and claimed that they were not offered a fair-market value for the property. As a result, they claimed that they were denied due process by the government to recoup the value of the half-acre of land that was being condemned by the city for the purpose of building a marina overpass.

In actuality, the government offered very little for the property. In fact, when the ordeal began in the early 1990s, the owners were offered about six thousand dollars for the land. The property owners were very angry because the land not only had a greater value, but would be used as a location for a casino. You can well imagine the projected income. The government did not agree that this property was a good location for a casino, hence the low assessment of the land's value. The relationship between the plaintiff landowners and the government was contentious to say the least. While the courts upheld the appropriateness of the government taking of the land for the overpass, court appraisers estimated the land to be worth closer to a million dollars.

The lawyers for the property owners had hoped to increase the value through a verdict award by at least several hundred thousand dollars. The focus group was the tool chosen to assist in case and theory development. It became clear that jurors were greatly affected by landowners' rights to do as they pleased with their property. This case happened to take place in the South, and the attitudes toward government power and land ownership may differ from attitudes in other sections of the country, rural or urban. The focus-group men and women were willing, in this situation, to see the government as wrong and acting improperly. One day of research gave the plaintiffs (with whom I was working) the guidance they needed, which resulted in an award at trial of five million dollars for the plaintiff property owners. I guess we could conclude that the focus group was well worth the time and money.

When the consultants meet with the jury after the deliberation, they focus their inquiry in order to gather a variety of opinions. We always ask the following questions:

1. What were the strongest arguments presented by the plaintiffs? The defendants?

2. What were the weakest points made by the plaintiffs? Defendants?
3. What suggestions do you have for the plaintiffs? Defendants?
4. Did you like the lawyers? Not like them? Why and why not?
5. What questions do you still have about this case? (Participants always want to know who brought them in for the research, but I guide them to the substantive issues. What is unclear or confusing about the case itself?)
6. Is there anything else you want the parties in this case to know?

Answers to these questions provide our clients with key information that may tip the scale in their favor. Again, to paraphrase Art Linkletter, *adults* say the darndest things. Over the years, I have seen jurors lose their inhibitions when they sense the research is over (which it is not), and let their hair down. "Well, I think that defense lawyer is awfully cute...is he married?" "Lose that tie!" "I thought that lawyer was an energy vampire. Whatever interest I had in the case, he sucked out of me in about ten seconds!" "Did he know his zipper was open? Because I couldn't stop staring at his...well, you know...." Some of these lines might be funnier if real cases weren't on the line.

Before we end the day with the jurors, we ask them to complete one final survey, which helps us gather their final and perhaps residual thoughts about the case. Finally, in many focus groups, the lawyers who have made presentations come into the room for a free-flowing discussion with the jurors. I always encourage my lawyer-clients to do this, even though their feelings may be all over the map about this part of the process. As I mentioned, some lawyers become so angry because of negative juror comments they do not even want to meet with them. Others simply want to tell the jurors all the reasons why they were wrong. However, most lawyers welcome the opportunity to clear up some issues in their own minds and then answer questions jurors may have for them.

Focus-group jurors always have questions, and invariably their first is, "Which side are you *really* on?" No matter what side the lawyer says, assuming they choose to disclose it, and most do, the jurors respond, "I *knew* it!" This is usually not true, because most lawyers do such a fine job of representing the other side that the jurors usually believe they represent the opposition. What is interesting is that many jurors spend much of the day wondering whether the two sides of the lawsuit are working together. I also find that many lawyers say at the onset that they do not want the jurors to know who has brought them to the research. But, after a long day of interesting and invaluable insights, once the lawyers join the jurors they will typically disclose the truth. There is a sense of trust and confidentiality that emerges from the work and the process.

The goal of the jury consultant is easily defined. We want to offer our lawyer-clients advice on case theme and presentation. We want them to know what arguments and theories worked and what did not. We provide suggestions and tips on what to do and what to avoid. And perhaps most important, we take a look at the results in concert with the community attitude survey results; all the data can now be integrated to provide the lawyers with some of the most powerful information of all: Who is a desirable juror in this case? We'll discuss the answer in the next chapter.

chapter 4

A Match Made in Heaven...Or at Least in Science

"How can you represent a guilty person?" This may top the list of questions people ask lawyers. It is a particular favorite of law students, many of whom approach law school as idealistic young people. Sooner or later they find themselves not only responding to the query, but wrestling with the answer, too. Of course, to criminal-defense lawyers, this question is essentially a no-brainer, but the problem is, most people neither like nor understand the answer.

The *real* question in a criminal case is not whether the defendant actually committed the crime of which he or she is accused. Most criminal-defense lawyers will admit that more often than not, their clients have done something wrong, and probably have committed the particular act or participated in the behavior or activity alleged. However, these assumptions aside, the real questions in a criminal case are:

1. What crime, specifically defined by a statute, does the conduct that is alleged to have occurred by the defendant actually constitute?
2. Is the prosecution able to prove every element of that alleged and defined crime beyond a reasonable doubt?

These questions are at the heart of every criminal case. For most people, the idea of a defined crime is where the confusion starts, but the concept is at the heart of the legal system. Suppose your friend Al taps, hits, or slaps you on the wrist. Even the particular word I choose to describe the conduct makes a difference. Let's say you hope the state will prosecute Al for the crimes of assault and battery—assault for putting you in imminent fear of harm or injury to yourself and then following through with an offensive contact or touch (the battery). Al says he doesn't even recall touching you until he sees the photo of the action, and then he clarifies some reasons for the touch. Perhaps he explains his action as one intended to protect you, or to show warmth, or for some other equally benign reason. He talks about your one-year friendship. All in all, he is stunned that he would be accused, much less found guilty, of any such crime.

When prosecutors analyze a set of actions, they have to process it through a framework that in a sense matches conduct with specific definitions of a range of crimes. In Al's case, they would start with a contact of some sort between Al's hand and your arm. However, what that conduct means or how is it defined or constituted under the law is the critical issue. You may allege that Al's action constitutes the elements of assault and battery as I defined them, but to prosecutors, Al's conduct (a mere tap) does not rise to the level of instilling fear of bodily harm. In order to charge and prosecute a criminal matter, the prosecutors would have to have a good-faith belief that Al's conduct could be shown to a jury or judge to rise to the level of "beyond a reasonable doubt." On the other hand, prosecutors may find a reason to look through all the statutes and definitions to determine what else they could call Al's action under the law. For example, you mentioned that after Al's tap you couldn't find your wallet, so Al's action could lead to a charge of robbery, with all the previous conduct being part of that larger alleged crime.

Obviously, I am simplifying the process, but the concept remains important. In a criminal matter, we don't start by defining and talking about the crime alleged; rather, we focus on the behavior, conduct, or actions as we attempt to apply to it the legal description or definition.

Second, the prosecution has the duty to prove beyond a reasonable doubt each element of the crime with which they have charged the defendant.

Trial consultants step outside of the specifics of the crime charged and take a more global perspective; that is, without the trappings of legal definition, we look at the facts of a case and consider alternative ways those facts might be interpreted by a judge or jury. There may well be viable alternative explanations for a set of events or actions. If the lawyers do not take time to explore the possibilities, then maybe the jury will do so when it counts, and that will cost one side or the other the case. Realistically, consultants who work in criminal cases become involved once charges are filed and the laws for which violations are alleged have been decided. On the defense side, the consultant can already see where the bar has been set, so to speak, and focus their efforts on alternative views of the facts.

In a murder case I worked on, the defendant was accused of committing a series of gruesome murders where he dismembered the bodies of his female victims, placed large objects in the vaginal cavities, and left the bodies to be found in a mutilated state. The defendant pleaded his innocence and had an alibi provided by his girlfriend, who said she was with him at the time of the latest murder, the one for which he was on trial. Given what was known about the time of death, and the whereabouts of the victim at various times that evening, it appeared that the defendant could not have committed the crime.

We worked with the defense lawyers to craft the opening statement that presented a timeline that kept the defendant away from the neighborhood in which the crime occurred. Ultimately, jurors would face questions of proof, wanting to see for themselves the telephone records, for example, that could confirm the defendant's story. Unfortunately, the defense team could produce no such records, which made the case much more difficult to present. It is not easy to craft an alibi without concrete proof that jurors can hang their hats on in deliberation. Yet this alternative view of the facts formed the critical element.

Why Are Charges So Complex?

You may have heard legal analysts discuss the criminal charges in great detail because the chances of winning or losing a case may hinge almost entirely on the charge filed. These discussions can become quite emotionally charged because great controversy can surround the charges themselves. For example, a murder victim's family may be appalled when what they assumed would be a first-degree murder charge is dropped to manslaughter. Most likely, prosecutors do not believe they have the evidence to prove the intent required for a conviction of first-degree murder, but they do believe they can prove the conduct can be seen at a minimum as reckless and therefore rising to the level of manslaughter. The punishment will be less than for first-degree murder, but achieving conviction may be much more certain. Meanwhile, the family may be emotionally attached to the idea that this was murder.

Is it Murder, Manslaughter, or Self-Defense?

The facts in an old case, *Crawford v. State,* illustrate the confusion surrounding actions and subsequent charges. Crawford was a forty-two-year-old man who suffered from nervous disorders. He lived in a rooming house and was constantly harassed by two young men named Farrell and Austin, who had robbed Crawford on more than one occasion. One day, they saw Crawford and they taunted him by saying they'd soon be back to get his disability check. Crawford called the police, but they could do little for him based on this threat. So Crawford took matters into his own hands. Before the letter carrier got to his house, Crawford stopped him and got his mail, including his check. He went to the usual place to cash it, but he kept part of the money so he could buy a shotgun from a pawnshop. Then he returned home. Sure enough, Farrell and Austin came to his room, one covering each of the two doors to the apartment. Farrell attempted to get into the front door. Crawford shouted a warning that he had a gun and urged them to leave. Farrell got his hand inside the door and Crawford, claiming to be aiming for Farrell's hand, shot and hit Farrell in the head, an action that killed him instantly. Crawford was charged with murder, but was found guilty of manslaughter in a bench (judge only, no jury) trial.

In this case, the judge decided that the prosecution couldn't prove all of the elements that were required to find that murder had been committed. While Crawford thought out and executed his actions, the judge was not convinced that Crawford intended to murder anyone, or that he had planned such a crime. Rather, it appeared (and was claimed by the defense) that the gun was intended for self-defense. Crawford warned Farrell and Austin to leave but they didn't take him seriously. Still, the judge found that Crawford did shoot the gun, that such action was excessive in the situation, and that Crawford should have realized what could result from his actions. These elements justified finding that the crime of manslaughter had been met beyond a reasonable doubt.

If you sat on a jury in this case, knowing the facts as I have related them, you probably would consider what you might do in the same situation and perhaps conclude that you might have shot Farrell out of fear for your own safety. Jurors will let these considerations run through their minds, too, but ultimately, the verdict must meet the standard of proof for every element of the crime. The issue comes down to credibility, in that Crawford is either trying to save his own neck, so to speak, or truly did aim for Ferrell's hand and accidentally hit him in the face.

In this kind of situation, a victim's family may be outraged that prosecutors cannot prove a murder charge, and individuals in the district attorney's office who are working on the case may agree, at least in spirit. But when prosecutors lose a case, analysts may point to what they call "overcharging" (of the crime) as the reason for the loss. In general, prosecutors prefer to get a conviction on a lesser charge than see a defendant walk free because they were unable to prove a case.

The actual point is that there is no reality except that which is created and argued, and in the Crawford case, the judge's verdict was appealed. On appeal, the higher court decided that Crawford should not have been found guilty of either manslaughter or murder. They determined that individuals have the right to protect themselves in their homes and have no duty to retreat from the place they live. Therefore, Crawford could take whatever action was necessary to protect himself while in his apartment. In the appellate court's opinion, Crawford's action was not excessive. The verdict was reversed and Crawford was released.

The actual events in Crawford's case occurred as described. Farrell and Austin harassed Crawford. He bought the shotgun. He probably warned them away and maybe he really did mean to aim for Farrell's hand, not his head. The facts are what they are, but what those facts constituted is an exercise of definition and proof. The prosecution believed the conduct was murder; the judge believed it was manslaughter, and the appellate court found it defensible action under the circumstances. Reality emerges from interpretation and perception.

Guilty of What?

Let's go back to your friend Al and his (according to you) ill-considered touch. Clearly, the prosecutors are unlikely to go forward if you ask them to charge Al with attempted murder. Putting the reasoning in legal language, prosecutors can't prove to a judge or a jury that Al "intended to have you die from his conduct and pursued and performed that action with such intent." So, even if they file charges against Al, they would likely go with a case that includes elements they can actually prove beyond a reasonable doubt.

In criminal law, decisions about what charges will hold up have consequences for all concerned, including the jury. You may recall the tragic case that became known as the "nanny trial." While I did not work in that case, I provided commentary for MSNBC during the proceedings, so I kept a close watch on the strategies and day-to-day events of the trial.

In that case, jurors were challenged to determine if the nanny, Louise Woodward, had, through actions that were related to "shaken baby syndrome," caused the death of eight-month-old Matthew Eappen, the younger of the Eappens' two children. The charges filed became critical to the outcome of the case because prosecutors advocated giving the jurors choices, including first- and second-degree murder and manslaughter. Manslaughter would have allowed the jurors to find that Woodward had abused the baby, but had not premeditated her actions or had the intention of hurting the child. However, the defense team pushed to have manslaughter removed from the possible verdicts, choosing instead to force a choice between the more difficult to prove murder charges and acquittal. At one point in the trial, however, the prosecution team asked the judge to instruct the jury on the lesser manslaughter charge. The defense then had to decide if they should oppose the prosecutor's request, thereby gambling that the jury would not find the evidence strong enough to justify a conviction on first- or second-degree murder.

In the end, the judge granted the defense's request to keep manslaughter off the table, and the jury's choices remained restricted. In a sense, both sides in this tragic case had to roll the dice, so to speak. If we examine the thinking behind the charges filed, we can see that prosecutors originally believed that they could prove that the nanny had acted with malice and extreme cruelty, elements of first-degree murder, but proving premeditation was a different story. Hence, they gave the jury the option of finding Woodward guilty of second-degree murder, in which premeditation is not an element.

A less experienced defense team, or solo lawyer, might not have seen the important strategy of keeping manslaughter off the table. If there was a strong fear that Woodward could face conviction of murder, the possibility of manslaughter would provide a point of compromise that, while subjecting the defendant to a prison term, saved her from a more harsh sentence associated with murder conviction. This defense team was fairly certain that murder was a long shot for the prosecution to prove. The sympathies of a jury worked in her favor as well. By keeping manslaughter out, the burden on the prosecution was in effect increased because they had nowhere to fall back on. In a real sense, it became an all-or-nothing case. The decision is strategic, shrewd, and, candidly, takes guts both on the lawyers' part and also on the part of the defendant Louise Woodward, who almost certainly had to sign off on the call. I suspect she made her decision more on her faith in her legal team than on her own sense or understanding of what charges she thought the prosecution could prove.

This case is important because it provides a look at the kind of decisions defense attorneys regularly make. Because it was a highly publicized trial, the strategies were dissected for the public on a daily basis. At one point, every evening news and commentary program on cable television had extensive analysis of the Woodward case. The defense team included the well-known lawyer Barry Scheck. Scheck had entered the public consciousness because he had worked on the Simpson defense team. Prior to that case, he had established a reputation as an advocate for DNA testing to revisit cases in which the convicted felons maintained their innocence. I have met Scheck on several occasions and I must note that he is a very sincere, dedicated man. He is often criticized for his efforts on behalf of certain defendants, which is not an unusual response when individuals are powerful advocates. However, Barry is an impressive man precisely because he is dedicated to making certain that the system works as it should and must.

In the Woodward case, Scheck and the rest of his team argued that their client was innocent of *any* charge related to Matthew Eappen's death. They could not accept a verdict of manslaughter because that would assign a degree of responsibility to Louise Woodward. The defense had established its position that Woodward was innocent and, therefore, could not engage in debates about degrees of guilt. Again, this position was strategic and risky, but the defense team climbed out on that particular limb.

The Woodward case also illustrates the way particular criminal trials become media events. This case contained many emotional elements that intensified throughout the trial. Obviously, the death of an infant is a horrible event and causes an intense emotional climate. In addition, Louise Woodward came from England, and the British press had a strong interest in the case and raised the issue of the fairness of the trial. In general, the British press proclaimed Woodward's innocence, and daily newscasts included footage of demonstrations in England that showed unfailing support for Woodward. As the case progressed, public opinion polls tended to run in favor of Woodward.

When the jury came back with a guilty verdict for second-degree murder, it looked as if the defense had gambled and lost. Second-degree murder carries a life sentence, but with the possibility of parole. Woodward was facing a long prison term and the defense team began planning its appeals. But then an odd thing happened. You may remember that Louise Woodward never went to prison because the judge exercised a seldom-used power and reduced the jury's verdict to manslaughter. Then he sentenced her to time served, which meant Woodward was free to go home—and indeed, she immediately returned to England. Naturally, the judge's decision triggered relief in some quarters and outrage in others. Of most interest, the very position rejected by the defense was the one that saved their client from serving years in prison. In other words, the defense, convinced that the jury would never return with a murder verdict, left the jury with no choice but to set their client free. The jury was not about to let Woodward off the hook. Yet, since they had no other option for conviction other than murder, it was the judge who had the power to set that verdict aside and determine the ultimate sentence for a lesser offense and determine that the prison time would be only the time already served. In effect, the defense won the case in spite of themselves; it was the judge who saved the day for Louise Woodward. The law works in mysterious, but legal ways.

So, was the jury wrong? Did the prosecutor overcharge the case in the beginning? Was the defense team's gamble a mistake? Who proved what to whom? Some jurors in the Woodward case spoke publicly about their dilemma. They believed the nanny was responsible to some degree for the death of the infant; these men and women might well have been satisfied to find her guilty of manslaughter, but they didn't have that choice. Jurors were stunned when the judge overturned their verdict, although he took pains not to criticize the jury's verdict. The prosecutors believed they won their case, regardless of what the judge determined.

The Eappen case illustrates how tricky the issue of filing charges can be. In another circumstance, with a similar set of facts, a case may never reach the trial stage. Every day across the country, prosecutors offer a manslaughter charge and the defense might agree to a particular prison term, thereby avoiding a trial. The prosecution could present the manslaughter charge, knowing that they could go to trial on a murder charge and stand a chance of winning. The defense accepts a plea agreement in order to avoid a trial and the risk of a life sentence.

Indirectly, the Eappen case leads back to the question of how criminal defense lawyers can represent guilty people. Because crimes must be defined and each element proved, then the question becomes, "guilty of what?" Despite popular opinion, the goal of defense lawyers is not to put guilty people back on the streets. Their role in our system is quite easily stated: their job is to ensure that whatever conduct occurred and however it becomes defined and charged by the prosecution, it must be proved beyond a reasonable doubt. Their job is to challenge each branch of the prosecution, starting with the arresting officers, in order to be certain that everyone involved with the prosecution has done what they are required to do. They make sure that every procedure is carried out properly, that is, within the technical and ethical boundaries of the law.

What Would Happen If…?

In some cases, such as the Eappen case, the criminal-defense lawyer steadfastly maintains the client's innocence, and the issue of plea agreements or negotiating for a lesser charge are not on the table. Regardless, their task is essential to the very existence of our legal system. Without this role, or without the burden of proof placed on the prosecution, any one of us could be taken into custody based on mere rumor and then jailed for life—or even executed. Looked at another way, the ordinary accidental-death case could be charged as manslaughter, or actions taken in self-defense could be charged as first-degree murder and no one would provide the "check" in our system of checks and balances.

A legal system that does not include the defense side is not a system at all, but takes on the trappings of a dictatorship. Or, it is a system influenced by fleeting public opinion and passions of the moment. Much of the world supports the overthrow of this kind of system, most recently in Afghanistan, where Taliban rule was just as I have described. Any rumor that individuals were in violation of a rule or law, and they could be instantly executed, beaten, or thrown into prisons. Of course, the Taliban did not invent such a system. Over the course of human history, harsh justice dominates. However, because we have put the defense component of our system at center stage, we must wrestle with the difficulty of preserving everyone's rights, even those accused of a crime.

Sadly, we can look back through all of political history, including our own, to see what happens when the prosecutor's burden is relaxed or when we allow public opinion to dominate a legal proceeding. Even with our legal protections and safeguards, the U.S. rounded up Japanese-Americans during World War II just because we were at war with Japan. Clearly, unjust arrests and convictions have taken place in our country, often because community or individual biases allowed these notable miscarriages of justice. If we instituted any less "muscular" burden of proof on the state, we could almost guarantee that countless innocent people would be prosecuted and convicted for crimes they never committed.

A criminal defense lawyer would argue that if a guilty person goes free because the police set him up improperly, planted evidence, or didn't properly handle evidence, then in this country that accused person *must* go free. When this happens, it looks like what victims, reporters, and the general public call a "travesty." Viewed another way, a strong message is sent to all arms of the prosecution team that they better follow proper procedures and protocol.

When the Penalty Is Money

In the world of civil cases, some people frown on plaintiffs' lawyers and refer to them as "ambulance chasers." Some believe that few people are actually entitled to monetary awards regardless of what happened to them. Along with this assumption, many individuals maintain that we are all responsible for our own safety and welfare, and therefore, civil trials are by definition just a way the greedy look for a free lunch. On the other hand, many citizens believe that our legal system is the only way an average citizen has any hope and chance of getting money (much less anything else) out of what they perceive to be cold and uncaring corporations.

I have worked in some of the tobacco cases that cause so much controversy. These cases broke new ground in issues of liability and personal responsibility and tended to provoke powerful emotions. In one, a smoker who died of cancer was awarded three billion dollars. Now that made a point.

Or, a man is driving along in his car and is hit from behind by another car. He claims he has serious injuries but he has no broken bones, no bumps, no bruises. In fact, he has no tangible evidence to prove the injuries except for his claim, along with testimony that he's been in pain ever since the accident. Ultimately he is awarded nothing for his claim. I have handled many of these cases in arbitration and in uninsured motorist cases. The point is that assertions involving the presence of pain are hard for decision-makers to accept without some objective finding or support for the injury. People do exaggerate their claims, as they know this hearing or trial is their one and only chance for an award. But, in reaching beyond what the evidence will support, they actually do themselves a disservice and end up with little or no monetary damages.

Or, let's look at the female forest-preserve police officer who alleged that male forest-preserve officers and supervisors sexually harassed her by placing pornography in her office mailbox and in desk drawers where all the officers worked. One time, she claimed that she pushed away a male officer who pressed his abdomen against her. She was afraid to complain and feared retaliation. Her lawyer asked the jury for $2 million in damages. Does this sound reasonable? Too low? Excessive? Less severe than a person who is injured in a car accident and gets nothing? In this forest-preserve case, heard in 2001, the jury awarded the plaintiff three million dollars. Clearly, they chose to send a message. After the trial was over, one juror said that the supervising department needed to learn that times have changed and it was necessary for them to "catch up" to the new world.

As I have said, there are checks and balances, and the court remitted, or lowered, the verdict in that case to $300,000, with the judge claiming that in his opinion, the evidence did not support the verdict. The judge broke down the award to $200,000 as compensation for emotional distress and $100,000 for damage to the plaintiff's reputation.

The judge, Arlander Keys, wrote, "The court is convinced that the jury missed the mark....The court will not sneak through the backdoor...." In other words, the judge acknowledged that the plaintiff may have proved her case to the satisfaction of the jurors, but emotions could not rule the day and lead to what the judge considered to be a verdict that was way out of line with what the evidence showed at trial. Yet, the jurors certainly did not consider their verdict to be excessive.

Compare this verdict to a New Orleans verdict where a plaintiff widow was awarded $1.4 million in a 2001 case for the wrongful death of her husband and son who were killed when their Winnebago motor home crashed into a tree.

I intentionally put these unrelated cases and verdicts together so you can see that cases, verdicts, and facts are all over the place. Low in some places, high in others. Some awards may seem excessive, while in others the monetary awards may seem inadequate. But each case takes place in its own courtroom where jurors hear a specific set of facts and do not have the opportunity to compare their case to others around the country, requiring them to focus in on the evidence in their own case and evaluate that evidence in accordance with the standards of that community.

I must also clarify that in our system anyone can sue anybody for anything. Ultimately, frivolous cases should get tossed out of the system, but it is amazing how the protections of our system can keep a ridiculous matter on the books for years. A case in point is one in which I represented the unfortunate defendant. My client, Richard, was sued by a man named Hill. Here is an excerpt from the Complaint (amended version, by the way, after the judge dismissed the first complaint and told the plaintiff to make a case) filed against my client:

> the plaintiff who as a victim of harassment and water contamination, is a victim of shocks> I was told by a nearolegist [sic] that I may suffer permanent permanent [sic] brain damages from been [sic] shocked! I was treated for drinking contamination from water from my faucet and injury to my hand and skin when the nerve gas can be fatal...I have been a victim of harassment and shocks to my head. During this time, I was in bed

when the defendant was shocking people with his computer. He should be made to pay.

I could not explain what the complaint said, much less respond to it as I would otherwise be required to do. No one in the courtroom, including the judge, could make heads or tails out of it, but that is not my point. The point is that the complaint itself was indecipherable. But our system protects the unrepresented and the case continued to remain alive in the system for a couple of years.

Time and again I would argue to the judge that the complaint made no sense; the judge would agree and he would dismiss the case, but always providing the unrepresented plaintiff the opportunity to refile an amended complaint in the next month. Time and again, the plaintiff would do so, with each subsequent complaint doing little more than reiterating what had been said in previous incarnations. I could never get the judge to just dismiss the case with prejudice. He would always give the plaintiff another opportunity to amend the complaint. In fact, the presiding judge of the court looked at me one day in court and said, "Expect to try this case, counsel."

"Excuse me, your honor, are you kidding?" I asked.

"No, counsel. But the only way this is going to go away is to try it and get a verdict, so plan on it."

What the judge meant is that he tends to resist ending an unrepresented person's attempts to properly state a legal cause of action and, therefore, would let the process continue. My client, not wealthy himself, could never handle the legal fees he would incur if he were being charged for representation. Even representing him on a *pro bono* basis, meaning waiving the fee, the case remains costly to everyone involved. These situations do indeed "clog" our courts. And so, the system, with all its good intentions, has its flaws. Fortunately for my client Richard, the plaintiff missed his filing deadline and never did file the fourth incarnation of the complaint. Through the work of my colleague Mark Smith, the case and Richard never heard from Hill again.

The protections are less tight in the civil arena because personal liberties are not in jeopardy and, theoretically, not an issue. Of course, if you asked my client how he felt about being forced to go through the motions of the legal process, he believed the entire ordeal was nothing more than harassment of his own personal liberties. But, the law must work through every case, from the simple to the complex and the justified to the indecipherable.

Different Requirements, Different Results

Let's take a moment to pull the criminal and civil worlds together. They are very different actions, but with very different burdens of proof. If you perceive the criminal and civil systems to be incongruent, then let's take a look at this issue by evaluating the seeming disparity of the verdicts in the two O.J. Simpson cases. The Simpson case helps illustrate the way in which jurors must deal with definitions of the law and apply these definitions using the appropriate standard. Even when compared to each other, the results appear to conflict.

Many people are convinced that O.J. Simpson got away with murder, and they can't understand how the jury in the criminal case found him not guilty. Yet, others found it strange that once he was found not guilty, a jury in the civil case could find him "guilty." Actually, in this situation "guilty" is a misnomer. The jury in the civil case found Simpson *liable,* or responsible, for the killings; they did not find him guilty. Lawyers must choose their words carefully, and when we all pay close attention to the words used, what initially appears cloudy can become clear.

In the criminal case, the court instructed the jury that the government had the entire burden to prove Simpson guilty beyond a reasonable doubt. Not "more likely than not" and not "beyond the *shadow* of a doubt," but "beyond a *reasonable* doubt." That represents a very high burden of proof. In a criminal trial, the court also instructed the jurors that Simpson did not have to prove anything at all. One can begin to see how the jurors in the criminal case were left with questions that provided what they considered to be a reasonable doubt. Does that mean that Simpson either did or did not commit the crime? No, it just means that the jurors were not convinced beyond a reasonable doubt. The verdict meant that the prosecution did not meet its burden to prove *every* element of the crimes of which Simpson was accused, and in the absence of doing that, he went free.

In fairness to the jurors, the prosecution drummed that message home to them for weeks and weeks during the jury selection, and during the presentation and arguing of evidence. I sat in that Los Angeles courtroom as again and again Marcia Clark looked at the prospective jurors and said: "If you look at Mr. Simpson sitting there and think he is guilty, then I don't want you here. As he sits there now, he is presumed to be *not* guilty." Television viewers didn't hear this portion of the proceedings, but those jurors sure did and they were sworn to follow the instructions of the court: a defendant is *always* not guilty until proven guilty.

In a civil case, the game has different rules, and the plaintiff's burden (in the Simpson matter, the families of the deceased) is merely to prove their case by a *preponderance* of the evidence. This means more likely than not, which to quantify it, means just a bit more than 50 percent. That is a significant degree below the standard in the criminal case. So, when the jurors found Simpson responsible for the deaths of Ron Goldman and Nicole Brown in the civil case, it is possible to make sense of this verdict, even in the light of what was seemingly an opposite verdict in the criminal case.

What Counts, What Doesn't

Different juries hearing the same facts will do very different things, which is why we, as jury consultants, recruit enough jurors for the focus-group event so that two or three groups of jurors can be created from the pool. (In some cases, even more juror groups are used.) Even though these people will hear the same case, one jury (in a civil case, for example) will award a large amount of money to the plaintiff, while another group just down the hall would send the plaintiff home with nothing. Similarly, in the real world, in order to attempt to predict what a jury will do, the individual dynamics of each jury must be considered. "Chemistry" varies from jury to jury, and demographic factors, such as sex, age, and race of the jurors, are the least predictive components in this process.

Understanding the life experiences of the jurors and even the dynamics of how they interact during the course of deliberations provides more cogent information about what the jury will subsequently do.

The Strange Turnaround of "Mr. Keys"

I worked in a civil case involving claims of racial discrimination against a hotel's management by one of its employees. The defense was pleased with the jury that ultimately was going to decide the case. But, something happened during the jury deliberation that no one could have predicted. One particular juror, a Caucasian man in his forties, had supervisory duties in his blue-collar job and on his belt he wore a key ring with many, many keys. This was a sign of his importance, but even more so, he wore this ring as a sign of self-importance. He was a supervisor and proud of it. During the jury deliberation, he made a comment that some of the black jurors interpreted as racist. This juror did not see himself as a racist, so he was apparently shocked at other jurors' reaction and felt the need to do whatever it took to set things right.

From the jury's reports, this is how the scenario played out: "Mr. Keys" had been a holdout for a defense verdict in the case while several other jurors were prepared to award the plaintiff some money. For most jurors, the dollar amount was an area of compromise, but this juror threatened to hang the jury. But then he made his comment. Some jurors took offense, and Mr. Keys instantly became the plaintiff's biggest proponent. Apparently, he thought the only way he could redeem himself in the minds of the other jurors (and likely to himself as well) was to now award money. So, thanks in large part to this lone juror, the jury returned with a multi-million dollar verdict in favor of the plaintiff.

A key ring full of keys may seem innocuous enough. However, I believe that for this particular person, those keys represented an *individual* characteristic that should have signaled potential trouble to the lawyers. This was a man who would be unable to put his sense of leadership and self-importance aside. So, when he made an error, his lack of education, perhaps combined with his social experiences, led him to conclude that a plaintiff's verdict would resolve the situation and restore his comfort level. This juror might have explored other avenues. For example, he could have apologized and added a statement that his comment, while not intended to insult anyone, would not lead him to compromise his beliefs and opinions in accord with the law of the case they were sworn to follow. This situation illustrates that predictions about juror behavior based on race or some other demographic factor alone often prove to be wrong or at the very least provide insufficient information.

Darrow Being Narrow

Historically (and in movies and novels, too), lawyers have always been concerned about jurors' life views and values, but in past decades that analysis was based on their experience, accompanied by some stereo-typing, assumptions, and gut instincts, with some good luck thrown in. The great trial lawyer Clarence Darrow wrote a great deal about what criminal-defense lawyers should do during jury selection in a criminal case. Darrow's "guidelines" covered men only, since during his time, women did not serve as jurors. Darrow noted that Irishmen are ideal because they are emotional, kindly, and sympathetic. But he also told us that Presbyterians are as "cold as the grave" but know right from wrong. Alas, these Presbyterians seldom find anything right. So, Darrow concluded, lawyers should get rid of Presbyterians before they contaminate the others. Darrow also urged lawyers to choose a person who laughs because Darrow found that jurors who laugh usually hate to find anyone guilty.

I am not contending that Darrow was entirely wrong. He was, after all, one of the greatest lawyers of the twentieth century. I am sure that, based on his experience, he believed such generalizations to be accurate enough to follow during jury selection. In fact, I imagine that many trial lawyers of Darrow's day enthusiastically followed his advice because he was so successful. But taken in global terms, this advice is about as solid as being sure that we don't walk under a ladder or doing an elaborate dance to avoid stepping on a crack in the sidewalk for fear of breaking our mother's back. Perhaps Darrow's advice falls under the category of "better safe than sorry," but none of his generalizations were scientifically grounded; as such, no degree of scientific certainty can guide, confirm, or contradict old assumptions and even instincts. Today, if confronted with a question about Presbyterian jurors, we would respond with something like: "Which Presbyterian? Living where? Sporting which bumper stickers? Reading what magazines?"

I know I frustrated many interviewers during the Simpson case, including Bryant Gumbel, who, during the jury-selection process asked if I thought African-Americans would be desirable jurors for the defense. My answer was always the same: "it depends." Now, that barely-a-sound-bite answer does not make good television. But what person's actions and decisions can be predicted by one single demographic factor? I have worked in criminal cases with African-American defendants in which the toughest jurors on the defendant were members of their own race. I recall one woman saying, "That defense lawyer figured that we would let his guy off just because we were black. No way. He's a bad egg and he needs to pay his debt. I know exactly where he comes from and what kind of people are there. He did it. He needs to pay." Interestingly, she related to the crime and the criminal in a way unlike the Caucasians and those of other ethnicity on the jury. In that case, the defense strategy to select the jury based primarily, if not solely, on the single demographic factor of race backfired in a major way. In fact, this juror was offended at the assertion or assumption that she would allow race to influence her verdict. Of course, that very reaction is a result of life experiences as well, and we will take a closer look at that concept in the next chapter.

It may seem that jury psychologists put aside instincts or gut feelings. But that is not the case. Rather, our work deals in sophisticated probabilities about what a lawyer is likely to find in a particular location for a particular trial. Jury consultants are not likely to specify generalities about the way specific groups of people will act in particular trials. Would every, even many or most, Irish people be sympathetic to criminal defendants? Are members of racial minority populations in the U.S. more likely to accept the testimony of a physician than the majority population? Well, some are, and some fall outside this model. There is little use in making broad, sweeping generalizations.

Individual behavior is often inconsistent as well. We saw this in the Mr. Keys example. Can you always be counted on to act in a predictable way regardless of the circumstances? Are there times you could find testimony from a physician credible and other times not credible at all? Our goal is not to decide how a person will act in every situation.

Generally speaking, demographics have historically performed poorly in social-science models. The problem is not with the characteristics themselves, but in the way social scientists looked at them in the past. For one thing, we live in a different world today, and by and large communities are becoming increasingly diverse. In an article I wrote with my colleague Ron Beaton, "Can You Judge a Jury by Its Cover?" we noted that it is indeed useful for lawyers to rely somewhat on surface characteristics during jury selection. Still, the key to successful jury selection is in the ability to discern subtle patterns that lie beneath the more obvious features of the juror's profile. So, while it is unlikely that any one demographic factor is predictive, the more factors we integrate into the consideration, the more accurately we can predict the way a particular juror will lean.

What is clear is that beyond a specific demographic factor, lawyers and jury consultants need to learn as much as possible about a person's life experiences if they are going to try to predict that individual's behavior as a juror. For that reason, we want to know whatever we can learn about potential jurors and about the case in question. So we want to gather information on gender, age, education level, employment situation and history, economic status, and social information such as the kinds of groups they join and hobbies they pursue, ways they use their free time, and on and on. Then we need to integrate that demographic information with information about the juror's life experiences, attitudes, and values. Not all Asians see life the same way, but an Asian woman in her seventies, a lifelong resident of New York City, with some high-school education, who was interred in an American detention camp during World War II, and who has built a small business through personal effort, sweat, and hard work and...you get the point.

Our life experiences shape our point of view and, in general, our worldview. If we have a bad experience with a group of people, we may assume all individuals within that group are bad. Children raised to see others of all nationalities, races, religions, and so forth are going to view life differently from those whose grandparents and parents have taught them to love some "categories" of people and distrust, fear, or even hate others.

The Process at Work

In one case, a school district sued the manufacturer of asbestos products for putting the dangerous material in buildings. During the 1950s and 1960s, asbestos was used in floor tiles, ceiling texture, and walls in many school buildings. Asbestos is nonflammable and was mixed into these materials to reduce the risk of fire in the schools. Some experts say the presence of asbestos-containing materials poses a health risk to students. Others say that if the materials are not disturbed, no health risk exists. This debate has been the basis for ongoing serial litigation for decades throughout the country.

Based on research using the tools discussed in this book, the ideal defense juror in that case proved to be a middle-aged or older, politically conservative, white (non-Hispanic) Republican person without children under eighteen years of age, and with an annual household income of more than $30,000. People who worked in the contracting field or construction industry who have witnessed the involved and costly process of removing asbestos-containing materials from buildings also tended to sympathize with defendants.

Ideal plaintiff jurors were nearly mirror opposites of this profile, in that they proved to be politically liberal, under the age of thirty-five, non-white, registered Democrats with a household income below $30,000, and also with young children. These people tended to have no experience in the contracting or construction industry. So, you can see how this works. Research points to demographic variables that suggest leaning, but life experience comes into play to help shape the juror profile.

Who and *What* Are on Trial?

In some cases, life-experience considerations can be key to selecting or deselecting jurors, and the correlation between the issues within a case and common experiences is direct. For example, even if you have never been in a car accident, you know they are common events. You may be appalled when a man kills his wife's lover in a fit of rage, but you know that is an age-old story. Sometimes, however, we find ourselves looking at an issue that has an unfamiliar twist, and it raises issues that go beyond the case itself.

Just as the Louise Woodward case became known as the "nanny trial," another Massachusetts case became known as the "hockey dads" case. The case provides another illustration of the decisions involved in filing charges, but the event itself also stunned the public. In essence, two fathers got into a fight in front of their children over an issue involving rough play in a kids' hockey game. The first fight ended, but the physically stronger dad went back to the arena and, according to the prosecution, initiated another round of fighting. The other dad ended up dead, and to make the whole matter more grisly, he died in front of his and other children, including the defendant's.

You may recall this case because it shocked the country. It brought up the issue of kids and sports and parental involvement—or over-involvement—in children's sports. This case had a life of its own in the media because it represented something larger than a situation in which a fight got out of hand. Parents attacking coaches and verbal assaults on opposing players and coaches by parents had reached alarming levels, and communities were looking for ways to prevent ugly incidents. The case gained national attention, we know from other research, because it tapped into the values and life experiences of the everyday parent. Who isn't involved in the activities of their kids? The horror of the event unfolding before the eyes of the children triggered the fear in the public that this could easily happen in their own community.

The prosecutors in the hockey-dads case filed manslaughter charges, and the defendant claimed self-defense. The jury found the defendant guilty of involuntary manslaughter. This meant that the defendant knew or should have known that he was endangering the other man's life by his actions. The judge showed no leniency and sentenced the defendant to a prison term that was twice that stated in the state's sentencing guidelines. The judge also reprimanded the defense for its attempt to characterize the victim in an unfavorable way. Some said this verdict and the sentence sent a strong message to parents and coaches and anyone involved in children's competitive activities.

When a relatively new social issue, or for lack of a better phrase, "crime scenario," is raised in a trial, how do we go about choosing jurors? Or, put another way, is the process any different from what we do in a case where the issues are familiar? Certainly, in focus groups one area we would study is the community's prevailing attitudes and feelings about the defendant. Is he a respected member of the community, seen as upstanding and honest? Would people sympathize with him? Could he be viewed as defending kids and not just defending himself?

As you can see, both the defense and the prosecution would be interested in these issues. Although they did not do this, the prosecution could have played the "send a message" card. As it turned out, they did not have to. They might have looked for jurors who would listen to the argument that intensity over kids' sports had resulted in a tragedy, and therefore, find the defendant guilty of the most serious charge, thereby sending a message that the community will not tolerate this behavior. The defense would prefer jurors willing to put aside these issues and look at self-defense. One man, a violent sort of fellow (they claimed), was behaving in a way that caused the defendant to believe he could endanger the kids, and it was not his fault when the fight escalated. He ended up having to defend himself against the assault.

In some parts of the country, hockey might have been on trial because it is a heavy-contact sport and professional hockey routinely includes fights. However, in a "hockey community," would that tactic work? Would either side run the risk of making the issue one of hockey fights rather than dad fights? One side or another might even consider asking for a change of venue. (This didn't happen, but focus-group work could have revealed advantages of moving the trial to another location.) Taking the long view, will the jury's verdict and the judge's sentence have implications for another trial in which parents have had some sort of altercation over their kids, sports-related or not?

Issues Matter

As you can see, each case raises many questions and variables. We know the background of the parties in the case matters. The actual charges filed by the prosecution matter a great deal when we set out to choose a jury. In addition, the background and life experiences of the community members matter in the creation of a juror profile. The very same set of facts presented to the suburban bedroom jury will be heard and responded to differently than the city jury. Just knowing some variables is not enough. We need to know about their life experiences to better predict their likely reactions and interpretations of evidence.

In the hockey-dads case, we may learn that an ideal prosecution juror is an avid hockey fan who has kids involved in the sport. They feel so strongly about protecting the integrity of the game that they want to throw the thug in jail. Ironically, an ideal defense juror may have a similar profile, but perhaps have a higher tolerance for violence in sports. He or she might subscribe to the "it takes two to start a fight" maxim, so calling the event a tragedy is one thing, but labeling it as a crime is something else again.

What We Can't Predict

If any case is presented a certain way, it can lead to a specific result. But as the prosecutors found in the Woodward case, other variables often interfere. In that case, the variable occurred after the jury reached a verdict, but the variables often take place during trial. For example, particular legal rulings may restrict admission of evidence or allow the jury to hear something that could appear to be irrelevant, but it dramatically shifts the "shape" of the trial and a different verdict results.

For example, consider the now-legendary event in the O.J. Simpson criminal case that prompted Johnnie Cochran's famous statement, "If it doesn't fit, you must acquit." Many legal experts agree this episode may have been the key element for jurors. You may recall that the prosecution produced as evidence the bloody glove purported to be worn by the killer of Nicole Brown Simpson. The prosecution made the decision to have Simpson put on the glove in front of the jury. This, they figured, would be a dramatic moment. The jury would see "the killer" wearing his glove. The problem is that through the course of time, moisture seemed to have caused shrinkage of the leather glove. Regardless, the reality that played out in front of the jury was a struggling Simpson who could not get his large hand inside that glove.

The prosecution then faced the shrinkage factor and brought in an identical new glove. That one fit Simpson. The problem is that the glove would likely fit anybody and everybody. In the jury's eyes, Cochran's argument rang very true. The glove found at the murder scene does not fit; this new glove would fit anyone, so what has the prosecution proved? Nothing. Do you send a man to jail because his hand fit into a new large glove? Or is the murder glove the only real test? As it happens, the whole exercise was futile, but the prosecution pursued this strategic miscalculation and had to live with the consequences.

Just what influence do lawyers have in the trial? I address that question next, but it is interesting to note that there is only one time in the entire trial that the lawyers actually are permitted to interact with jurors. Throughout the course of the trial, lawyers talk *at* jurors; during the jury-selection process, they actually get to interact *with* the jurors. It is a task not to be taken lightly, so let's take a look at the work of lawyers during the phase of the trial known popularly as jury selection, but defined more realistically as juror deselection.

chapter 5

If Men Are from Mars and Women Are from Venus, Then Lawyers Are from Uranus

Most people do not understand what lawyers are all about, perhaps because they are intimidated by the notion that these professionals strategize and *argue* for a living. Or, maybe people are put off because it has become such a visible profession, one that by its nature involves speaking on behalf of others. Lawyers are paid to be the mouthpiece for a person who would rather not be in a position to need any such thing. No one ever wants to retain a lawyer, just as no one wants to see a doctor. So, given the perception that lawyers are paid to argue on behalf of people who wish they did not need them in the first place, the seeds are sown for mistrust and skepticism.

Observing Lawyers at Work

One setting where the public has an opportunity to observe lawyers, many for the first time, is when they are seated in a jury box and considered as jurors for a trial. This situation is often mystifying and ends up appearing adversarial. By necessity, the prospective jurors are under oath to tell the truth, but few are prepared for the notion that they must respond to questions that often require them to reveal personal and sensitive information about their lives.

Even with all its inconveniences, it may be difficult to fully appreciate the foresight of those who saw the value of having a group of individuals defined as a defendant's peers and drawn randomly from the community. Perhaps the most powerful components of the system are the relative anonymity and the fact that jurors are not accountable for their decisions at the time of trial or at any time thereafter. Puzzlement and even outrage over some decisions aside, most of the time, lawyers and average citizens have a degree of reverence for the jury system, and all parties take their potential service seriously, at least once they are in the courtroom.

Although we have become a very casual society, and generalizations about attire may be risky, we can sometimes see the respect for the system itself by the way potential jurors are dressed. Remember when people used to dress up when they went "downtown"? Well, some people put on their best clothes to go to court. I recall one elderly woman who cast disapproving glances at a particular young man. Others noted this disapproval, and in time we learned that she did not like that he was dressed in shorts and a T-shirt. She, on the other hand, wore a suit and a dressy hat. The generation gap was apparent. Eventually, this woman sat on the jury and was vocal in her opinion that one should dress for court like one would dress for church. "It's a matter of respect," she said. Younger people do not necessarily match clothes with the seriousness of a situation, but many still do, and courtroom attire provides a clue about individuals and their attitudes. Serious dress may not always equal a serious attitude, but it is certainly one indication that the person is aware that we imbue the legal process with a degree of dignity.

Common Sense Turns Out to Be Common

Matters of attire aside, what gives anyone the ability to hear a set of facts and come to a proper determination that effectively concludes a dispute? In short, common sense. Indeed, it often guides the process. The court system, both in philosophy and on a practical, day-to-day basis, expects common sense to be the guiding force. With all the lawyers' maneuverings, selective evidence, and best arguments, over time, we have learned that jurors try very hard to do the right thing. If a possible verdict goes against their sense of common decency or logic, they are unlikely to go in that direction.

Sometimes, however, in matters that deal with First Amendment issues, jurors will rely more on logic and principle than "decency." In other words, people will look to constitutional protections of otherwise offensive images or speech. They may not like the material in question, but they act in a manner that protects free speech because the principle is more important than their personal reactions. The key question for the lawyers is gaining a sense of how the jurors in the case at hand will react to the presentation of facts, and what common sense means for *those* jurors.

By the day of jury selection, the lawyers may well be armed with juror profiles created from the community attitude surveys and pre-trial focus groups. When jury selection begins, their task is to figure out how the jurors who show up in court compare to the profiles. The goal is to find individuals who align with the desirable juror profile and eliminate (or deselect) the people who fit the profile of the other side.

For most cases, jury selection begins without fanfare and notice. People who have received their notice to report for jury selection come to court in the morning, report to a clerk, and settle into an assembly room where they wait (and often wait...and...wait...and...wait) their random turn to be called into a courtroom. Unfortunately, for many this can end up being a very boring day, unless they are engrossed in a good thriller.

Nowadays, it is amusing to see so many jurors waiting with all the trappings of modern life, from cell phones to laptops to pocket organizing devices. Between the beeps and rings and buzzes, the assembly room can sound like an office. Of course, many men and women sit all day and never are called for a jury at all. Depending on the policies of their local system, they may be required to return the next day and go through the waiting game again. In some venues, if they have not been selected on that day, their service is complete for at least one year. This system is called "one day, one trial." If you have been involved with this kind of system, then you know you can be called for one jury, but if you are not selected, you go back in the assembly room and wait to be called again that day as part of the pool for another jury. If you are not selected for a jury that day, you have done your duty. If you are chosen, you must serve for the entire course of that trial, regardless of how long it lasts.

What's with the So-Called Media Circus?

As you know, some trials attract a lot of attention, and the selection of the jury is viewed as the "first big day." A major media event, photographers mill around snapping photos of everyone (and anyone) who walks into the courthouse, and network reporters stand in front of the courthouse. These reporters usually call out questions, try to get quick comments, or request an interview. Anything for a sound bite is the rule of the day, so reporters use any tidbit to make or create news. Sometimes it really does seem like a circus.

I have been on both sides of the media frenzy. As a commentator during the jury-selection phase of the O.J. Simpson case, I tried to be a careful observer, always prepared to take to the airwaves at a moment's notice to answer questions posed by the news anchor. One day, I took a walk with my colleague Jo-Ellan Dimitrius, the in-court jury consultant for Simpson. We could not walk three inches without television cameras being shoved in our faces, while reporters yelled at her. We were on our way to a bookstore to pick up a book tangentially related to the case that was released that morning. (It happened to be *Nicole Brown Simpson: The Private Diary of a Life Interrupted*, by Faye Resnick, one of Nicole Simpson's friends, and it created a stir of anticipation.) Wind of the book's release came during the trial, and the case was recessed to give all the "players" a chance to read the book. This is not a typical reason to call a recess in a trial, but as you know, this was not a typical trial.

As it turned out, the media folks had scooped up most available copies before we could get one. Jo-Ellan and I walked through the mass of reporters and tried to ignore the fuss. Then, at some point during our walk, the reporters just dropped back, apparently deciding to end their hunt for a comment. Perhaps someone perceived to be more "hot" in terms of news was rumored to be in the area. Reporters often move in "herds" during these high-profile trials, just as they do during major crisis coverage.

It's Difficult to Be a Good Citizen When....

I have asked myself how the prospective jurors in the Simpson case must have felt as they arrived at the courthouse and saw the cameras and reporters, from both electronic and print media. Literally hundreds of men and women were called to the courthouse, and suddenly they were celebrities-in-waiting, stars of the moment. In this situation, the generally respectful atmosphere I described earlier begins to slip. Is the presence of media responsible for that? I think so, although that trial and a handful of others produce more than their fair share of frenzy. Most trials attract almost none.

During the jury-selection phase of the O.J. trial, we saw Andy Warhol's premonition become reality. All these potential jurors were in contention for their fifteen minutes of fame, whether they liked it or not. It was an unreal scene, as much for most of the lawyers as for the jurors. All you needed to do was see the new budding professionals: the sellers of O.J. Simpson T-shirts, key chains, and even "squeeze the Juice" exercise balls you could squeeze to both strengthen your grip and take out your frustrations against Simpson, if you had any. I still have a series of mock press credentials that picture Simpson in a clown out-fit. Enterprising folks could not create memorabilia and sell the items fast enough. Yet, this was to be the seat of justice.

As much as I believe that most jurors do feel great respect for the system, it is also true that in the real world, most men and women who show up are those who could not find a way to get out of jury duty. Worse yet, at least from a lawyer's perspective, among the large pool are individuals who *want* to serve in the worst way, and this may or may not serve the needs of either side. For potential jurors, the practical reality looms large, from concerns about work responsibilities, finding sitters for the kids, and juggling appointments, and for many, address-ing the critical issue of who will walk the dog.

We certainly observe a range of personality types in the waiting areas. Some individuals are frantically making phone calls, huffing and puffing around while looking at their watches every few minutes. Some people believe they are far too important to waste time with something as trivial as jury duty. Others may pace around, but they are ready and willing to serve if they are chosen. And a few people are taking it in stride—these are men and women engrossed in a novel, enjoying a legitimate day away from the office.

What Is Typical Anyway?

As I have said, not every case has had a community attitude survey or focus group performed. In the vast majority of cases, no research has been conducted, either because of budgetary constraints or because the lawyers in the case do not think the research offer any value to them. In addition, the presence of available profiles does not simplify the task of selecting jurors. Knowing what the research means and being able to find the desirable people from the pool can be tricky. This is why we must take great care in crafting *voir dire*—jury selection—questions, and then conducting the jury-selection process in such a way that we can attempt to uncover the life-attitude components of the profile. The term *voir dire* translates from the French literally as "to see, to say," but practically speaking, means, "to speak the truth while undergoing an examination by lawyers to test one's competence and bias for the purpose of serving as a juror."

In addition, no one is actually selecting anyone. By that, I mean that the jury-selection process is better defined as a system of deselection. All parties want to remove the undesirable jurors from the pool. Assume both sides have the same level of research and even similar profiles of "positive" and "negative" jurors. Unlike recruiting for a sports team, lawyers do not get to pick the jurors they like and put them on the jury. We attempt to identify the undesirable jurors and remove them from the panel through a process called "challenging the potential juror."

Lawyers challenge a potential juror in one of two ways. First, lawyers can make an unlimited number of challenges for cause. This means that the lawyers identify, through information in the juror's background, life experiences, or answers during jury selection, anything that confirms that the juror cannot be objective and fair. In other words, the lawyers learn that a particular individual likely will be unfairly and clearly biased in the case. Of course, everyone is biased in some way, but in this situation the person appears to show bias so deep and so relevant to the case or subject matter that the parties won't get an even hearing. For example, in a case in which the subject matter dealt with same-sex pedophilia, jurors who held very strong convictions against all homosexuals would not likely be able to maintain a sense of fairness and would not even be willing to listen to the defense of the case.

One obvious example of deep bias is if the person does not believe in the death penalty for any reason. That person is never going to be chosen for a jury when the prosecution is keeping the death penalty as an option. It does not matter if the person's belief is motivated by religious or ethical considerations or is purely a political, practical matter; this person will not stay in the jury venire.

The judge has the power to grant or deny a challenge for cause. When the bias issue is clear, the judge likely will grant the motion. However, I have observed many judges who resist releasing jurors for *any* reason. I once assisted with jury selection in a case in Chicago in which the trial judge asked the jury as a whole: "Is there any reason under the sun that you cannot be fair in this case?" As long as the jurors acknowledged that there was no reason under the sun, the judge would not entertain any challenge for cause.

This judge called me up after the jury selection he railroaded through and said, "Now *that's* the way you conduct a jury selection. You can forget all those fancy research efforts that those jury consultants use!" Because I was introduced only as a member of the legal team, he did not know that I was present as a jury consultant. When I tell this story to my lawyer audiences, most just shrug and grimace. They have been there, so they know what I mean.

In another case, I worked with the plaintiff where the judge demonstrated a clear bias in favor of the defendants. He would not grant the lawyers' challenges for cause (meaning that the judge would not accept the specific bias or prejudice that the lawyers pointed out) as reasons to excuse a juror in the case of two individuals in the venire, one of whom claimed it would be quite difficult for him to award a large sum of money, and the other who thought plaintiff lawyers were generally ambulance chasers. The judge exercised his right to rehabilitate the jurors, and got both of them to indicate that their answers and predispositions aside, they could and would be fair.

My client had exhausted his peremptory challenges (a set number of challenges permitted to each party, which allow them to reject, without specifying a reason, any juror, so long as there is no pattern of excusing that would be protected by law, such as race or gender). The judge affirms the number of peremptory challenges, often in consultation with the lawyers. The number varies based on the numbers of parties in the case or its complexity. For example, in a case with multiple defendants, the judge allows each party a certain number of peremptory challenges, such as four or five. The lone plaintiff is given the number of challenges the judge considers fair in relation to those granted to multiple defendants, such as a total of six to eight.

In the case just mentioned, we worked late into the night in a fierce scramble to write a new opening statement. We had to establish the plaintiff's lawyer as a person to be respected and admired, and we emphasized the conservative nature of the request for damages that would be made in the trial. We came up with the careful and appropriate metaphors to assist the jurors to understand the case, and we mentioned the lawyer's admirable experiences. Although they elicited an objection from time to time, we made statements such as: "In my thirty years of trying cases, I have represented some of the finest citizens in the country, but none as deserving as Mr. Jones."

These kinds of strategies are often required because of the apparent bias of certain judges. These judges do not necessarily show these biases in inappropriate ways, but rather are simply reflecting their own life experiences. However, these judges sometimes forget that they were once practicing lawyers who liked to actually interact with the jurors themselves. Once on the bench, many judges become convinced that they are the best inquisitors, and lawyers are best left out of the process, to whatever extent is possible.

Regardless of the judge's attitude, lawyers will have a say in which jurors are removed from consideration from the panel. If the judge does not allow their challenge for cause, then they resort to another type of challenge to ensure that they can, for the most part, remove whomever they believe must go. As I've said, this additional type of challenge is the peremptory challenge. In common parlance, we would call this getting "bad vibes" from the prospective juror. Limitations exist, however. Our courts have stepped in to make sure that lawyers cannot systematically remove jurors on the basis of race or gender, for example. As time goes on, it seems that the court will extend the list to protect other groups, but essentially these restrictions serve to limit the freedom parties have to remove any jurors they wish, and further reduces the lawyers' influence in jury selection.

In general, our courts are called on to balance two sets of rights. Minorities and the sexes have the right not to be discriminated against in any situation, while a criminal defendant or state prosecutor has an interest and duty to seek a fair and impartial jury based on any model they wish as they pursue their case. Over the years, challenges have been made to lawyers who appear to systematically remove jurors for some reason. Race or gender exclusions were first challenged, but the list of cases has even included an attempt to remove male jurors with beards. This ends up being a perpetually tough issue. We need to strike a balance between a party's right to remove anyone he or she feels will not give them a fair hearing, but at the same time, doing so in a way that does not compromise civil liberties or rights. This area will continue to evolve on a case-by-case and issue-by-issue basis.

The Juror Questionnaire

When we are fortunate enough, judges permit the lawyers to have the prospective jurors complete a juror questionnaire. I say "fortunate enough" because many judges believe that such activities thwart the attempt to produce a fair trial and believe some trickery is going on behind the scenes. In reality, a juror questionnaire is nothing more than an effort to explore the attitudes, values, leanings, and biases of the prospective jurors. In cases where the lawyers have conducted pre-trial research, such as community attitude surveys or focus groups, the juror questionnaire becomes the final exam.

The questionnaire is the test by which the profiles for desirable and undesirable jurors can better be identified. For that matter, the survey permits the lawyers to identify those who are likely *not* to listen to one side of the case. So the search for a partial jury is on.

The juror questionnaire is a valuable tool because the courtroom setting can lead jurors to answer questions in a way that is socially acceptable but not necessarily truthful. In a public setting, most people feel the need to say the proper thing, or at least the so-called "politically correct" thing. The questionnaire permits honesty and prevents public embarrassment. These questionnaires have the flavor of the community attitude survey and the focus-group documents because we attempt to achieve consistency in the way the research is conducted.

A particular juror questionnaire was used in the Heidi Fleiss case. My partner, Richard Gabriel, designed and wrote the questionnaire and gave me permission to discuss it. You may recall that the Fleiss case was known as the case of the "Hollywood Madame," and it sent panic waves through Tinseltown. Fleiss had run a discreet prostitution service, but unfortunately for many famous people, not discreet enough, because she boasted to an undercover cop about being the top "Madame" in town. Many famous names appeared in her little black book, and many well-known men did not relish the thought that these names would become public knowledge. Fleiss told *Los Angeles* magazine that all she did was set up rich guys with girls who were willing; according to her, she was, in effect, an agent.

Fleiss was caught when LAPD officers arranged a sting, resulting in the arrests of three or four women at a hotel. The women met with the officers. Later, Fleiss was arrested at her home, and her records were confiscated, including the black book containing the names of her clients. Hollywood's elite went into panic and denial mode because they feared revelations about their identities. Her trial included charges of five counts of pandering and one of narcotics (cocaine) possession. In December of 1994, she was found guilty of three counts of pandering and not guilty of the other counts, including the narcotics possession charges. She received a three-year jail sentence. But, the story is not that simple.

I recall running into Richard Gabriel in Albuquerque just as I was on my way to the NBC studio to provide some Simpson analysis. The

Fleiss jury was still deliberating. As I passed Richard, we stopped long enough for me to ask him what he thought was going to happen in the case. "She's going to win this one," he replied as he dashed off. Ah, but then came the verdict: "guilty on the charges of pandering."

I called Richard that night to both share concern, and, to be honest, kid him a bit about his overconfident prediction. He was very angry. "Something went wrong," he said. "This makes no sense. That jury just wasn't going to convict. Something has to be up." And right he was. This was the beginning of a two-year legal battle that led to an overturned verdict due to juror misconduct.

Shortly after the verdict, the defense requested an opportunity to interview the jurors. It quickly became clear to Richard, who conducted research for the Fleiss team, that there was, in a legal sense, misconduct among the jurors. The jurors admitted that they began to deliberate about sentencing and the fact that they didn't want to see her do any jail time. But, juries are specifically instructed not to talk about sentencing; that is the job of the judge, not the jurors. Remember, too, that to criminal defense lawyers (and the jurors who hear the case), it is not so much a question whether or not their client committed a particular act as it is about whether the arms of the prosecution and trial process act properly and appropriately. The issue of preserving the sanctity of the system and the rights of the defendant is always paramount.

Heidi's conviction was reversed on appeal because of the juror misconduct. Why did Gabriel have such a strong sense of what the jury would do and an even stronger sense that something was amiss when the verdict was delivered? It was because of the insights he gained from the jurors when they completed the juror questionnaire. These insights led him to advise the team to delve more carefully into the jury's activities. Without that pre-trial work, his instinct regarding the need for post-trial follow-up may not have been triggered and the conviction could have remained in force.

When the jurors arrived for jury selection for the Fleiss trial, they were asked to complete a questionnaire that asked the usual demographic information. They were told to describe their educational background and occupations, and also for their partners/spouses and children and grandchildren. Then, through questions about hobbies and past and current organizational memberships, the questionnaire probed into attitudes about politics, religion, law enforcement, and so forth.

Some of the questions can certainly be personal. The term "living arrangements" can cover considerable ground, from single individuals living alone to married spouses to unmarried, same-sex partnerships and opposite-sex, unmarried partners. No single question reveals potential attitudes and tolerance or intolerance toward prostitution in general or Fleiss in particular, but a combination of answers might provide important clues. For example, one question asked: Do you belong to or associate with any groups that have crime prevention or law enforcement as a goal? Another asked if the individual has ever had a leadership position in such an organization. Memberships in organizations might provide clues, but not necessarily obvious ones. What might members of the NRA (National Rifle Association), the ACLU (American Civil Liberties Union), and the Sierra Club have in common? More specifically, what would membership in these organizations signal to either the prosecution or the defense teams in a prostitution case, as opposed to a land-use matter or a product-liability issue? Different kinds of cases call for different "bedfellows."

In a non-celebrity case involving "private behavior," a liberal ACLU type and a conservative, self-described libertarian were both seated as jurors, and their influence went exactly as we had hoped. Neither liked the idea of anyone having the power to investigate sexual activity between consenting adults, and their disdain of "big brother" carried the day and convinced even those jurors with strong religious convictions that the case was about the Constitution, not about sex.

In the Fleiss case, Gabriel designed questions that directly asked jurors about their attitudes toward undercover operations and law enforcement "disguising" itself. It is quite possible that men and women with political attitudes resting firmly at opposite poles could easily end up on the same side when it comes to any issue that raises constitutional issues. Like our ACLU member and the libertarian, many people dislike the idea of law enforcement probing the private sexual lives of citizens. Some people do not use drugs, but they feel strongly about what they consider to be a waste of public money spent prosecuting adults who use marijuana, or perhaps even other currently illegal drugs. This kind of person would have been a desirable juror in the Fleiss case.

In a case dealing with sexuality, religion inevitably becomes an issue. In addition to asking jurors if they practiced a religion, and if so, how important is it in their lives, Gabriel's questionnaire asked point blank: is their anything in your religion or religious practice that has any belief or attitude about prostitution and drugs? He went on to ask more about that issue in order to assess the degree of influence religion is likely to have in the way an individual would hear the evidence in the case. Understanding religious attitudes among the jurors may play a role in crafting a theme for the case. While some people may be morally opposed to prostitution, they can accept it as a reality in society and may not wish to see money spent to investigate or prosecute what some call a "victimless crime." Others want to punish anyone who does anything against the law at any time.

Most cases attract no media attention whatsoever. In only a few cases is prior media exposure an issue, but when celebrities are involved and extensive coverage of the people or the case itself emerges, then we may well need to ask jurors if they have already formed an opinion about the case. In fact, some people might indeed take the position that "Where there's smoke, there's fire." Or, some men and women harbor unconscious resentments against the rich and powerful and enjoy seeing them in the hot seat. They may not have formed an opinion one way or another, but they if they are channel surfing, they stay with a program that is offering the latest tidbit of gossip about the accused and the lawyers and perhaps even potential witnesses.

The Fleiss questionnaire also asks about what magazines and newspapers these individuals read, as well as what television programs they watch. In this case, the Fleiss team was interested in jurors' exposure to programs such as *Inside Edition*, *Hard Copy*, and *A Current Affair*. Did they also watch "cop" shows or other programs that focused on law enforcement?

I recall a woman in another case (involving an accused "con man") who freely told us about all her media habits and biases. She watched all the tabloid shows and reality "cop" programs, and had followed various murder cases closely. You might say she was a Court TV junkie. Our case did not involve murder, but was about fraud and con artists. It had weak links to celebrities, which is why it became fodder for the tabloid shows and newspapers. This juror liked to believe the worst about celebrities, but she did not show great respect for journalists either because she did not believe they were above lying about any person. This woman (who if you try to picture her in your mind's eye, you need only think of "Aunt Bea" from *The Andy Griffith Show*), was a good choice for the jury because she was used to listening to stories that took many twists and turns. Our con-artist case had plenty of detours. Unfortunately, the other side saw these qualities, too, and deselected her. We hated to see our perfect juror walk away.

Sometimes it is better to have jurors who know all about a case—or at least think they do. If they are honest about impressions, but they know these impressions have not been formed through actual presentation of facts, then they may have open minds. In highly publicized cases, if a juror answers no to a question about hearing any pre-trial publicity, then the person is probably lying. Unless they have been on a mission to Mars, camping in Patagonia, or marching to Pretoria, there is no way anyone could have missed media coverage of the Whitewater matters, Monica Lewinsky, Chandra Levy, Bonny Lee Bakley or Laci Peterson murders.

Just to summarize, Richard and the defense legal team were after the prospective jurors' views on the issues relevant in the case: prostitution, drugs, and notoriety of the defendant and the case, including the pre-trial publicity that surrounded the case. Interestingly enough, the attitudes and life experiences of the downtown Los Angeles jurors in that case were such that they were not particularly bothered by the issues of pandering, which is nothing more than a fancy and legal way of saying pimping, or influencing a woman to become a prostitute.

As it turned out, it appeared that the jurors did not take poorly to Ms. Fleiss at all. Such was the basis for the juror misconduct, because by addressing the strategy of keeping her from doing much jail time, the jurors were overstepping the boundaries of their duties and responsibilities. You can assume that if Ms. Fleiss had been tried in a more socially conservative state (such as Alabama), she would have been convicted on every count if only because of the nature of the environment. Again, I do not want to stereotype, but where a case is heard can make a dramatic difference when the issues involved trigger fundamental human filters.

The Fleiss case took place at the time the O.J. Simpson criminal jury selection was taking place. Her trial was going on in the same building, just a few doors away, and it attracted attention, too. Between media representatives, street hawkers, and interested bystanders, that courthouse area was a sight to behold.

In some situations, and the Fleiss case is a good example, the attitudes about the alleged criminal activity are critical. However, in other situations, jurors' attitudes about certain kinds of evidence and even the profiles of witnesses are likely to be of greater importance. Take DNA evidence, for example. Some people believe they cannot be good jurors unless they understand DNA evidence. They do not trust what they do not know. Yet, even lawyers agree that understanding DNA is not an achievable goal for most of us. Let's face it, perhaps Barry Scheck and his partner Peter Neufeld understand DNA and helped half the country comprehend the basics during the O.J. trial, but 99.9 percent of lawyers do not know much more about DNA science than the average person.

No lawyer expects jurors to understand complex scientific information. Depending on the case, and the side we represent, we need individuals willing to trust experts to explain the evidence and give jurors reasons to either believe their interpretation of the evidence or distrust the evidence itself. Sometimes, especially when a science is new, lawyers want jurors who lack faith in the evidence or the expert witnesses. Odd as it may seem, individuals do exist who do not believe in scientific methods—I have interviewed potential jurors who distrusted carbon dating because they believed that nothing on earth was more than about 6,500 years old. Usually, the distrust is based, if not on religious grounds, then on a lack of understanding. I have also found that some of these jurors who distrusted science can come to accept its findings once they are taught what they need to know from the experts who come into the courtroom to teach them.

What Happens to the Information?

The information gathered in the juror questionnaires is maintained as part of the court record and shared among the lawyers. As a rule, the court seals the records, which means that the information is not open to the public; the identity of the prospective jurors remains protected, at least until the trial is over. Then, jurors are free to do and say as they please, unless specifically ordered not to by the judge. Even in many high-profile cases, you will hear television commentators refer to "juror No. 2" or "juror No. 7" whom they can identify by their appearance in court and what is learned from what they say during jury selection. Other than that, their identities remain protected by the court. In cases of little or no profile, the judge may permit the lawyers to refer to the jurors by their actual names and have them state their addresses in open court. This occurs usually in matters where there is no press present anyway, and the need to protect the identity of jurors is not an issue.

We always come back to the phrase "fair and impartial" because we know the concept is part of the foundation of our judicial system. Yet, we also know that a player in any case would be crazy to want such a thing. The parties want sympathetic, empathetic, absolutely partial people who will hear the case in the way most favorable to them. You can see how the juror questionnaire in the Heidi Fleiss case helped to uncover jurors who might consider the evidence in a particular light because of existing values about what Fleiss was accused of doing. Or, even without specific attitudes toward her, perhaps the men and women have certain attitudes about what law enforcement had to do to "catch her."

Let's say I'm a criminal defendant who is also Native American. I have been victimized, and I believe this led me to do whatever I'm accused of doing. Or, in a different situation, I believe my ethnicity led to the *accusation* that I committed a particular crime when I did no such thing. Do I want people with open minds? No. I want people who have been victimized, people who relate to me, men and women who are more likely to accept my view of the world because they have lived it, too.

All This Work, and Look What Happens

On occasion, the pre-trial work can be rendered unnecessary, again, based on the thinking of a particular judge. As a practical matter, judges want trials to move as swiftly through the system as possible, and do not want a trial to last even one day more than is necessary. I recall a case in which the judge made no secret of his disdain for the matter, and specifically for the plaintiff's case. It appeared that the case would go on for at least six months. Each day, the judge grew less and less tolerant of the testimony, specifically the seemingly weak expert testimony. Sure enough, although the case involved major entities and accusations of fraud and antitrust violations, the judge did not take long to grant what is called the motion for directed verdict.

A directed verdict granted at the end of the plaintiff's case means that the judge has decided no legal basis exists upon which a jury, having heard all of the evidence presented by the plaintiff, can rightfully find in favor of the plaintiff. In fact, it is the judge's way of ruling that if a verdict were to be rendered in favor of the plaintiff, the judge would have to reverse it. While this motion is routinely made by the defendant in every case at the conclusion of the plaintiff's case, it is rarely granted.

I had one case in which one of the charges (called counts) in the complaint asked for punitive damages, claiming the behavior of the defendant was willful and intentional. The defense made its motion for directed verdict at the conclusion of the plaintiff's case, arguing that no evidence presented by the plaintiff during its case-in-chief (meaning all of the witness testimony, documents, and other evidence presented that constitutes the support of all allegations made in the case) that support a finding by the jury of willful and intentional behavior. The judge agreed, granted the motion, and effectively eliminated from consideration by the jury the issue of willful and intentional conduct.

In most cases, the motion is denied because the court will find that the plaintiff has presented evidence sufficient enough to permit a jury to address the question. When denied, the motion for directed verdict is renewed by the defendant at the conclusion of its own case in every trial as a way of saying to the court, "If you denied this motion before, now that you have heard our side of the case, it is now a legal certainty that no jury can appropriately find in favor of the plaintiff and we once again request that you end the trial now, and find in our favor." At the end of the defendant's case, the plaintiff also routinely makes this motion. The plaintiff requests the judge to find that the jury could not legally find in favor of the defendant because the defendant's response to the plaintiff's case was not sufficient enough to counter the case as a matter of law.

In one case, both parties made their motions for directed verdict to the court. The motion made by the defense was fascinating because in this personal-injury suit, the lawyer for the plaintiff failed to offer any evidence at all about future damages and expenses that would be incurred by the plaintiff. The judge granted the defense motion with regard to future injuries and instructed the jury that they would not be allowed to award any money for future damages.

To lawyers, it would seem clear that the plaintiff's lawyer made a mistake, plain and simple. And for the client, a future action for mal-practice is likely in the cards. This is a terrible situation because this plaintiff clearly suffered from injuries the jury found to be a result of the wrongdoing of the defendant doctor. And yet, because his lawyer neglected to offer testimony that addressed the difficulties this person would face in the future, such as additional surgeries, constant out-patient therapy, special braces, and other needs, the rules of the game called trial say that the jury cannot do anything about the future. If this seems unfair, it really is not. We do not want jurors basing decisions on information *not* presented to them. But the result is that, in a case like this, an injured man will have to rely on the damages awarded to him by a jury for the situation he had been in up to the point of trial.

As a rule, judges hesitate to pull a case from the jury and know that they face scrutiny on appeal from granting a motion for directed ver-dict. In the case just described, the judge granted the motion for directed verdict in favor of the defendant at the conclusion of the plaintiff's case. This situation illustrates that many ways exist for the *absence* of "fair and impartial" to rear its head at trial.

Different Venue, Different Rules

Currently, lawyers' freedom to conduct *voir dire* is being tightened. For example, in the federal system the right (and I use the word "right" intentionally) to question prospective jurors has been essentially removed from lawyers. Instead, the judge conducts the questioning as he or she chooses from questions submitted by the lawyers from both sides; the lawyers make their decisions on the limited information retrieved through this tightened process of *voir dire*.

This truly amazes me. Questionnaires aside, lawyers want information that only direct interaction can produce. However, these federal judges now appear to assign a bigger priority to moving the case along, and they are convinced they are the only participants capable of keeping the process short and sweet, as if short and sweet is the greater value. As we know from other areas of our "open society," speed may be efficient, but it does not necessarily protect the parties involved in a case.

In some state courts, lawyers are still allowed to do their own questions, but in many states, judges have reached the same conclusion as their federal colleagues. They are now taking the position that only they can conduct an effective *voir dire*. In some cases, it is likely these men and women have their sights set on a federal judgeship one day anyway, so by tightening *voir dire* they send a message that they can play the same way.

Actually, part of a lawyer's preparation involves learning as much as he or she can about the judge. For example, does the judge tend to lean one way or the other in her rulings? Lawyers are very sensitive to this information, and it gets shared between them. Recently, I helped select a jury in a case, and before we even started, the lawyers told me they thought the judge had no sympathy for their client's position. "She doesn't really want to hear this case," they said, "and we are afraid her rulings will all go against us."

As I sat in court for the jury selection, I recognized that the judge was indeed tough. But she was tough on everybody. Her clerk came out prior to her entrance telling everyone where they could and could not sit and exactly what the judge expected of them. In fact, the judge sent the message to my clients that "the jury consultant" could not sit at counsel's table. So, I moved back and took my own notes. Fortunately, the judge did let me interact with the jurors for a few minutes prior to asking the lawyers for their decisions on which jurors they wished to strike.

Even if lawyers are allowed latitude in conducting *voir dire*, judges often limit the time. Some will say, "Each side will get one hour, so use the time wisely." Finally, in some places, the lawyers still get to do whatever it takes to satisfy all parties in seating the jury. In one recent case, the judge let the lawyers know that the jury selection would begin at 9:00 A.M. and be concluded by 11:37 A.M. We figured that the end point time was arbitrary and that the judge was trying to make the point that she would push the process through. Strange though, she brought the process to conclusion about 11:52 A.M. Close enough, so I am guessing she was not sending a humorous message. The point is that judges have different temperaments, and lawyers get to know what they are dealing with in each courtroom.

I see the greatest difference between judges in state and federal courts. The proceedings in federal court, as a rule, are the most formal and judges allow the least amount of leeway for lawyers. Maybe because these judges are nominated by the president and confirmed by the Senate, a bit of ego comes with the appointment. Maybe it is the fact that they do not face election and, therefore, do not have to worry about the lawyer's bar associations published evaluations and ratings of them. Whatever the reason, they do not need to concern themselves with how tough they are to the players in their courtroom domain.

Not surprisingly, I think lawyers ought to get whatever time they believe they need to conduct a thorough jury selection. However, I am a realist, too, and I do not mind that judges find it necessary to impose a time restriction. Frankly, many lawyers do not know what to do on *voir dire*. Their mission is to understand what makes the potential jurors tick, but they cannot learn this in law school because the academic environment does not offer any courses on that topic. Only trial experience can provide such insight, and because so many lawyers are inept in *voir dire*, judges may feel justified, even forced, to impose limitations, which then limits opportunities to gain the needed "real world" experience. The situation is made worse because some lawyers do not use or even believe in any pre-trial research, preferring to "go with their gut," which is essentially a combination of intuition and experience…and in some cases, mistakes.

Keeping Up with Change

A few years ago, I presented a trial-advocacy seminar in Minneapolis. During a break, a lawyer in the audience came up to me and said: "I've been practicing law for twenty years. And for the first fifteen years, I had a great trial record. I would win and do a great job for my clients. But, for the past five years, I haven't won a trial. I can't seem to win anything anymore." I asked him what he was doing differently. "Nothing. Nothing at all." Well, that was the problem. The lawyer had not changed in the last twenty years, but jurors and the system have changed, and this lawyer let the changes pass him by.

It *is* a different world today. Jurors are more educated about the legal system. One cannot underplay the importance of the influence of legal programming on television and, of course, Court TV. Many viewers have come to believe they are almost lawyers themselves. They may have picked up ideas about strategy and tactics. So, by the time they show up for jury duty, they have their legal television degree (their "LTD") behind them. They not only want what they see on television, they expect it. Today's jurors do not expect to be bored, so they are often in for a rude awakening. Actual trials are often very boring.

When Court TV first came on the air, I wondered who would have the patience to watch these televised trials. As I thought about it, I realized that if there are people who can sit through televised golf, then there are those who probably enjoy staring at slow-moving trials. On the other hand, many viewers enjoy the "human drama" involved in a trial, slow going or not. And television programming provides for breaks from the creeping pace by hiring commentators to explain and debate and even argue heatedly about what they just heard in court.

Many of today's jurors also read political and legal fiction and non-fiction, and may see the participants in a trial as "characters" playing their parts. My point is that lawyers must be aware of the rapid changes in public sophistication—even if it is pseudo-sophistication.

Some lawyers are armed with the research, but they go forth on their own, still without a clue about what to pursue on *voir dire*. I can identify this type because they ask many "What are your hobbies?" and "What do you do in your free time?" questions. These lawyers do not know what to do with the information they get, which is why they may hold tight to their pet phrase, "Give me any twelve people and I can convince them." These lawyers have no systematic evaluation process to guide what they do.

I have seen too many lawyers try to stereotype jurors. For example, information about television and reading habits may be important, but some lawyers use the answers to pigeonhole jurors, and none too subtly at that. One lawyer all but told a woman that because she reads the *National Enquirer,* she was hopelessly unsophisticated and certainly not as smart as the woman he had just interviewed who read the *New York Times.* I have seen lawyers laboriously explain what an opening statement is. Jurors are often not shy about rolling their eyes and appearing insulted by the condescending attitude.

When we eliminate the lawyers who have not kept up with trends and those who claim they do not believe the research anyway, whom does this leave? In essence, we are left with the lawyers who are armed with prior research, a profile, and the ability to ask the kinds of questions that reveal deep levels of life experience, and who have moments of insight into what the jurors *may* do. These lawyers have an ability to establish trust and credibility with jurors, individually and as a group, and the ability to get a valid sense of the jurors' underlying values and ideals.

What is it about trial lawyers Gerry Spence and Johnnie Cochran, to name two among many, that contributes to their consistent success? Without question, it is their ability to make jurors believe that they understand their life experiences and their suspicions about the process. This allows them to relate to the jurors' experiences. These lawyers possess the ability to influence jurors because they exude a sense of "I am one of you" to the panel. At the very least, their message is: "I get it, and I respect you, and I love you as a human being." Underlying the message is a lack of visible ego and an ability to close the distance gap between jurors and lawyers. They also display an intrinsic sincerity about the case and the client. The foundation of the relationship with the jurors is their compassion and empathy for the client, and this translates to passion in presentation.

As you may have seen firsthand, both Gerry Spence and Johnnie Cochran show great passion in the courtroom or when serving as commentators on television. This display of emotion gives them the ability to speak directly to the jury and make them feel important. I work with a lawyer-client who is very much the same way. He is so passionate about his client, his case, and the value of the legal system that his pride and honesty shines through his entire presentation. The most telling moment occurred after a case he lost, when the winning party came up to him and said, "If I ever need a lawyer again, I am calling you! You did a heck of a job and I wonder how much better I would have done had you been my lawyer in *this* case."

The Skill and Art of Asking Questions

Most lawyers would acknowledge that they do not actually "select" a jury; rather, they want to identify those potential jurors whom they believe will be harmful to their client's position when it comes time to deliberate. In other words, lawyers do not get to tell the judge which jurors they want to keep; all they can do is remove the individuals they do not want.

In a case involving allegations of religious discrimination in hiring and firing, my clients were the plaintiffs. We believed that professional people would prove favorable because they understood when lines were crossed in employment-related decisions. But, these same people may have faced charges from their own employees or people whom they interviewed for positions. They may have dismissed the charges as nonsense. So professionals made sense unless they had ever been accused of improper hiring or evaluation methods themselves. The defendants liked professionals, too, especially those who had been wrongfully accused of improper hiring practices.

In the end, we both eliminated professionals, based on our impressions. However, one retired professional remained. He had owned a business, so the defendant liked him. In the end, he decided for the plaintiffs. It turned out that he ultimately sold his business to his employees, whom he believed made him the wealthy man he had become. These facts had not emerged during jury selection, and we were happy about that.

When all is said and done, the parties are left with a jury that consists of people who have either hidden their bias well, or at least have not tipped the scales of fairness sufficiently one way or the other to lead either side to remove them. The difficult part is determining how to ferret out the jurors who are both negatively and positively predisposed to your case and the "story" you are about to tell the jury on behalf of your client.

In forming questions for jury deselection, the lawyers consider various demographic factors when they determine how to interact with each individual. To be truly effective, they must learn to use language that is congruent with jurors' experiences.

Unfortunately, many lawyers seem to find this task too difficult. Sometimes jurors seem amused when lawyers ask them about "exiting vehicles" and "ascending stairs" rather than "getting in and out of cars" and "going upstairs." They may talk about "expiring" rather than dying and ask jurors about their "offspring" rather than their children. Most people silently wish these lawyers would talk like human beings rather than robots. Gerry Spence and Johnnie Cochran would never use legalese, which may amuse some jurors but make others feel a bit ignorant.

Part of my job is coaching lawyers in the art of using ordinary language. I have taught patent lawyers to describe complicated scientific processes as similar to making pancakes. I have worked with municipal bond lawyers to "dumb down" their presentation so that laypeople can understand the complexities of bond issues by comparing them to home mortgages.

I once helped a prosecutor in a complicated stock scheme to compare the case with concert ticket scalpers. My client was the prosecutor in a stock fraud case and we had difficulty trying to teach the jury why the practices used were illegal and should be punished in a scheme where lots of "victims" made money. These types of cases are known as "penny stock" cases because stocks were bought and sold for pennies, but the actual buying was controlled and predetermined, thereby keeping market forces out of the process, which is something you just cannot do. My client presented his argument to the jury by comparing the event to a concert ticket scalper who bought out the house and sold and resold tickets to make a lot of money. Not only did the jury get the point (and ultimately convict the defendant, a story I discuss in more detail later in the book), but it was great to read the morning headline that compared the defendant to a ticket scalper. If the newspapers liked it, we figured the jurors did, too.

Some lawyers downplay the selection part in favor of "lecturing" about the case theme, often going on and on in legalese, which only magnifies their fundamental mistake. I once saw a lawyer talk to potential jurors about family secrets and skeletons in closets, which made good television drama, and eventually would have been an effective case theme. This was a murder case that involved a grown son murdering a father. It was a whopper in the sense that it had all the "gothic" elements of dark old houses and secret wills and backyard pet cemeteries. The lawyer, however, was unable to restrain herself from weaving so many interesting and fascinating elements into the *voir dire* discussion that she had a tough time getting people to admit they were biased. As a result, she had trouble getting many jurors dismissed for cause.

Lawyers caught up in their theme too early are usually working hard to sell their cases. Some behave as if they are presenting a closing argument rather than concentrating on what is going through the minds of the jurors about the issues in the case. These lawyers often are uncomfortable with the relationship component of jury selection. All they want to do is argue the case at hand—this jury-selection business is a necessary evil, after all. They pass up the opportunity to learn everything they possibly can about the jurors.

Traditionally, jurors seem to view plaintiff lawyers as more likable, especially when compared with a very "corporate" appearing defense lawyer. I once worked with a plaintiff's lawyer who was typically unprepared for trial. He had an active evening social schedule and relied a great deal on the fact that he was a likable guy. His opponents were often the stodgy older lawyers who argued that their corporate clients did not do anything wrong. More often than not, my plaintiff lawyer-client won his case. Jurors liked him, and while research does not typically support the lawyer's personality as a crucial factor in jury decision making, this lawyer was one strong exception. At least he understood the importance of building a relationship with jurors.

Seek and Hide

If I identify a juror who I believe is "good" for our side, I try to hide that advantage from the other side. In order to keep our opponents in the dark, I provide my clients with advice I learned from two colleagues, Robert Hirschhorn and the late (and great) consultant Cathy Bennett. These professionals advise lawyers to ask all the jurors a number of questions so that the opposing counsel becomes confused. In one case where I was assisting the defense, we liked the background and demeanor of a prospective juror. We were convinced he would not easily go along with a big award in the liability case. We asked all the jurors the same questions and several jurors some specific questions, but we left this fellow fairly much alone. In other words, we clouded the desirable juror by keeping the focus off of him. The other side let him remain and he turned out to be our hero—and even the foreperson.

We sometimes try to make a desired juror look negative by asking questions and then, regardless of the answer, having the lawyer feign concern. The goal of this feigned concern is confusion for the other side, who may think we know something they do not. If we look worried, they figure they are supposed to be happy. I recall one young attorney who said, "All I know is that if the other side doesn't want a juror, I do and if they want someone really bad, then I don't." This may work some of the time, but not when a lawyer's calculated reaction throws a monkey wrench into the analysis.

Our attempts to cloud issues and pretend to be concerned must be balanced with the more important task of establishing a sense of truth. We can make the mistake of feigning so much concern that the potential juror is offended or wonders who we really are, which blocks our attempts to build rapport—the kind of bonding Johnnie Cochran and Gerry Spence are so good at establishing. A simple principle of communication, in any setting, holds that it is easier for people to do what you want them to do when they like, trust, and believe you. That is really what rapport is all about.

Rapport and Beliefs

So much of what trial consultants do involves an effort to understand people. Then we work with our clients to establish the most effective ways for them to enhance rapport with the jurors. Jurors, like all human beings, will seek a verdict that does not conflict with their beliefs; they will resist attorneys' overt attempts at persuasion. For example, lawyers are prohibited at trial of violating what is known as the "Golden Rule." In the law, this means that you cannot, through argument and example, put the jurors in the shoes of the parties. For example, you cannot say to the jury, "Imagine if it were you who suffered this terrible fate." That takes away from the objective role of the jury to evaluate the evidence as presented. You see the objectivity issue play out in jury selection as many prospective jurors come to realize that their own experiences will not permit them to hear and evaluate the case fairly.

In a case alleging religious discrimination in the workplace, I recall one prospective juror who had lost relatives in the Holocaust. While she was a relatively young woman in her twenties, she told the judge that she had very strong views on the subject. In addition, she was in a biracial marriage, which made her very sensitive about allegations of discrimination. The plaintiff prayed she would nevertheless claim she could be fair and stay on the jury (because ultimately, every bone in her body would guide her to favor their clients), but the woman said she just could not keep an open mind and was excused. Another prospective juror told the judge that he was an atheist. The plaintiff loved him.

The judge asked if he could be fair, comforted by the fact that his own religious convictions or lack of them were irrelevant to the case. He seemed to look inside himself and said, "Your honor, I really don't mind doing jury service and I am not trying to get out of this, but I just can't give the defense a fair ear." Off he went.

So, while the jurors must (supposedly) be able to put their personal values outside the decision-making process, the reality is they cannot. In our system, we do not want lawyers making the situation even more difficult by permitting them to "place" the jurors in their client's shoes during their opening or closing arguments. The case must stand on its own without playing with jurors' emotions in a blatantly unfair way. Regardless of how persuasive they are, lawyers know that what they say to jurors is argument, not evidence. During trial, lawyers try to deflect attention from themselves and turn the jury's focus to the witnesses, who are experts or other individuals who support the story of the case. These individuals often provide the emotional overtones the lawyers are unable to provide.

The *voir dire* questions are designed to reveal bias because certain leanings may indicate emotional responses later on during trial. If someone asked you whether you were biased against a particular race or the other gender, would you admit to it, even if you realize that you harbor certain prejudices? Most of us resist revealing the truth, especially if we know it will embarrass us in some way. Of course, men and women who want to get out of jury service might deliberately attempt to mislead the lawyers during *voir dire*. They all but announce that they will have difficulty being fair. They listen to what other jurors say that leads to their being excused and try to tap into the same argument. However, judges can usually see through it.

I recall a multiple-murder case in which the judge recited one vicious, grisly killing after another. The jurors groaned—audibly. We all heard a few say, "I gotta get outta here…." When asked if they could be fair, most all said, "No, I can't." They did all they could to withstand the court's efforts to get them to put their feelings aside and serve as fair and impartial jurors. This process is called rehabilitation. It is the judge's effort to take any juror who says, "Your honor, I just can't be fair because…" and get them to reverse their stance to "OK, I can put my strong personal convictions aside and just listen to the evidence."

Bias and Publicity

Sometimes the judge is successful in getting the prospective jurors to say they can be fair and will not let their own attitudes get in the way, but lawyers rarely trust this outcome. Once the bias becomes clear to the lawyers, they will find some way to get rid of anyone whose views are not to their liking. I recall one juror in this murder case who said he knew of a person who had been murdered and the crime remained unsolved. He was frustrated with the justice system and the police in particular, but claimed he could put those feelings aside and judge this case on its own merits. The defense must have figured that far from an open mind, this person would use the case to get revenge on the system, and their client would be the victim. Ultimately, they excused him.

The illogical idea that we can right some past miscarriage of justice with a verdict in a current case may become an issue in certain cases. Shannon Runnion, whose five-year-old daughter, Samantha, was abducted and murdered, lashed out at the jurors who in a previous trial had acquitted the man who was apprehended and charged with the murder. She expressed her anger on the Larry King program on CNN. Snippets of King's interviews often make their way into newscasts the next day, even on other networks. Sure enough, the mother's impassioned words were repeated many times over the course of the following few days.

Meanwhile, in a courtroom in the same part of the country, Southern California, David Westerfield was on trial for a similar crime, the kidnapping and murder of Danielle van Dam. His lawyers became very concerned about the publicity in the other case and wanted the jury sequestered so they would not be influenced by Ms. Runnion's feelings or the community's concerns that child abductors were going free. The public discussions included speculation that the jurors would confront the sad reality that if the previous jury had found her daughter's killer guilty, he would not have been "on the street" and therefore able to commit another heinous crime.

The Runnion situation pushed numerous emotional buttons and occurred during a period when there seemed to be a rash of abductions of young girls by strangers. It was too late to do anything to influence the seating of a jury in the Westerfield case. However, even with admonitions on the part of the judge to avoid listening to all the publicity about the missing girls, the defense realized that good intentions cannot wipe away the subtle pressure on the jury to "not make this mistake again."

Lawyers deal with these issues all the time, and it is difficult at best to choose a jury when pre-trial publicity is intense. When emotional issues occur during a trial, lawyers must do the best they can to keep the jury focused on the facts at hand. It truly is illogical to take the mistaken verdicts in other cases and then, in some twisted way, "right the wrong." Interestingly enough, while these child abductions were occurring and the Westerfield trial was winding down, a man who had been wrongfully convicted of rape was released from prison after serving eighteen years. DNA testing finally exonerated him. This was a serious miscarriage of justice, too, which some might conclude could put other juries on alert as well. Many individuals may fear putting a man in prison based only on eyewitness testimony, with the specter of the innocent man walking free after eighteen years of incarceration guiding their desire not to make a similar mistake.

Try as They Might

Jurors must be careful what they say if they want to be removed and are willing to do just about anything to make that happen. If they are caught lying, the court can charge them with contempt, which leads to fines and even jail time. Some individuals stick with the conventional reasons and plead that they cannot miss work. Most judges simply say, "That's not a good enough excuse. We all have our civic duty." Seeing that the work excuse was ineffective, the next juror in line says she has family obligations. Not good enough.

Only an inability to hear the case fairly or an inability to follow the law as presented by the court represent viable means of getting out of jury service. It is much more difficult to fool the court than some people think. On more than one occasion, a celebrity or business executive has called and said, "Paul, help me get out of this. I don't have time to do jury service." In fact, many of these individuals are in a better position than most people to take the time to serve, so I spend most of my time trying to convince them that jury service is important, not to mention fascinating. The response usually is, "Yeah, right," but I say it anyway because I really do believe it.

People will say all manner of things to avoid being seated for the jury, but they do not realize that much of what they hope will get them excused is not going to work. I constantly hear, "Your honor, I can't be away from my job. I am indispensable," or, "Judge, my spouse is ill and I really need to be around in case I am needed." Some judges are more sensitive than others, but typically judges will emphasize that jury service is essential, and having to deal with some hardship may come with the territory. Some jurors believe their medical conditions will provide automatic grounds to be excused, but they often find the court is willing to be most accommodating about the time they need to take medications and such. In fact, many judges bend over backwards to accommodate special needs. Sometimes, the judge will schedule a day or two off during trial if a juror has a personal commitment that even the judge agrees cannot be missed, but is not necessarily sufficient reason to excuse the individual from jury service.

This process is not unlike what happened back when we still had a military draft. Some men would say just about anything if they thought they could be declared "unfit for service." In these situations, individuals prefer to be deemed stubborn or prejudiced, or even a bit of an oddball, rather than serve. The bottom line is that if you do not want to serve on a jury, you better have a physical condition that prevents you from seeing or hearing evidence, or you better have underlying values that are so strong that they will keep you from hearing and evaluating the evidence fairly. Finding reasons not to serve is easier said than done because the judge will push the issue, and you are under oath to tell the truth.

Looking beyond the Words

Sometimes the potential juror shows a predisposition to suspect everything about the case, which reveals a "generic" bias. This type of person may have heard something about the defendant he did not like. Perhaps his experiences with police officers have left him with a lack of trust in the prosecution, too. He sees smoke and fire everywhere. I recall a man who believed that law enforcement wanted to accuse certain people of crimes, and therefore, police officers set up these individuals. He assumed that the defendant was one of those people. On the other hand, our suspicious juror also harbored a deep distrust of foreigners, and the defendant in the case did not speak much English. This juror had serious suspicions he found nearly impossible to overcome. The judge will challenge this juror with a series of questions, usually starting with something like: "Do you understand that in this case, the parties are entitled to a fair hearing and your personal values do not belong as part of your analysis here?" Ultimately, the lawyers on one side of the case are not going to be comfortable with this juror and will request that he be excused.

The other type of bias is specific bias, or a particular leaning or reaction the juror may have to elements of the case, such as the guilt, responsibility, or liability of a party in the case. In one case, the plaintiff was a former bartender. One juror had been in a relationship with a bartender, coming to believe that all bartenders were likely to exaggerate and even lie. That was enough to trigger the eye and ear of the lawyer and jury consultant to begin the process of exploring bias. "Is there anything about your experiences with a bartender that would get in the way of your listening to the evidence in this case? Do you understand that these parties are entitled to fairness and an open mind?"

If this sounds like we are trying to trick the jury pool, you need to understand that our job is to reduce defensiveness and uncover underlying attitudes and values; we need these to "leak" through. For example, it is not enough to know that a juror is an atheist. I want to know how that value, and any other related values, influences his decision making and life views. So, I might have the lawyer ask: "In this case, you will hear from witnesses who have deep religious convictions and who are devout. Will you give their testimony any less weight or more weight just because they have religious values that are different from your own?" Then I listen to what they say and watch their behaviors as they speak. A show of discomfort in a turned-away gaze, for example, may suggest that the answer "I can be fair" might be said in good faith, but unachievable in reality.

As a jury consultant, I design questions that are seemingly unrelated to the relevant attitude. For example, by asking jurors seemingly innocuous questions about what they read or the bumper stickers they have on their cars, we gain insight into degrees of personal or political attitudes. A person who reads the *Wall Street Journal* and *Forbes* usually is a different kind of person than one who reads *The National Enquirer* and *People* magazine. (There can be a crossover, however, so this is not a foolproof distinction.) Religious or political bumper stickers make statements; no sticker at all may say something else, such as "I am unwilling to 'wear' my opinions." These individuals may have strong convictions, but they do not have an "in your face" attitude about them. Again, there may be crossover, but what I call the "bumper sticker wars" that go on in many communities reveal a particular kind of person. In fact, that is the point of these stickers in the first place. Choosing a provocative bumper sticker is a way to telegraph exactly the kind of instant judgements we all make when we see them on other people's cars.

The point of asking these questions is to discover a juror's meaningful life experiences and attitudes that may serve as metaphors for that individual's life values. If I am looking for someone with a socially liberal leaning, I might ask what she does in her spare time and then follow up with specifics to get a sense of the leaning. So, "I like to watch television," might be followed up with, "What is your favorite show?" If I get *Will and Grace*, I am in good shape. If I get "anything with Charlton Heston," I am in trouble.

Watching how people react to the questions they get is informative as well. I recall a lawyer asking a prospective juror to describe his work duties. The juror paused for awhile and said, "That's really personal and I don't want to answer." Strangely, once the court ordered the juror to respond, he was a bookkeeper with not much to hide. The concern for my client was that if this juror found basic employment questions intrusive, how would he react to the very personal matters, including sexual dysfunction claims, which were going to come up at trial? My client, the plaintiff's lawyer, excused this juror.

Jury consultants are consummate people watchers, and we look for clues in clothing and accessories, including the kinds of pins and other jewelry, handbags and attachés, or even in the lunch bags they may have brought along. I have had my clients ask the jurors about a pin or T-shirt where a message was clear. In one recent case, a juror wore a pin reading "God Bless America." Before September 11, that might have been an awkward area to probe. Wanting to find out if the juror was motivated by patriotism or conservatism, the lawyer asked about the pin and what the message meant. The answer was emotional and involved, but it clarified that the juror was more liberal than conservative, and had lost a friend in the World Trade Center.

Favorite jokes, books, and movies also provide clues to what drives a juror. Asking a juror about favorite childhood stories can uncover powerful underlying drives and needs. Consider the kind of background a person might have whose memorable childhood story is *The Ugly Duckling* or *The Secret Garden*. Locked inside these stories are major life themes, memories of pain and loss, and identification with hardship and isolation. If I am representing a plaintiff in a sexual-abuse case, this juror can perhaps identify with childhood pain and loneliness.

Asking about movie personalities can be revealing as well. I recall a juror who was fascinated by Julia Roberts because she had everything that this juror did not. The interaction almost became akin to a therapy session in that the juror never felt called upon to do much of anything that was important until the jury trial. She was convinced she would be fair and would listen to the evidence because she wanted to do something that mattered. We kept her, not necessarily because she was a favorable juror, but we knew that a strong case and argument could bring her into our court.

It sounds esoteric, but understanding the metaphors that represent a juror's life can help the lawyers shape case strategy and guide the manner in which evidence is presented. One juror had been laid off after fifteen years of service to a large company. She felt bitter, angry, and revealed a sense of having been betrayed. The defendant in the case for which she was called was a large corporation, and we asked her several questions to see if she could distinguish between her experience and this clearly unrelated case. She consistently claimed she could differentiate, but peppered almost every answer with statements about what a great employee she was and how her efforts went largely unappreciated. We did not want her to serve on the jury either. Regardless of the way in which it is done, a good lawyer knows that the differences among jurors are worth exploring.

I encourage my clients and seminar participants to sample a wide range of popular media, including tabloid papers and the latest television shows and news networks. Their potential jurors are likely sampling the same range of information and entertainment. A lawyer who is "above" watching *Seinfeld* reruns, *Frasier*, or *The Simpsons* is likely out of touch with a great majority of the potential jurors coming into the courtroom. I do not like rap music, but I make it my business to have a sense of Eminem's latest songs. Again, our juries are not people who have nearly identical experiences every day of the week. Today's jurors may watch C-SPAN one evening, but tune into the latest reality TV the next. Their children may be hooked on MTV, and the "water cooler" talk at the office may alternate between terrorism alerts and what was on *Oprah* the day before.

Usually, time is quite limited, so lawyers are unable to delve deeply into the issues I call life's metaphors. However, when time does permit, it can be an enlightening information-gathering process. For example, a lawyer can ask a juror to complete the sentence: "To me life is like..." An array of answers might follow, including such phrases as, "a rat race," "a struggle for survival," "hard work," or "a challenge to excel," all of which suggest different driving forces.

I once had a juror compare her life to a race, so she might appreciate or understand certain kinds of language and illustrative comparisons. She can relate to phrases like "speeding up," "pit stops," and the place where "rubber meets the road." Another juror thought of life as "play," so he related to the idea of loss of freedom, restrictions imposed by injuries, or doing something just for fun. This person would respond emotionally to a personal-injury case in which the person had lost the freedom to live normally and was physically restricted. The basic tool involves listening to the language and phrases jurors use and integrating such phrases in their dialogue during jury selection and in arguments. I recall one juror who answered questions with "absolutely" as opposed to a simple "yes." My client-lawyer began to use the same word and made a strong connection to the juror.

Too Much Blah, Blah, Blah

Too many lawyers talk too much and listen too little. I remember a lawyer who was so busy thinking up his next question that he completely ignored what I called "cues of hate" coming from a juror. The lawyer leaned over to me at one point and asked what I thought of the panel.

"Have you seen Mr. Armstrong?" I asked.

"No, I haven't noticed anything," he said.

"Well, look at the way his eyes narrow and he frowns; he was looking right through you while you were looking at your notes!"

Minutes later he whispered, "Oh my, he's outta here!"

I'm not sure why so many lawyers find it difficult to stop selling, arguing, and persuading (the three blahs in blah, blah, blah), but if they do not let jurors do the talking during *voir dire,* they limit what they learn about the jurors. When lawyers really listen to what jurors say, not only with their words but with their facial expressions and body movements, they can learn an immense amount of information that reflects what that person is truly thinking.

The Obvious May Be Subtle

While judges still command a certain respect, jurors do not necessarily feel that way about the lawyers in a case. More than one individual has become upset and said, "These are stupid questions." This type of remark is actually quite common. Some jurors frown or sigh or shake their heads, all of which are meant to send a "I can't believe this" message. Many lawyers react quickly and think, "Let's get rid of 'em!" They immediately want to use one of their peremptory challenges and dismiss that juror.

When this has happened to me, I usually say something along the lines of: "It seems I've done or said something that you're not comfortable with. Can you help me understand it?" It is the rare individual who refuses to elaborate. In fact, one person said, "Well, I felt like you didn't like my last answer, but I was just being honest." I not only assured that prospective juror that I respected her response, but I also reminded myself to be aware of the cues that I was sending as well. In this situation, the exchange with the juror revealed that she was positively predisposed to our side, and perhaps she thought we did not recognize our symmetry. We did, and by matching her vocal tone with an added sense of apology and appreciation on my voice, she got the message. More importantly, she visibly got more comfortable as she straightened up in the chair and smiled. It was like a kid who got a puppy when mom and dad had yelled at her unfairly and then wanted to say they were sorry.

Jurors watch everything that goes on in the courtroom. They try to attribute meaning to anything they observe. A lawyer's frown is often taken personally, and certain tones or gestures may be interpreted differently in different parts of the country. For example, making a statement with an upward intonation in the voice may be seen as polite in the South and a sign of stupidity on the East Coast.

In general, we like people who are most like us. In an earlier chapter, I mentioned the case I tried in a small town in Illinois where everyone knew everyone else. I not only did not dress like everyone else, I spoke more quickly, so both verbally and nonverbally I managed to block rapport in every conceivable way. This occurred early in my career, before I realized that stress and anxiety could get in the way of what would otherwise be natural adjustments in style and demeanor in order to create similarity with others.

I like to pay attention to words and phrases that are distinct to particular jurors and then use them myself (or have my clients use them) in argument or even when interacting with a witness. I remember a case where a juror had, during jury selection, often stated, "Well, that's the way it looked to me," as a tag line after several answers. During opening statements, my client would borrow that phrase and suggest "the way it will look to you..." After a while, jurors subconsciously accept the phrases as a reflection of reality, because it is what they would have said and how they would have said it. What is more real than that?

Every Step Counts

Ideally, the rapport building that starts at *voir dire* continues to develop throughout the trial. If the jurors appear uncomfortable because the courtroom is hot, a lawyer can create commonality by telling the judge that the room is notably warm. If the courtroom is noisy and the sounds appear to disturb the jurors, the lawyer can indicate that the noise is disturbing everyone. As a consultant, I have my eyes everywhere. I am always watching for reactions, movements, and gestures on the part of jurors, the judge, the lawyers, and witnesses. It is a lot to monitor, but it is crucial. In one case, I saw a few jurors stare at my client as he would constantly tap his pen on the table, or click as the ball point protracted and retracted constantly when he was deep in thought. While my client was oblivious to the behavior, the jury was not, and I leaned over to bring his attention to this unconscious behavior.

It may seem odd that some lawyers need to be reminded or even taught basic principles of communication, but law-school training does not provide this kind of insight that can be easily adapted to the courtroom. I see my role sometimes as the teacher, and sometimes as the nudge or reminder to my clients not to lose their sense of fundamental rapport.

The Inconsistent Juror

I recall two jurors who met in the courtroom and appeared to bond instantly. Sure enough, during post-trial interviews they constantly referred to each other and talked about the super intelligence of their new "best friend." This illustrates the point that lawyers must pay attention to all the jurors, finding a variety of points of similarity, along with noting inconsistencies. Particularly when judges permit lawyers only limited *voir dire*, a lawyer must be very focused and concentrate on inconsistencies that emerge between what in the communication field we call jurors' verbal and nonverbal cues, or "incongruence."

I recall a juror who constantly paused and shifted with discomfort with any question that asked if he could side with the plaintiff if he felt the evidence warranted it. The verbal said "yes," but the nonverbal clearly said "no." In this case, he nodded his head, but he crossed one leg over the other and looked away. This is a bit like a person who says yes but shakes her head in the negative, from side to side. In this kind of situation, the lawyer must ask more questions and do what she can to get the juror to admit his inability to give both sides an equal ear. In many instances, a judge may determine that the verbal "I will be fair" answer is sufficient to withstand a motion to dismiss for cause, but the lawyers better monitor the use of their peremptory challenges, the ones they can exercise for nearly any reason they wish.

We also "hear" incongruence when an affirmative answer is stated with a rising or questioning intonation. Sometimes this can be perceived as sarcasm. I remember a juror who told the lawyer during jury selection that she was familiar with his reputation, but also knew of a person who claimed he was an unethical lawyer. No matter what the lawyer asked, the juror nevertheless stated that she would not let that person's experience color the way she would hear the evidence in this case. Again, the words said, "fair," but the voice said, "You don't have a chance with me." He removed that juror. In another case, a juror said "socially appropriate" things to the defense lawyer, but after each answer, she adjusted herself in her seat and let out a nearly audible "harumff," sending a strong suggestion that the affirmative answers did not mean much.

Incongruence often is felt or sensed. Our reaction might be to think or say, "Something doesn't add up here." We may not be able to pinpoint the incongruency because it may be quite subtle, unlike the examples used above. Most of us eventually learn to trust the subtle sense we call gut feelings. And, since the majority of trial attorneys still rely on their gut reactions to guide their deselection process, it is not surprising that jurors act precisely the same way when they evaluate an attorney and the story presented by a lawyer both during the trial and deliberations.

Using All the Senses

As I mentioned before, my friend and colleague Jo-Ellan Dimitrius is a well-known jury consultant who has worked on several hundred trials. To satisfy public curiosity about the way she carries out her work, she wrote the popular book *Reading People.* Her book is also intended to help readers learn how to become more perceptive about the individuals they encounter. She explains many elements of jury selection that may seem intangible and hard to pin down. For example, as she describes it, she uses all her senses. She watches for the subtle expression on a potential juror's face, and she listens to tone of voice. There are fine distinctions in tone between anger and sarcasm, or between commitment and uncertainty; lawyers mired in the heat of battle may miss these distinctions. The presence of heavy perfume or other cosmetics can suggest a juror more egocentric and focused on the burdens that the trial is placing on her social calendar than in paying close attention to complex evidence. An odor may accompany certain medications, which sends a warning to the court that it should be certain that none of the jurors are so concerned about a personal medical condition that they are not focused on the trial. I recall, for example, one juror who asked to see the judge and lawyers in private so she could inform that while she was happy to do her duty, she had little control over her bowels and could have to go the restroom frequently and with little or no warning. She was excused by the court.

The jury consultant pays attention to the style of dress of the jurors as they show up in court. Those who show up in business attire may hold their responsibilities with great seriousness, as the judge will confirm in her opening comments, which usually emphasize the importance of the juror's roles in the system. Conservative dress may also indicate that they tend to adopt beliefs we may label as conservative. Jurors who show up in jeans or very casual clothes may not be as serious about their duties, or they may just be a bit more open minded and liberal in their leaning. We pay attention to the way potential jurors move around in their chairs. Squirming can suggest discomfort with an issue in the case that is being discussed. On more than one occasion, I have seen jurors squirm as they learn that sexual dysfunction is an element in the case, or when they see graphic and gruesome photos that will be part of the evidence. We even watch the way jurors breathe; deep breathing can suggest that the evidence may be more than a person can handle, or more importantly, evaluate fairly.

You will recall the case I mentioned in which a juror sported a hefty key chain, full of keys, keys, and more keys. While the keys could, on the surface, represent someone of significant authority and power, they could also be the ego boost for someone who can open up a lot of unimportant doors where he works. So the lawyers must ask questions to see which way the pendulum is swinging; my job is to note the cues and try and decipher their meaning. Any of these characteristics, idiosyncrasies, or small mannerisms may not be important individually, but taken together with surveys and verbal interchange, they may lead to what is called a gut response (or more bluntly, a good guess) that is actually an informed reaction. This is where voodoo science is replaced by grounded research and analysis.

One reason jury science can seem to some like "hocus pocus" is that many people do not understand that the ability to read nonverbal cues and patterns is a learned skill. Certainly, jury consultants with the track record of Dimitrius may seem like highly intuitive individuals, but that ignores the fact that so many disciplines within the social sciences and psychology come together to create these informed evaluations and decisions.

It is clear that jurors (and everyone else, too) enter the courtroom filled with their particular preexisting biases about the world around them. These biases may be expressed verbally and/or nonverbally. The attorneys who concentrate their efforts on forming a connection with jurors are better able to assess these preexisting biases and the windows into them. Then, at the end of *voir dire*, the existing rapport results in the attentiveness of the jurors as the real storytelling part of the trial gets underway with the opening statement. A great deal of my time is spent working with lawyers in crafting and shaping the arguments they will present as they both open and close the case. We will explore that process in the next chapter.

chapter 6

"First Thing We Do, Let's Kill All the Lawyers…"

The day lawyers deliver opening statements is not exactly like the opening night of a play, but often, that is how it feels, jittery hands and all. However, trial lawyers generally have the kind of personality that craves the "performance" component of the law. Most believe they are at their best when they stand before the jury giving an opening statement or closing argument, and they live for it. I have heard young lawyers say these moments are the reason they went into law in the first place. "I don't make much money as a public defender," a friend of mine said, "but what other job allows me to be in court every day, running from courtroom to courtroom, always preparing for a new trial? I live for this." It may not be everybody's idea of a good time, but for my friend, the day of opening statement is the opening act. But how much of a difference do those "soliloquies" in front of a jury really make?

Is the Party Over before It's Over?

Many observers of the legal system, and some lawyers, too, assume that the "show" is over by the time the lawyers conclude their opening statements. They believe the myth that in 80 percent of cases jurors make up their minds on the verdict by the time the lawyers have completed the opening statements. Every time I present one of my seminars, I ask the lawyer-participants how many of them have not only heard this "truism," but believe it, too. Many hands go up because that is what they were taught in law school. This myth was presented as fact.

However, this so-called fact is actually an old myth, and is based on the misrepresentation of information in a legal text, *The American Jury*, published in the 1960s and written by jury-research pioneers Harry Kalven and Hans Zeisel. However, Kalven and Zeisel never even used the phrase "opening statement" in their book, let alone devise the 80 percent myth. Some years ago, I contacted Professor Zeisel at the University of Chicago and asked him about the attribution. He was not sure how the mistaken information began circulating, but he confirmed that it was erroneous and he actually believed that jurors definitely do not make up their minds by the time opening statements are completed. In fact, he was conducting research at the time to confirm his belief.

If you stop and think about the 80 percent figure, it becomes clear that it is ludicrous. Do you believe that nearly all jurors have made up their minds before they have heard *any* evidence? Or do you believe your friends and neighbors are typical jurors, and for the most part are rational beings who will try to carry out the judge's instructions, which include such details as listening to the evidence? Of course, they will not listen with a fair and impartial ear because such an "ear" does not exist, but that is not the same thing as throwing away the principles of the legal system, which mandate proving guilt or responsibility for an action.

Once the 80 percent rumor started, it became stubbornly difficult to reverse. A colleague of mine, Ron Beaton, and I became curious if some grain of truth exists in this particular myth, and we did some investigating of our own. We found that people do not reach a conclusion without further consideration, but they do begin to lean in one direction or another. This makes perfect sense once we accept that each juror comes to the table with attitudes and biases.

Logically, each juror is likely leaning one way or another once they gain even a modicum of understanding of the case—and that includes what they have heard during pre-trial publicity. In less publicized cases, the jurors hear the case summary from the judge at the onset of proceedings; others gain a good overview of the facts from the lawyers' efforts to explain the case during the *voir dire*. Ultimately, the jurors get a clearer sense of the case from the admittedly biased retelling of the case—or story—at opening statement.

Listening with a "Leaning" Ear

Our research indicated that some jurors begin to lean during jury selection, others during the openings, and still others did not begin to lean one way or the other until they heard evidence presented. Once a person begins to lean in a direction, he or she will try to hear the evidence in a way that supports their initial point of view or leaning. This makes sense. A leaning is not the same as a point of view; the latter term implies a greater degree of conviction behind the stance. Leanings can be likened to moving toward one side or another, but new information can nudge a move in the other direction.

Initial leanings generally fall in place based on specific belief systems. If you believe, as many people do, that where there's smoke there's fire, we expect you to have a pro-prosecution or pro-plaintiff leaning and you will listen with an ear that is receptive to evidence that proves the presence of fire. If you believe everything happens because of destiny or fate or because the Supreme Being willed it, you will find an explanation for virtually everything, from damage done by a hurricane to a death in the family, that fits that belief. Or, perhaps you believe a scientific explanation exists for every phenomenon. In that case, you listen with an ear that is influenced by facts and what you define as proof. Jurors listen in their individual ways at trial.

So, while the trial is not over with the opening statements, the lawyers' understanding of the jurors' existing attitudes and values guides or shapes the "story" and the way it is told. Since all lawyers want to help jurors lean in their direction, they must speak to the "receivers," who are already conditioned to hear and interpret information based on a frame of reference.

Three Sides to Every Question

Most of us accept that there are two sides to every question, but parties in a lawsuit are apt to forget the reality of the *third* side, which is the truth of what happened. Usually, the reality of what happened in a case is some combination of everyone's point of view. We tend to see what favors us and block out what does not favor our side of an argument. Parties to an auto accident will each immediately blame the other for causing the collision. Two corporate defendants will cloud a civil liability case to their own advantage, and the plaintiff may have a complex set of facts to live or die on, too. Parents warring over custody of their children rarely see that the truth lies somewhere in between their version of what is absolutely right. The parties involved are not necessarily lying; they are reflecting a natural process called "slippage." This means that over time, certain details of our experiences are lost from memory; our minds reshape other details.

Experts on human memory agree that we create memories that include causation. This means that we will add in a memory we do not really have in order to place the cause of an event somewhere—and usually, not on ourselves. For example, in a study conducted by eyewitness-testimony expert Dr. Elizabeth Loftus, individuals were shown pictures of Disneyland with Bugs Bunny in front of it. They then reported memories of having met Bugs themselves when they were at Disneyland. Since Bugs Bunny is a Warner Brothers character, he would not be caught dead at Disney! But people remember things as they think they should. They do this because they try to be honest. Therein lies the problem in reporting what might otherwise be an adversarial truth.

Lawyers know their clients will delete details from the first retelling of events. From the beginning, then, lawyers need to recognize that they cannot re-create in the courtroom what actually happened. Rather, the lawyer's role is to create a new reality, one that is consistent, appealing, and, ultimately, compelling in the jury's eyes. This process begins in the client interview, extends through depositions and other discovery, and must be established without a flaw at trial.

We expect jurors to compare the competing stories told by the lawyers during opening statements and attempt to sort out the truth from everything heard in argument and subsequent testimony. Lawyers know that jurors listen to their statements with a jaded ear. Jurors know that each side is engaged in persuasion and argument, and equally important, they remain aware that lawyers are paid to present their clients' cases in the best light. So, a self-serving opening statement is hardly a surprise.

Memories, Stories, and Truth

The concept of a story sometimes makes many of us uncomfortable because we do not want to believe that a trial could simply be about telling a story. A story could be fiction, mere fabrication. Jurors want the truth, but all lawyers have is a story. Once an event is over, however, we have only biased and tainted memories of it, and these constitute the stories we tell ourselves in our lives. We have an argument with someone and we tend to recall that the other person started it and is at fault. That may be blatantly false, but it is what human beings do.

Many times the facts of a case are uncovered, not from the client who may knowingly or unknowingly block facts as they tell their account, but from the process of fact discovery that goes on in lawsuits. Reality emerges from reviewing documents and photos, DNA results and ballistics reports, and other items discovered through what are called production requests in a lawsuit. Witness statements, depositions, police reports, and so forth all provide additional sources of facts that may contradict a client's own memory of what happened in this particular story.

In the courtroom, storytelling is crucial because jurors listen to the competing stories of the event. This is why we have the trial. In essence, the jurors' job is to determine which side's story makes more sense. In our minds, the trial really starts when the lawyers establish the story in their opening statements. You will not hear lawyers talking about stories; rather, they use the terms "case continuity" or "account," because, as I have said, a story sounds too much like fiction. They understand that the stories they craft are framed in a strong sense of reality, but "account" grounds their words in the nonfiction world.

A popular model of storytelling lawyers use views the story/continuity as the vehicle by which we organize information that enables the jurors to perform two interpretive operations. First, jurors locate the central action in the case, and second, they construct the most credible inferences between the bits of information presented through testimony and evidence. As they listen, jurors are looking for a way to explain events that are in dispute. The only way to do it is through comparison and contrast of the accounts presented.

Rarely do we see a last-minute witness that unravels one side's case and clears up everything, usually making the jury irrelevant. This makes good television drama, but it is far from the norm. In day-to-day courtrooms, jurors look for connections between the elements of testimony presented at each stage of the process as they attempt to figure out if a set of events could have occurred in ways suggested by the lawyers and the evidence. This is why framing the information in the form of a consistent story is so important.

Looking at the Central Action

Every story and every real event contains a central action, which is the glue that frames the continuity of events and keeps circumstances in context. The central action also serves as the gauge for inconsistency and is a tool to evaluate circumstantial evidence. In one case discussed in my book *Courtroom Power*, the following was presented at trial.

The plaintiff, Brian Mertz, was injured while using a Sharp-Cut saw to perform simple carpentry jobs around his house. He had used one before and read the instructions. He can now no longer work or perform daily functions.

Certain surface-level inferences could be made by the jury from the testimony: Brian cut his hand while using Saw Company's dangerous product, and as a result, he experienced and continues to experience pain, suffering, and financial loss. The central action, or what specifically caused the plaintiff's injury and what the defendant could have done to avoid it, is unclear at this point. If Brian's lawyer failed to establish each of the story elements, he would be unable to meet his burden of proving every allegation.

The jury went on to learn that the Sharp-Cut blade had a safety guard that was known to snap off while the product was in use. The blade guard of this particular saw was missing from the product after Brian was injured. By establishing the central action, namely, that the plaintiff's injury was caused by a flaw in the defendant's product, of which the manufacturer had notice, the story became more complete for the jury.

The defendant countered the plaintiff's story with an alternative explanation. For example, the defendant's expert testified that the safety guard was designed properly and worked properly, but the plaintiff misused it. The defendant went on to show that its product's safety guard had never injured anyone before. Through some witness testimony, they raised the possibility that the plaintiff had been drinking when he used the product; therefore, it was possible that Brian was not using the product correctly, in a proper state of mind, or for its intended purpose.

The above scenarios are typical of those presented in product-liability cases. The jury is left to weigh two potentially credible accounts to determine what really happened. You can see why it is crucial for the trial consultant and lawyer to work closely together as they form the story. The case theme becomes critical, and each lawyer needs to anticipate and prepare for any counter-explanations.

In another case involving very lengthy opening statements, our firm was hired to provide a mirror jury, which is a group of people who are recruited to sit through the trial, just like the actual jury. We talk with them following every day of trial to get their reactions and perspective on how the case is going. In this particular case, the opening statements took two full days, one for each side. It was unusual for a judge to allow so much time, but there were many parties to this class-action lawsuit and plenty of allegations regarding antitrust violations and fraud, among other things.

As we spoke to our mirror jurors after the plaintiff's arguments, they were swayed. "Pretty strong case" and "I can't wait to hear what the defendant has to say to all this" were among the comments. Just twenty-four hours later, after listening to the defense, these same jurors were saying, "Wow, now I'm not so sure" and "The defense really addressed the concerns I had, so I have to listen to evidence to figure this out." Well, that was fine and exactly what they needed to do, but it highlights the power of effective lawyers to at least temporarily influence jurors.

Sometimes, part of the jury consultant's job is to help clients be certain they do their best to craft the competing story, the one their opponent is likely to tell the jury. Then, we work with them to be certain that their own story incorporates the arguments that will be made by the other side and address the points head-on. For example, in the case in which Brian suffered an injury while using the saw, the manufacturer of the saw argued that "these tools are dangerous—of course you are going to get hurt if you don't use them properly and carefully read the instructions." Because we knew they were likely to say this, Brian's lawyer was careful to emphasize that Brian had, indeed, read and followed the instructions.

What if we had known for a fact that Brian had *not* read the instructions? Then I would have had to address that problem with my client and craft an argument to explain why it was not necessary for Brian to have read the instructions. For example, we may have had to argue (assuming the evidence would support it) that Brian had used many of these kinds of tools on several occasions. There was nothing special about this saw and he relied on his familiarity and expertise with the tool, as well as his expectation that the manufacturer properly designed and created this particular tool. Fortunately, Brian had spent time with the instructions and we did not have to go in this direction. The point is that we must not leave the other side's arguments hanging out there—we tackle them head-on in the opening.

Promises, Words, Atmosphere

Underlying the facts of the story, the theme is the backdrop that is introduced during the lawyers' arguments. And so, with all the preparation behind him, the lawyer begins:

> Ladies and gentlemen of the jury, during this opening statement, you will hear the story of my client, Maude Fridgen, who fell on some ice in the hallway of the Cowan Hotel. This is my opportunity to talk to you directly about what the evidence will show. Once the evidence is in, you will see that my client is entitled to a substantial sum of money.

With these words, the attorney believes he or she has captured the jurors' attention. Do these words grab you? Or, more likely, have they put you to sleep? Since we do not want snoozing jurors, we shape the statement to contain drama, surprise, and other story elements. The opening statement, although it does not absolutely determine the final outcome, as the common myth holds, does set up continuity. Jurors listen closely to the promises lawyers make and they listen for consistency and, equally important, inconsistency. Consider the same case opening this way:

> A cold, dark hallway, left unattended, with a constant stream of water dripping and freezing almost instantaneously when it hits the floor. This is the dangerous scene that awaited any unsuspecting hotel guest. And in this case, it was the condition that met the plaintiff, Maude Fridgen, who broke her leg and continues to suffer pain from an incident that should have never happened. Let me take you to the beginning…."

In the second version, the jury is more likely to be intrigued, ready, and interested to listen to the unfortunate circumstances the plaintiff encountered. Same case, same facts, but the second scenario is far more effective. Let's discuss what makes an opening statement effective.

Here Comes the Judge

During opening statements, the jurors are also becoming acquainted with the presiding judge. Most jurors defer to the judge's lead at every stage of the trial because he has leadership authority and sets the tone in the courtroom. Jurors have faith in judges to keep the proceedings fair, but they also listen for clues about what is going on beneath the surface. Many jurors watch the judge during the proceedings, and most are affected by the judge's position, the robe, the gavel, and the position of the bailiff, not to mention the ever-present flag, all of which are intended to add to the dignity and sober nature of the proceedings. And of course, judges are usually seated much higher than anyone in the room, which is a classic method to create an aura of authority, as well as establishing respectful distance. These distinctions are not lost on jurors.

I recall a juror who passed the judge on the street and came back to comment to his jurors, "The judge is much shorter than I thought. He looks so big up there. Kind of like a trick they use in the movies." Whether the judge really looked taller in his chair or whether the overall atmosphere influenced this juror remains open to question, but I cast my vote for the latter. Since more than 90 percent of the impact of the information transmitted in a courtroom occurs at a nonverbal level, it is not surprising that the judge will usually enjoy a high level of rapport among the jurors.

Judges may speak only a relatively few words during a trial, but everything else they do delivers powerful nonverbal messages. A simple "Counselor!" said in a stern tone from the bench to a lawyer talking with an associate at counsel's table can bring the trial to a halt. I recall a judge warning a lawyer to, "Watch where you are going with this line of questioning...." Then, as the lawyer seemingly took a step too far, the judge took off his glasses with a brisk motion and stopped the lawyer in the middle of a word. "I'm not going there, Judge," the lawyer said sheepishly. Of course, the judge never said he was, but that movement alone told the story.

I advise lawyers to consider adopting some of the judge's postures and general motions, while avoiding blatant mimicry, both during their own opening statements and while listening to the opposing side's opening. It is not uncommon for some of that juror-judge connection to slip over to the lawyer who fits the same mold. People like people who are like themselves, so what better person to align your behavior and demeanor with than the person who rules the courtroom?

It may sound odd, but in the courtroom, lawyers can use their hands and body to place truth and untruth in different locations. For example, when referring to the truth of what the jury will hear from witnesses, the lawyer can emphasize the point by standing in a particular spot or by pointing to a specific place in the courtroom. The jury observes that truth is placed in one location and untruth in another, although this is not necessarily consciously absorbed information.

The technique becomes even more powerful as it is repeated throughout the course of the trial, in testimony, and again in closing argument. Soon the jury will understand what is true and what is not, merely by watching the movements of the lawyers as they repeat or trigger the "anchor" for the jury. For example, a household saw, a safety device, and an injured arm may be indisputable facts. But the condition of the saw, the instruction book, and the intended use of the saw may be in dispute. So, the lawyer in the "saw" case worked hard to "set" each of these facts in different areas of the courtroom using different physical postures or gestures. He walked around the well of the courtroom as he talked through the proper steps taken by his client in preparing to use the saw. In this way, the unconscious message continued to get anchored in the jurors' minds.

I recall one case involving a roof leak in which the lawyer discussed the leak by pointing to the courtroom floor as though the roof and its dangerous leak were right there. He did this unconsciously. Then I watched several jurors walk toward the jury room during a break and consciously avoid stepping on the area of the perfectly fine floor where the lawyer had effectively placed the leak. That demonstrates the power of anchoring. The jury consultant's job is to make sure the clients we work with understand the power of these basic communication techniques. If these sound like theatrical techniques, we need only remember that live theater is one of the most powerful communication mediums ever created.

Consultants might also help lawyers introduce words and phrases in the opening statements (or reinforce them from *voir dire*) that serve as verbal triggers. Terms such as "ripped off," "smashed," and "crashed," or "responsibility" and "accountability" can be anchored and triggered throughout the opening statement, and then through testimony at trial. If they originated from a juror's mouth, these words serve as especially effective anchors. In actuality, every phrase that comes from jurors in *voir dire* has the potential to serve as an anchor for the lawyer. The jury consultant can step back from the flurry of trial preparation to synthesize the theme and the key words that can reinforce the desired response.

Even idiosyncratic remarks can become anchors for specific responses. For example, the phrase (accompanied by rolling eyes and a sliding tone) "There you go again!" is forever associated with Ronald Reagan. In his presidential campaign, Walter Mondale used the phrase, "Where's the beef?" the immortal phrase spoken by Clara Peller in Wendy's television commercials. The phrase made its way into common parlance, which means it sends a universal message most jurors will understand. Most recently, the phrase "Let's roll," uttered by Todd Beamer of the fated September 11 flight that crashed in Pennsylvania, seems forever to ignite courage and strength in action.

Promises, Promises

A lawyer's opening statement is supposed to be a road map, and is particularly important because throughout the trial and into deliberations, the jury will remember what they are promised in these opening statements. Lawyers must be careful about what they promise to prove because the jury expects the promises to be fulfilled. The opening becomes a gauge the jury uses to assess reality as they listen to the testimony and the "story" of the case. If a lawyer fails to do or produce what is promised, the lawyer loses the jury's trust, and quite possibly the case.

I have noticed that fans of televised trials keep track of lawyers' promises, too. One of the reasons viewers become "hooked" on a trial is that they want to see the lawyers deliver what they promised in opening statements. Where is that witness who will say he sold a half-dozen cans of kerosene to the defendant? Where is the witness who says the defendant distributed a bunch of spare kerosene cans to the neighbors to use in their heaters during a power outage last winter—maybe even several cans? They do not expect that kind of crucial testimony to be cut into with commercial breaks.

I advise my defense clients, for example, to refer to the promises and expectations they believe the other side needs to prove. They can remind the jury of the prosecution or plaintiff's burden by saying, "Hold her to it. Be sure she shows you through the evidence every element, because if she does not, then we cannot be held responsible. Watch the evidence. You won't see it here."

Blah, Blah, or Ah Ha!

Thoughtfully processing information goes beyond hearing the words; to effectively listen, jurors need an internal "map" they can relate to the case. Just as lawyers consider how the other side will tell its version of events, jurors think ahead and often do exactly the same thing. They ask themselves how the other lawyer would respond. For example, in one case discussed earlier, a pedestrian crossed in the middle of a busy street and was hit by a public bus. The conflicting stories involved the account of the negligent bus driver who was improperly and inadequately trained by the bus company. That's the plaintiff's version. In response, we heard the account of the defendant, which is that no one, even a careful driver like in this case, can avoid a "dart out" in the middle of busy traffic by a man who is not looking where he is going.

An effective opening is persuasive, yet simple, which sounds obvious. The problem is that many lawyers are boring and their stories are not compelling enough to listen to thoughtfully, much less consider credible. Many lawyers present their cases in a way that makes sense to them. They listen to their own story as if they have a really open-minded jury in front of them. "I'd believe it," they say to themselves, "makes sense to me." Well, whether it makes sense to the jury, the only people who count, remains to be seen. Trial consultants can step in to "refresh" a theme or a story that lawyers have become too comfortable with because they have been living with the case for a long time, often for many years.

For some reason, many lawyers waste the first moments of the opening statement. They get caught up in defining to the jury what an opening is, the purpose it serves, where the trial goes next, what role the lawyer will play, and on and on. With any luck, they finally begin to discuss the case several minutes into the presentation. Unfortunately, by that time the jury likely is tuned out. I once worked with the lawyer for the plaintiff who brought an action for wrongful employment termination based on religious discrimination. When I first sat with my lawyer-client and asked her to present her opening statement for me, she began: "My name is Terry Johnson and I represent Dave Brady in this action against Marchant Consulting. This is my opening statement; my opportunity to tell you what we believe the evidence will show. Now, the law does not allow an employer to hire or fire someone just because of his or her religious beliefs. Specifically, the law states…"

At that point, I cut her off. "I'm sleeping, Terry. This is boring." A bit harsh perhaps, but I needed to make the point.

"What should I do?" she asked. "I don't know any other way to start."

I pulled one of the corporate documents that had religious verses all through it and said, "Here, start with this."

She began again. "My name is Terry…"

I cut her off. "No, Terry. I said start with the document. I don't need to know your name. The judge told me your name. Just start reading."

She began again. "'The Lord is good, a stronghold in the day of trouble; He knows those who commit themselves to Him.' Ladies and gentlemen, you may think I am reading from the Bible to you. Well, the words are from the Old Testament and specifically from the book of Nahum. But the document I am reading from is a corporate document sent by the defendant to all employees in his company. 'Awake, awake, put on strength, arm of the Lord! I, I am He who comforts you; who are you that you should fear mortal man, or the son of man who shall be made like the grass?' This biblical passage was also found in a prominent place in a corporate planning document. You will see and hear many corporate documents in this case, all of which will demonstrate that this is a company whose owner made every decision, from hiring to firing, solely on the basis of religion."

This was so much more alive—and we won the case.

The first version of Terry's opening statement started in the wrong place because she grounded it on the wrong foundation. Some lawyers know their case so well and then act as if the jury also must be quite familiar with the facts, too. This is a little like a physician using technical terms to describe the stage of a tumor before the patient fully understands that the doctor is trying to tell him he has cancer. You and I know that a speaker, any speaker, has to hook an audience. The same is true with opening statements. Their job is to hook the jurors and grab their attention.

In the religious-discrimination case, Terry refocused her opening statement and began at an emotional high point. In fact, it perhaps was a bit of a shock. However, by reading those documents at the onset of her opening statement, the jurors knew exactly what her point was going to be. And they quickly learned that they would have to pay special attention to the myriad corporate documents with religious messages that made up a great portion of the evidence in the case.

Am I Going to Hear the Whole Case?

I recall working with a lawyer who had memorized every small detail of the case. This may be useful, but the opening statement is no place to expound on a trail of small facts. This lawyer talked about the year a television was manufactured and a computer was purchased as he went through a laborious list of items that had been allegedly stolen. Who cares? The theme of the case involved a dispute over whose property the items were in the first place. This was actually a domestic dispute, not an armed robbery. Another lawyer droned on about toxic chemicals, essentially giving the testimony of the expert she planned to call. Then she droned on even longer as she presented and disputed the arguments she expected the defendant's expert to present.

These lawyers go too far in creating a compelling case and become bogged down with so much detail that the jurors begin to wonder if they are hearing all the testimony at once. Jurors may dread having to sit through it all again. Like the rest of us, jurors have a short attention span. If a lawyer knows that most students have trouble listening to a two-hour chemistry lecture, they should understand that adults will have the same problem with a two-hour opening "lecture," no matter how critical each fact is. Jurors may listen intently for the first few minutes, but soon they begin thinking about the last episode of *The Practice*.

So, What Should an Opening Statement Sound Like?

An effective opening statement starts with a powerful phrase, one that captures the tone and message of the case. My colleague, jury consultant Richard Crawford in his book *The Persuasive Edge*, tells lawyers to fire the "silver bullets."

Consider the following examples:

- In a personal-injury case, the plaintiff's lawyer says, "This case is about safety on the job, about a man who lost his hand while just trying to do his job, about a man who worked for the same company for fifteen years, and now a man who can no longer do his job. But this case is much more, because we will show that this man, Mike Charles, did not need to lose his hand, that this man had his hand taken from him because he was asked to operate a piece of equipment unsafe for anybody to use. When Mike Charles was asked to operate the machine, he did not hesitate because he had a good-faith trust in his company, a trust which made him believe he would not be sent to a job with equipment that would harm him."

- From a defense perspective in the same case: "A little care and a bit of caution. That's all it would have taken to avoid the unfortunate accident that occurred in this case. A little care in reading the instruction manual and assembling the machine; a little caution in turning the machine on and beginning to work properly with it. But when you rush, and you don't pay attention, then you end up in court pointing fingers at the company that encouraged that employee to take the time, care, and caution in the design, manufacture, and use of what everyone will admit is a dangerous machine."

These opening statements provide themes the lawyers can return to again and again throughout the trial. The lawyers have determined the theme through a combination of the facts they have to work with, community attitudes, juror profiles, and so forth. Now, with the opening statement, they have the opportunity to plant that theme in the minds of the jury in the opening statement. They then go back to the theme many times because this is the essence of the "story" they will tell.

In some situations, physical gestures can have just as powerful an impact in opening statement as visual aids, such as charts and photographs. For example, in one case, the lawyer wished to create the impression of a small, near claustrophobia-inducing room. He spread his arms wide to describe more reasonable rooms, but he crouched into himself to create what it was like to step into the room involved. He used this physical "aid" throughout the trial whenever he wanted to remind jurors about the small room.

"Noise" of a Different Kind

Delivering an effective opening statement is an art, and as in all the arts, to be good at it, you have to practice. This is why trial consultants help clients to keep moving to the next level, as the saying goes. When an opening statement is done well, the lawyer's client, either a plaintiff or a defendant, becomes a real human being, not just a name, or worse, just a corporate entity with no face at all. And the lawyer has done this in spite of all the competing "noise" that may fill the jurors' heads. What I mean is, jurors get bored, inattentive, and distracted. I have seen boring lawyers reduce juror attention to counting the number of "uhs" the lawyer says rather than focusing on the points presented. I recall a juror who said she found it hard to listen to a particular lawyer because she could not keep herself from paying attention to his wrinkled shirts and torn jacket, which, unfortunately, he wore day after day.

Distraction can also take the form of the juror's internal dialogue in his head, such as continually wondering what the constant objections mean and intense curiosity about what is being said in the sidebars going on between lawyers and the judge. A lawyer who is unable to maintain and retain the jurors' attention after such moments is losing valuable opportunities to relate to the jury.

I advise clients to talk to the jury as they would to an acquaintance. Rather than saying "We submit, ladies and gentlemen," they should say: "You know what happened here? This man walked into the bank and…." This conversational tone does not compromise either the necessary respectful formality of the courtroom or the importance of the case. But it does establish a person-to-person rapport with each juror, and even more important, it keeps the jurors focused on the case, not the trivial details.

When "Guilt" Is Not the Issue

Imagine a case where the defendant admits he is in the wrong, (i.e., is responsible for what has happened to the plaintiff). If the defendant admits he did something wrong, then why is this case being tried in court? Usually, this occurs because the defendant and plaintiff disagree on how much money is appropriate to resolve the dispute. Take a case in which two plaintiffs are driving along in their car and, while waiting at a red traffic light, they are hit from behind by a truck. This is a classic scenario where the defendant admits responsibility. But how much does it take to care for an injured plaintiff? If they cannot agree on terms, then the case goes to trial on the issue of damages. The jurors are told that, as a matter or law, the defendant is responsible. They are told not to consider that question at all. The only issue for them to consider is how much money is the appropriate award for the plaintiff.

In this case that follows, details are changed but the case is real. I have shortened the arguments and details to both make my point easier to understand.

So, the plaintiffs' lawyer tells the jury:

> Just two days before Christmas, on December 23, 1998, Danny Deveening and his daughter Theresa had been out doing some last-minute Christmas shopping. Theresa, just seventeen years old, and Danny, then forty-eight, were stopped at a stoplight on Northbound Road. Theresa was driving and her father was sitting in the front passenger seat. The defendant, Leo Nardo, was operating a semi-tractor-trailer that was coming further down Northbound Road. Theresa first saw the defendant's headlights in her rearview mirror. Mr. Nardo approached the stoplight. Then came a loud horrific boom and the sound of metal crunching metal as the defendant did not stop for that light. He continued driving, crushing right into and demolishing the Deveening car at thirty miles per hour, propelling it out into the middle of the intersection like a man being shot from a cannon. [That analogy lets jurors see pictures of the accident scene and Deveening car.] As a result of this devastating and violent

collision, Danny suffered permanent brain damage and a spinal-cord injury resulting in paralysis and constant pain. Theresa suffered facial cuts, head and neck injuries resulting in chronic headaches, chronic neck pain, scarring, and disfigurement. You will hear evidence in this case about the accident and the damages that resulted from it.

Let me tell you a little about Danny Deveening before the accident. You'll see through the evidence in this case that he was a proud, intelligent, independent, and hardworking family man. He worked for Parker University as a computer technician. Needless to say, Danny has been unable to return to work and will not be able to return to work there or anywhere else for that matter. All of his treating doctors will tell you he cannot work in any capacity. As a result of this accident, Mr. Deveening's calculated lost wages, fringe benefits, and loss of household services total about 2,250,000 (two and a quarter million) dollars. Following the accident, Danny and Theresa were taken by ambulance to Springfield Hospital. Theresa was lucky. She was treated for minor abrasions and released. Danny was diagnosed with permanent brain damage, paralysis to the right side, and spinal-cord damage. He continues to be in constant pain, experiences a loss of balance and control, and remains in a state of severe depression.

Listen carefully to the evidence, ladies and gentlemen, and you will see that an award in excess of several million dollars from the defendant who has admitted fault in this case is more than appropriate.

The plaintiff's lawyer did not need to focus on the details of the accident and fault; everyone agrees the defendant must pay. But if you are the defendant, how do you respond? Where do you begin? Here was our suggested approach given the evidence in the case. It was quite lengthy, and perhaps more detailed than I suggested most opening statements should be. I've summarized some of it (my comments are in brackets), but hang in with it—you may be surprised:

A tragic accident happened three years ago on December 23. We are not here to contest that. We are here today willing to compensate Daniel Deveening for his injuries. We have accepted responsibility for his injuries and want to provide for him for the rest of his life. We are willing to do this; it is only right. We are willing to provide him with enough money so that he can live comfortably for the rest of his life. What is a reasonable amount of money? How much money is enough?

You heard the plaintiff's story. It is a compelling story with many chapters. Their story, however, is not the complete story. We are here to hopefully help you see the complete story and to find the truth.

What is the truth? Who is the real Daniel Deveening? How can we find the truth of the value of his injuries? We can look to the care and treatment of the plaintiff through the course of his recovery. The truth, ladies and gentlemen, is what the medical records show. The truth is in the gains Daniel has made in the months following the accident as he worked to recover. The truth is in the testimony heard in this courtroom. The truth is in the evidence of how the plaintiff is doing today.

The plaintiff claims that he suffered a traumatic brain injury. What is a traumatic brain injury? How do we know if someone has a brain injury?

The evidence will show that the first indication of the nature and extent of a brain injury is the level of consciousness after the impact....

[At this point, the defense lawyer went into some detail about the kind of medical tests used to assess brain injuries. These tests indicated that the plaintiff's injuries were not previously described accurately by the other lawyer. The lawyer would use a visual report to confirm his claims. They would use other medical reports as well. Daniel's state of consciousness immediately after the accident was an important issue.]

The paramedic report indicates that Daniel may have lost consciousness at the scene. But when the paramedics and firemen were rendering medical treatment to him, he was conscious and moaning. At no time did the plaintiff slip into a coma; he remained stable. [More medical reports were discussed.] Contrary to the plaintiff's contentions, the evidence is clear that Mr. Deveening was not in a coma.

A traumatic brain injury or brain damage is the result of the brain getting jarred during a violent impact. As a result, there could be swelling or bruising of the brain, which may result in brain damage. [The lawyer showed the report on the ELMO— a projector that enlarges a document and allows the jury and others in the courtroom to view it simultaneously.] There is no objective evidence that there were any lesions, bruises, or swelling on the plaintiff's brain; no test that any doctor can show you where the damage was. All we can rely on is what the plaintiff tells his doctors and what they observe. And that will be the testimony and evidence you hear in this case.

[At this point the plaintiff's rehab process was discussed, including a discussion of testing. His doctor was named and specific types of testing were referred to. You may note by now that the defendant was putting great amounts of information forward. The lawyer made it clear that his client had nothing to hide.]

We have evidence that Daniel talked to his treating physician and told him that he felt his mind was not different as a result of the accident, but he did recognize a difference in his speech, which is slow. He also reported that he felt less tolerant and more irritable since the accident. Otherwise, he felt his functioning was unchanged. Neuropsychological tests of problem solving show a pattern of mixed abilities. [More neurological testing results were shared.]

To be clear and fair, ladies and gentlemen, you will see and hear the evidence that confirms that the plaintiff's cognitive functioning remains strong, and no other significant residual cognitive deficits were evidenced. In fact, Mr. Deveening was found to be a good candidate for rehabilitation. He showed signs of good insight and awareness of his problems; is extremely, if not excessively, motivated to participate in treatment; and retains much of his cognitive functions, including memory and problem-solving abilities, which he can bring to bear. In therapy, he would be able to work directly on increasing his mental speed as well as on his speech and language deficits. And because his accident was recent, his deficits may improve significantly in the next several months as he continues in the recovery process.

[Again, remember what we know about brain injuries, that most gains are made in the first six months after the injury. This is important because this is not the only testing the plaintiff has. And like all good stories, Daniel's story has a twist.]

What do we really know about Daniel Deveening? What does Mr. Deveening want you to know about him? While it may be offensive to some, in order to present the truth to you in this trial, ladies and gentlemen, video surveillance was conducted of the plaintiff. After all, these are allegations of very serious injuries and serious damages. You are entitled to see the real Daniel, the Daniel Deveening the plaintiff and his lawyers did not want *you* to see. A picture is worth a thousand words, and it is important to see him when he does not know he is being watched and when he does know he is being watched. The video evidence you will see show the true nature and extent of his injuries. After all, the plaintiff may be able to fool his doctors and his lawyers, but he won't be able to fool you in this court of law.

What else don't you know about the plaintiff? The evidence will show that he still drives. He even renewed his driver's license. What we do know is that the plaintiff, the private Mr. Deveening, is never seen using a cane, wheelchair, walker, a person, or any other assist device. He walks with a limp; we are not denying that. His gain, however, is at a comfortable pace and with a minimal amount of apparent discomfort.

Plaintiffs have told you about the severity of the injuries that resulted from this accident. He sustained such injuries that would prevent him from doing everyday things without great assistance.

If that is how bad it is, then he would not be able to go out shopping, drive, and do all the things that our video camera, and our injury verification team, saw him doing. Cameras don't lie. The truth is the truth. The evidence will be very clear here.

The plaintiff has looked at what he thinks is fair and reasonable to take care of him for the rest of his life. We too have looked at all of the medical records, reviewed the videos of his daily activities, and talked to doctors, economists, and other experts to come up with truthful figures. I would like to take you through those now.

You heard about the plaintiff's annual earnings. [The lawyer then went into some calculations used to determine settlement amounts. These calculations dealt with potential earnings, lost income, etc.] Can the plaintiff ever work again? He says no. The video camera proves otherwise. We know that Mr. Devenning can go to the store, bend down and reach into a large cardboard bin, and select a large watermelon and put it into the cart. We also know that he is able to load and unload a grocery cart. We saw him on the video lift large items, palming honeydews and rearranging the groceries in the trunk. A recalculation in present-value dollars, and consideration of the plaintiff's ability to undertake various forms of employment, the lost income would be viewed, not near one million dollars as the plaintiff suggests, but one closer to $75,000. What do our eyes tell us?

[You can see where this argument was going. The lawyer moved on here to the future costs of Daniel's medical care and much of the information was based on standard calculations.]

So, as you listen to the evidence in this case ladies and gentlemen, watch and listen closely. The plaintiff has been injured, but what you see in this courtroom, and the evidence will confirm, is a man who has made a remarkable recovery. A man who hopes to parlay a terrible accident into a lifelong lottery so he never has to work again. We think you will find that a very reasonable amount of dollars will adequately and appropriately compensate the plaintiff.

Imagine the surprise of the jurors when they heard the defense claim that they have heard lies. Was the plaintiff a seriously and permanently injured person? Or was he recovered to the point that he could resume a reasonable life, but saw this lawsuit as the opportunity to get a lot of money? Lawyers take a great risk when they accuse a person their clients have injured of lying and fabricating the facts of his condition. But the evidence of this man's fraudulent claims was compelling enough to allow them to take this kind of risk.

Toppling the "King"

Earlier I mentioned a complex financial case that we simplified by likening it to ticket scalping. At the time, financial-misconduct cases seemed more complex than interesting, but nowadays, many attract attention because the investing public feels it has a stake in these cases. The case I mentioned earlier was known as the "Penny Stock King" case, *U.S. v. Meyer Blinder,* and I assisted the U.S. Attorney's office in Las Vegas with their prosecution of the case.

This "Penny Stock King" case was important to the government because Blinder had bought up stocks, controlled their price, and subsequently made millions of dollars at investors' expense. Blinder was charged with securities fraud and racketeering. Today's jurors might be more sophisticated about these cases after the Martha Stewart scandal, but pre-trial publicity may tend to make seating jurors more difficult. In the Blinder case, singer Wayne Newton was on the list of possible witnesses, and this raised the potential for eventual publicity.

When we compared Blinder's activities to those of a ticket scalper, we knew that many individuals would relate to it, and most certainly residents of Las Vegas. The lawyers, Joseph Dion, a special prosecutor with the Securities and Exchange Commission at the time, and Howard Zlotnik, the chief of the criminal division, chose to present the case using the ticket-scalper theme, around which they formed their opening statement. The case was off to a good start because the jury was spared the need to listen to complex financial information.

The jurors came to understand that what Blinder did violated federal laws, and the jurors ultimately understood the principle and convicted the defendant. Blinder was quite surprised by the verdict because he believed he could never be convicted. At the sentencing hearing, what may have been a light sentence ended up quite stiff because the defendant lunged for the prosecutor in open court. It was a bad move, not to mention a defense lawyer's nightmare.

In one civil case, I represented a major-city newspaper in its defense against a plaintiff who was shot by one the newspaper's drivers. Notice, I do not say he was allegedly shot, because he was and the driver did do the shooting. However, it was our position that such behavior was completely outside the scope of job responsibilities or even reasonably anticipated conduct. In fact, no one on the staff of the newspaper had any knowledge that any of the drivers carried guns, or at least that is what all the deposition testimony confirmed.

The plaintiff's lawyer had the job of getting the jury to hold not only that the newspaper driver, who we will call Randy O'Sims, was responsible, but in addition, the lawyer needed the deep pockets of the large-city newspaper. How could he create the necessary link? He said:

> Accountability and responsibility. When you are accountable for the actions of someone, you must be held responsible for their wrongdoing. On the night of December 22, two years ago, my client, Charles Bailey, was without warning and for no reason shot and permanently injured by the City Newspaper through the reckless act of its driver, Randy O'Sims. The evidence will show you, ladies and gentlemen, that the newspaper *knew* its drivers carried guns in the face of a policy against carrying guns, and that it did nothing to properly train and prevent its drivers from recklessly shooting people. When you take aim, you gotta take the blame.

The money in that case was going to have to come from the newspaper because the driver most likely had few resources. If the plaintiff spent all his time focusing on the driver, then the case and theme could lead the jurors to feel strongly about the driver. But the only significant verdict comes from a finding against the paper.

How did the newspaper respond? I knew the paper was the target defendant, so I had to meet the argument head on:

> If an employee is going to break a rule, no matter how much you train and urge them to follow the policies and rules of the company, then they are going to find a way to do so. The City Newspaper couldn't have done more to ensure that its drivers took every precaution to be safe and to ensure the safety of others. In this case, ladies and gentlemen, you will see that the newspaper had and continues to have a serious and extensive policy that prohibits its drivers from carrying guns on the job. It is undisputed that employees know that the consequences for violating this policy are grave indeed. The plaintiff knows this as well, but he knows that while the newspaper has done nothing wrong, they do have one thing he wants, money. And being a large corporation, ladies and gentlemen, is not reason enough to declare responsibility when you haven't done anything wrong.

I had to address the policy in the hope that the jury would align with the position. Would the newspaper be seen as trying to escape the case? Or would the jury find that employers, so long as they have done everything in their power to properly train and care for their employees, should not be held responsible for an act so outside the scope and expectation of known or anticipated conduct that it would be unreasonable to do so?

Starting at the End Point

We will explore the role of witnesses and evidence in the next chapter. For now, though, let's look at when the case is completed, and the lawyers return to the stage and pull it all together in their closing arguments. Often thought to be a moment of high drama, it is the moment that many lawyers wait for to create the solidifying element for the case. Court TV viewers all tune in for closing arguments, and sometimes the cable networks will break in to cover this portion of the trial because viewers want to see the loose ends neatly tied up.

Many lawyers write the closing argument before any other trial preparation, following the adage: "You have to know where you want to end up in order to figure out how to get there." However, the power of the closing argument rests strongly with the manner in which the evidence comes in through the course of the trial. Jurors remember the promises the lawyers made during the opening statement. In a sense, the closing is a summation of all the promises kept, and perhaps a reminder of the failure of the other side to keep their promises.

Lawyers must evaluate each step or point in the trial. Were the witnesses perceived to be as credible as they had hoped? Did the substance of what was offered through these witnesses have a positive impact on the jury, or did the jurors find the case presented less than compelling? Essentially, the closing argument is the culmination of a trial, which should have been in the planning since the case first came into the office.

Shaping the Meaning

The meaning of evidence is perceived by the jurors, but is shaped by the lawyers. In other words, lawyers need to understand how the evidence is being accepted in the jurors' minds as they shape the closing arguments around their perceptions. The power of the closing argument is established through the cross-examination of adversarial witnesses.

The jury expects direct examination to confirm the story that was forecasted in the opening statement. Therefore, they especially want to hear from witnesses supposedly there to testify against that lawyer's case. Those witnesses are tested through cross-examination.

The best modern example of effectively using cross-examination is the closing argument delivered by Johnnie Cochran in the O.J. Simpson criminal case. Who can forget the image of Johnnie standing in front of the jury with a ski cap on his head as he discussed not what the defense witnesses said, but information presented by the prosecution? This was a strong technique. The mostly African-American jury understood how some people, and especially the police, may rush to judgment in assuming identity just because a black man is in a ski cap.

As Cochran said, "In a ski cap, I am still Johnnie Cochran in a ski cap."

An even more telling moment in the closing was the defense's attack on the fateful attempt to tie Simpson to the bloody glove found by the police. This was probably the single most costly mistake the prosecution made in the case.

Does the Closing Matter?

According to existing research, closing arguments matter when the sides are fairly even in terms of the substance presented during the trial. They also matter when the dueling lawyers are equally skilled and prepared. When the jury is balanced in their preexisting attitudes, the closing argument strongly influences the ultimate verdict. They matter less when one side has a much more solid case than the other. Contrary to popular movie images, if one lawyer really is substantially more skilled than the other, and the power of the evidence is strong, then the case can be won or lost in closing argument.

A case in point may be the Martha Moxley murder case, a highly publicized matter, in which a Kennedy family relative, Michael Skakel, was convicted of a murder that had occurred decades earlier. He was convicted on primarily circumstantial evidence, and many commentators agreed that the jurors were strongly swayed by the prosecution's closing argument.

You will recall that Mickey Sherman, Skakel's lawyer, told me that he viewed the case as a fairly simple and common murder case, except for the aura of "celebrity" surrounding it. He was right. And the prosecution was able to pull the pieces of circumstantial evidence together in such a strong fashion that the jurors were convinced beyond a reasonable doubt of Skakel's guilt. Legal analysts pointed to the prosecutor's (Jonathan Benedict) ability to link a motive (jealousy), opportunity, and subsequent alleged admissions of guilt. He pointed to all the alleged "holes" in the defense's presentation, and even after twenty-six years, Benedict's "story" of the crime apparently provided a cohesive version that swayed the jury. This was accomplished without a parade of experts and virtually no forensic evidence. In this case, most legal analysts doubted if the prosecution could win, so the verdict surprised many in the legal community. Without question, Mickey Sherman is highly skilled, but it appears that a tightly constructed argument by his opponent carried that day.

Persuasive power means reaching into the reality of the jurors and not attempting to fit the case into the lawyer's version of reality. One reason lawyers use jury consultants throughout trial is that they rely on the consultant's skill to constantly read the jury and make adjustments in presentation along the way. (A mock trial going on behind the scenes may also help gauge progress and suggest adjustments).

I recall a lawyer who never felt as if he had the jurors on his side. The case presented some complex issues about banking, and the lawyer assumed that if he understood the case, so would the jurors. I had a tough time getting him to create visual aids or to "dumb down" his case at all. However, day after day he saw the glazed-over looks on the jurors' faces. Finally, he said, "I need help....I'm going down fast." We spent a very long night creating a series of visual aids and slides that he could use in the trial and again later in his closing argument.

These visuals shed the light of day on his case. He was lucky to have caught their lack of attention early, and he had time to bring the jurors back. Their response was visible. They smiled and nodded as they finally grasped information that had previously confused them. Jurors should not have to struggle to understand evidence; if lawyers cannot explain their cases, they should probably find another line of work.

Since lawyers cannot ignore what has transpired before the closing argument, they often find themselves scoring points, losing points, and creating new strategies. Commentators may open discussions of current trials by saying, "It was a good day for the prosecution" or "The defense scored big today with strong testimony." (No wonder no one really believes that a trial is a "search for the truth.")

Then there is the issue of "burden of proof." Despite the way media consultants commonly use the terms, a lay juror may be unfamiliar with the real meaning of terms like "preponderance of the evidence" or "beyond a reasonable doubt." The attorney needs to explain the appropriate burden and explain the facts of the case in light of that burden. The closing argument is the place we can do this.

We're Old Friends, Aren't We?

A key function of the closing argument is to reinforce the core message of the case. It is also the time lawyers try to renew the relationship and rapport they developed with the jury throughout the trial. Attorneys are not confined to arguing only what is in evidence. They can address common sense, general knowledge, and understanding. This is easier to do when the jurors are predisposed to feeling commonality with the lawyer.

The final words must bring together the story, theme, and message, all of which have been running through the trial. Remember that unlike direct and cross-examination, the lawyer is in total control during the closing argument. It can be the most powerful moment, but it is a moment that should be planned, not from the onset of the trial, but from the beginning of the case.

In the Danny Deveening case, the plaintiff's lawyer closed with a powerful plea for a large number of dollars:

> Why are we here? What is this case really about? We can't bring Danny back to the way he was before the accident. All of Danny's doctors believe that he will not make any more improvements. Danny Deveening will experience these permanent impairments and disabilities for the rest of his life. What is most tragic is that Danny knows he is not the same man. He knows that he cannot think as he could prior to this accident. He knows that he sounds different when he talks, looks different when he walks, and has become totally dependent on his family just to do daily activities. The defendants have admitted that they are responsible for what happened to Danny Deveening and that they need to compensate him for his injuries. Our judicial system provides that the only way to try to make a person whole again is to compensate them with money. There is no amount of money that will bring Danny back to the way he was, everyone agrees to that. What we don't agree on is what is reasonable amount to compensate Danny for his permanent injuries.
>
> The law recognizes that, while it is impossible to truly put a dollar value on a person's life, there are ways to look at that

person's life and to value the types of loss and damages a person has suffered. The law allows a person to recover for these different types of damages.

[The lawyer then went on discuss the details of the actual medical expenses and lost wages Danny incurred that were presented through testimony. He described the main facts, knowing that while the experts had explained in detail where all the terms and calculations came from, the jurors likely dozed off (or zoned out) during the testimony. It is the lawyer's job to pull difficult and complex testimony together and make it come alive. And so, the lawyer continued.]

What gets to be a more difficult, but doable, calculation is his rightful compensation for his permanent disability and impairment if his disability has significantly diminished his quality and enjoyment of life. Danny is entitled to compensation for the remaining days of his life. We don't have a crystal ball to look into to see how long his life will be. What we can do is look at the mortality tables, which give us an indication of what the average life expectancy would be.

[The lawyer reviewed the testimony the jury heard about Danny's life expectancy and how they would be able to calculate the damages the lawyer was arguing that Danny was now entitled to through the verdict. Again, reviewing what was very detailed (and quite boring) expert testimony, it is now the attorney's goal to make the complicated information more palatable and meaningful.]

Danny is also entitled by law to receive money damages for his pain, discomfort, and suffering. He was hospitalized, where he underwent surgery, numerous tests, procedures, and extensive rehabilitation. He will forever experience physical and shooting pains.

[The lawyer confirmed what he believed he could strongly argue that the evidence proved: Danny was rightfully entitled to a sizeable sum of money for his discomfort, over the course of his life. And then, as he reaches his final moments of the closing argument, he wants to grab the jury's attention and see if he can ground them in his favor, if, in fact, any jurors are still sitting on the fence and have not decided which way their verdict will go.]

Believe me, Danny Deveening would much rather be able to return to his job, get on with a normal life, and put a bad accident behind him. But that is not possible. He will endure the pain and suffering of physical, emotional, and social pain for the rest of his life. For Danny, this existence is his future....It is his life. The only thing anyone can do for Danny is award him the money that will permit him to be cared for the rest of his life. To ensure he gets the medical care and has the best quality of life that he can given....To be sure Danny has the best quality of life possible given what the defendant has taken from him.

Remember that the defense in this case had attacked the calculations and put evidence forth suggesting that the plaintiff had not been telling the truth to the jury. In this case, the defense presented video evidence of the plaintiff doing things he had claimed he could not do. Yet, the defense had admitted liability. We got the following closing words from the defense:

Ladies and gentlemen, we said at the beginning of this case that we would take care of the plaintiff. That he was entitled to compensation, and he is. But as you have seen the evidence in this case, it is clear that the plaintiff has not leveled with you. In fact, it is in many ways offensive that he would take a terrible accident and attempt to turn it into a lottery. The evidence has been clear that there have been medical bills and lost time from work. He is entitled to compensation for pain and suffering, but he clearly has the opportunity to return to a good life. He can work. He can play. He can make something with his life if he chooses to do so. And I believe that you, ladies and gentlemen of the jury, need to send him a message that tells him how important it is that he make something with his life. An award of $100,000 to $150,000 will more than adequately care for the plaintiff while encouraging him to go forward and to return to the working world....

The defense appealed to reason. By encouraging the jurors to keep their feet on the ground and to compensate without awarding inappropriately, the jurors were presented with a tough task ahead of them in deliberation. Actually, the case settled for more than one million dollars before the jury returned. It made sense, since the defense was prepared to pay some money and the plaintiff feared the results of his conduct being caught on videotape. Settling the case removed all doubt and risk for everybody.

In the civil newspaper shooting case, I expected my opponent, the plaintiff's lawyer, to pull the evidence and case together by placing an emotional emphasis on the civic duties of the defendant newspaper. The driver certainly received his share of attacks of alleged (and from my point of view, provable) wrongdoing, but we expected the lawyers to hammer home that the real blame had to be placed on the newspaper. After all, it had to be the fault of the corporate entity, the newspaper, whose management had to know (or so the argument went) that its drivers were out in bad neighborhoods at late hours. They argued that no reasonable person could expect the driver not to carry a gun for safety, and the paper should have anticipated the very likely possibility of reckless use.

O'Sims needed his own lawyer because the newspaper's strategy ultimately included pointing a finger at the driver. If the jury held the driver responsible, the paper hoped to sidestep their tie to him. The newspaper emphasized their no-gun policy, and supervisors could offer testimony that affirmed the policy, along with their lack of knowledge that any employee would carry a gun because that meant losing his job.

I handled this case while I was still in practice, and the facts are fairly close to what happened, with some changes. However, I won the case on behalf of the newspaper *before* trial. The judge was persuaded by the policy against guns and the uncontradicted testimony of all newspaper employees about the policy and the consequences for violating it, and he granted our motion for summary judgment. This means that the judge decided as a matter of law that the facts were clear and there was nothing for a jury to consider.

I think the judge was wrong. In my heart, I believed that a jury should have been able to hear the case and decide whether the newspaper really did not know its drivers might carry guns. But, my client and I were pleased that the decision held up on appeal. Since we all experience our own version of reality, I figured the judge and appellate judges saw the matter differently from me. But who was I to complain? Ultimately, my client was happy and we won fairly.

Clearly, lawyers want to know how the case is going to end and hope that the evidence will be presented in a coherent and logical way. But things do not always go the way we want. Plan as we might, sometimes witnesses go off on their own and, one way or another, they can make or break a case. From laypeople to experts, these people present testimony that must support the stories being told. You might be surprised to learn just how much impact a lawyer, with the assistance of the trial consultant, can have on the way in which words come from the mouths of witnesses. This is the focus of the next chapter.

chapter 7

Nothing But the Truth...Sort Of

The lawyers deliver the "prologue" in their opening statements, and then the real show begins. Having concluded their opening statements, the prosecutors in a criminal case and the plaintiffs in a civil case call their first witness.

I call this the *real* show because, as the judge instructs the jurors, what the lawyers say is not evidence, but what the witnesses say *is* evidence. For lawyers, who have spent months or years preparing, the trial often seems like the "beginning of the end." This is also a time when lawyers must rely on others, specifically the witnesses who will be "going public" for the first time. And as we all know, no one has complete control over what other people will say and do.

In addition, while what witnesses say is important, how they say it is equally significant, as is the way they appear before, during, and after they take the witness stand. Trial consultants play an important role in preparing witnesses to testify. We work with witnesses to make sure they are as effective as possible when they take the stand and are subjected to questions from both sides.

I recall a very nervous witness who constantly played with a paper clip or pen, a habit that made him look as if he was hiding something. We worked with him to put the clip down, and when the day came to testify, the lawyers made sure his pockets were empty. Wouldn't you know that even the best-laid plans sometimes fail? When the witness took the stand, he found a rubber band and played with it through the entire testimony, to the great frustration of the lawyer. Who thought of doing a search of the witness stand before putting someone up there? Unfortunately, no one.

It Comes Back to Communication

Throughout this book, I have mentioned principles of communication because when it comes down to it, examining a legal matter that results in a trial is much like working in a human-communications laboratory, from interviewing witnesses and potential jurors all the way to closing arguments. One of the basic tenets of communication is the presence of a sender and a receiver. When I witnessed an accident, I sent what to me was straightforward information: "I saw that car slam into the truck because the driver didn't stop at the stoplight." In essence, this is how I expressed what I saw happen at the intersection. The receiver then filters this statement through his or her life experience. This principle has everything to do with the way witnesses testify.

If the receiver of my statement is a lawyer or an investigator, the thought process might go something like this: I'll have to check on the position of the light; I wonder if it was dark or the sun caused glare; and where was this witness driver sitting? My neighbors might filter this information in an entirely different way. They believe what I said because they think of me as an observant person, they have known me for years, and they might assume that since I have no "dog in the fight," I have no reason to embellish or misstate what I saw. They do not think about time of day or where I was positioned. A few people might think about how easy it is to miss the stoplight. Soon, their thought processes are off and running and they are complaining about the city council, which has not responded to community demands and repositioned the stoplight. Meanwhile, law enforcement, investigators, and lawyers are checking and rechecking all the versions of the accident, some of them no doubt conflicting with what I reported.

So Many Different "Truths" to Sort Through

Sometimes people negatively interpret information about senders and receivers, which sometimes translates into making witnesses afraid they will be accused of lying because their story shifts over time. Well, stories do shift over time. It is the way it has to be in human interaction. Most witnesses do not understand why what they say can be looked at from so many different points of view. Too often, we become invested in what we think of as facts and then conclude that these facts add up to the truth. Lawyers know that facts are not always facts, and the absolute truth is illusive—or nonexistent.

Witnesses are often nervous and uncomfortable because they live with uncertainty about what is going to happen to them. Some individuals run from any accident or crime scene because they do not want to get involved. Or, they may avoid stepping forward and offering information because they believe they may end up in trouble.

I worked on a case in which potential valuable witnesses disappeared because they were smoking marijuana together behind a building. The prosecuting lawyers believed these individuals could have seen the man who attacked a woman behind another nearby building. They did not necessarily need to call all these individuals, but a positive identification could bolster their case. In this situation, the witnesses' fears were understandable. If there is a legitimate way to attack the witness on cross-examination, then the witness does face a difficult moment. Smoking marijuana, for example, could easily interfere with accurate perceptions, and would be fair ground for the cross-examiner to address.

In the spirit of "no good deed goes unpunished," I remember taking a series of depositions of eyewitnesses to an accident, and my opponent asked one of the Spanish-speaking witnesses, "Are you here in this country legally?" I immediately objected and asked the purpose of that question. "Well, uh, if he's not here legally and they catch him, he'd be deported and unavailable for trial." That is certainly one way to get rid of a potential key witness during the pre-trial stage.

I told the witness that he had the opportunity to get a lawyer, since neither my opponent nor I was serving as his lawyer and protector. The other side's lawyer decided to drop the tactic and move on. The situation really disturbed me. Fair is fair, but this witness was doing nothing more than trying to help and tell us what he saw; he should not have been put in that awkward situation because it had nothing to do with the issue at hand.

Whose Words Did You Put in My Mouth?

From a lawyer's point of view, it is even worse when witnesses are resistant to being prepared to testify. Since they will certainly tell the truth on the stand, they think, then why do they need all this extensive preparation? Some people take it a step further and believe it is unethical and manipulative to prepare a witness to testify. How dare we shape testimony? How dare we put words into a witness's mouth? Isn't that playing with the truth? These questions, perhaps better called suspicions, represent a fundamental misconception about what trial consultants (and lawyers for that matter) do as they work with their witnesses.

Ethical lawyers and trial consultants do not tell witnesses what to say. Most certainly, they do not change testimony. What they do is review the account of information the witnesses have to tell and assist them in telling that story in the most effective way possible. Consciously or not, they prepare witnesses with the concept of a "sender and receiver" in mind. In a jury trial, we are dealing with a group of "receivers," so preparing a witness helps us shape the way relevant information is sent.

Telling and Retelling

One of the reasons cross-examination can be so challenging is because in nearly all cases, the testimony given at trial does not mean this is the first time the witness has given his or her story. They have likely given a statement to a police officer at a scene, an insurance investigator when insurance is involved, and in a deposition when the lawyers get involved and conduct the discovery phase of the case. As a rule, the lawyers have taken the deposition of every witness and party who will take the stand. Sometimes witnesses become legally unavailable for trial. Civil matters can go on for many years and witnesses die or become disabled because of illness or are otherwise unavailable and out of the legal reach of the court. In these situations, the deposition can become the testimony that is read to the jurors, and is all the jurors will hear from that witness.

Lawyers can use every recorded statement taken from a party or witness to test or impeach what is subsequently said at trial. If a witness changes his or her story from statement to deposition and/or deposition to trial, then the cross-examiner can use this information to challenge the discrepancy. Sometimes the discrepancies are small and do not rise to a level that leads to impeaching the witness, but at other times, these discrepancies can have a significant impact on the case.

In one case, a plaintiff had testified in a sworn statement that he was not feeling too bad within a couple of days after the car accident. He did not return to work, but that was because he had been laid off. Now, at trial, he chose to change the story to claim ongoing severe pain and an inability to work. The lawyer let the contradiction go unnoted in the testimony itself. However, at closing argument, the defense lawyer laid into that plaintiff: "Amazing that at the time of the statement, only days after the accident, the plaintiff was fine and ready to go. I wonder what happened between then and this trial, when it appears we hear about pain and suffering for the first time. Unless it is because he thinks he can trick you ladies and gentlemen into buying his eleventh-hour tale of woe." The jury agreed with the defense and sent the plaintiff home with nothing.

Note that the skilled lawyer will rarely point out the power of the discrepancy during the testimony. Most likely, the lawyer will let the inconsistency occur and then save the drama of pointing it out for the closing argument, when the witness cannot offer his or her own explanation.

The Right to Be Ready

For many years, I have spoken to lawyers' groups on the topic of witness preparation. I always address the topic of ethical witness preparation and point out that every witness story is subject to cross-examination by a skilled and talented lawyer. When the day comes that witnesses are allowed to say what they have to say and step down, then I will say it is unnecessary for trial consultants to work with witnesses. That day will not come as long as we have the adversarial system of justice that allows people to confront their accusers and to test the veracity of every witness's account. Testing witnesses' testimony—and other evidence—helps put the jury in the strongest position to reach a fair verdict. In other words, preparing witnesses is healthy for the justice system, and these individuals have the right and duty to be up to their task.

Will the Lawyers Outsmart Me?

Almost all witnesses fear a situation in which a skilled lawyer will unnerve them, and frankly, lawyers do indeed have ways to do this. For example, they can ask questions that make strong testimony sound weak and confident witnesses look uncertain. I recall one witness, we will call him Mr. Zachary, who testified during his deposition as follows:

> I sign every invoice that is paid and I never received or saw the invoice that the plaintiff says we refused to pay.

This sounds straightforward enough, but the boxes of documents turned over during discovery served to provide the skilled cross-examiner with several options for an attack on this point. We were prepared to have her read this testimony to the jury once she had made the point there were, in fact, contradictions to the testimony. She might have followed up in a number of ways:

1. There was a paid invoice that the witness had not signed, which was produced after having been found among the hundreds of documents turned over in discovery. "So, what about this document, Mr. Zachary? This was paid, wasn't it? And it does not bear your signature, does it?" As the witness tries to explain how and why that occurred, the cross-examiner would plan to resist the long explanations with a simple, "Thank you for your response. You have answered my question."

2. There was also an invoice uncovered that had been signed but never paid. "But you don't actually write the checks, do you,

sir? In fact, you sign the invoice and then trust that your staff will pay it, correct? And it is possible that an invoice comes in and is received but doesn't make it to your desk, isn't that correct?" Again, the witness would be forced to scurry to figure out an explanation that the cross-examiner would likely dismiss as too little too late.

It turned out that she used both tactics. The witness sat there looking bewildered and confused. He had forgotten the testimony he had given in his deposition and felt a bit boxed in. But my client came to the rescue, or tried to do so. On redirect examination, he asked the witness, "Now how many such invoices do you review in an average month?"

"Maybe a hundred or more.…I don't know for sure, but it's a lot."

In this way, although the cross-examiner had caught the witness in a contradiction, the direct examiner did a fine job of recovering by showing, in effect, that witnesses are human. Anyone who reviews hundreds of documents is entitled to be wrong a time or two. The jury, however, did not forgive the contradiction. The verdict illustrated that they held the witness to the contradiction, but he was not perceived to be the intentional liar that the cross-examiner was trying to portray.

During direct testimony, the other side's lawyer takes notes and gets ready to attack the testimony on cross-examination, so the better the witness is prepared, the better he or she can handle even the best cross-examining lawyer. When trial consultants or lawyers prepare witnesses, we are, in essence, teaching them the game, which means they come to understand that they cannot win the battle of cross-examination; they merely need to withstand the siege. We prepare them to hold their own ground and not be led into contradiction, confusion, or areas in which they lack knowledge.

Witnesses befuddled on cross-examination are favorites on television. Ah, the viewers say, that person is not so honest after all. Maybe she's the killer and poor honest Sam is taking the rap. Thankfully, in actual courtrooms, witnesses are rarely taken away in handcuffs once they leave the stand. Usually, that is *not* the adversarial lawyer's goal.

I recall a witness who seemed very nervous throughout the preparation session. Finally, she confessed that she was worried she could and would be asked whether she had ever used drugs. While the case had absolutely nothing to do with drugs or drug use (it was a product liability case), she was so fearful that her previous drug use (occurring years before) could come out, it was apparent she would be ineffective, at least until we cleared up her concerns. We found out she was afraid of having her past mentioned because she was now a schoolteacher with two young children. Her fear of personal humiliation was palpable.

This fear of "ambush" probably nags at witnesses because they see such things on television. They recall a drama in which the "evil" lawyer asks a witness embarrassing personal questions, all of which the judge strikes from the record, just before she sternly warns the lawyer that she will throw him in jail for contempt. Still, the information is out there, and the audience knows the twelve jurors will likely see it as key to the case. Our schoolteacher witness came with a suitcase full of television-induced fear, along with real issues she did not want exposed. But when she understood that she would not be asked questions about her personal past, she fulfilled her role as witness without fear of the sudden dramatic moment.

Dress Rehearsal

In some ways, preparing a witness to testify is akin to a rehearsal. It resembles the situation in which a politician has staff members ask questions in preparation for a debate with the opposing candidate. Generally, a witness's lawyer asks the same kinds of questions that likely will be asked on both direct and cross-examination. Nowadays, the process is generally videotaped and the tape is reviewed with witnesses so they can get a sense of how credible they appear. It is the trial consultant's job to help witnesses feel and appear comfortable and confident. No one in the process ever tells the witness what to say. The story is the witness's story alone and it is unethical to cross the boundary of substance.

After many years of experience, I have learned not to let witnesses view the tape until we can show some marked improvement. Otherwise, we are faced with the uncomfortable experience of showing witnesses how poorly they appear without being able to balance that image by showing improvement. The challenge of making a witness comfortable is an issue in itself. At a minimum, I have witnesses lean forward and place one hand on top of the other on the table or witness stand. This position alone creates the appearance of comfort—and strength—and usually elicits a positive reaction when witnesses see themselves at least looking confident, even if the internal feeling does not quite match the external appearance.

It is not permissible for a lawyer to feed information or attempt to coax a witness into saying she saw the defendant's face, for example, when she did not. This would be counterproductive anyway, because witnesses have been questioned before they appear in court. Every new "fact" or impression brought forth is evidence of inconsistency and is subject to tough cross-examination. When trial consultants prepare witnesses, we take what we have and try to form the questions that cast the information in a way that is favorable to us. Each side must do this, or the civil client or criminal defendant would be cheated.

Lawyers know that most people stand by what they see and experience, and they usually do not take kindly to the idea that their memories are not accurate or are tainted in some way. Automobile accidents are so common, unfortunately, that they lend themselves to examples of typical scenarios. Let's say you were an eyewitness to an automobile accident. You saw the whole incident, and being a good citizen, you approach the person who you believe is the wronged party, as I did when I witnessed an accident. Keeping it simple, you say: "You know, I saw that other driver run the stop sign. I was standing right there. I'll testify for you if you need me." You and the other person exchange business cards, and within a couple of days an insurance investigator calls you and asks you for your version of the story.

You were walking your dog Winston when you saw a car approach the stop sign, come to a complete halt, and proceed through the intersection. All of a sudden here comes another car, rushing right through the stop sign. You saw the collision, and the "innocent" car was hit broadside. It was just after dinner, so it had to be early evening because you always take Winston for his evening stroll around the block at the same time every evening. So, were you walking around the block? Well, not exactly. You changed your routine that day and you walked three blocks up the street, which is how you happened to be at that intersection, but it *had* to be around 7:00 P.M.

You have the best intentions possible, but the fact is, the accident actually occurred around 7:45 P.M. The investigator notes this, knowing it may or may not be important information. A few days later, the investigator and insurance company's attorneys call you again and ask if you will reconstruct your story at the site of the accident. It is inconvenient for you, but you agree because once in the situation, you believe it is your duty to see it through. You point out the exact spot you were standing when the accident happened. By this time, you wish the other driver would just settle this matter. Clearly in the wrong, his insurance company should pay for the damage and end this thing. You are becoming a disgruntled citizen by now who blames the bad driver, his insurance company, and the lawyers for all this trouble.

Meanwhile, another witness has stated that the person you see as the wronged party did not come to a full stop at the sign, and the other driver did. Oh boy. And that other driver is the one who ended up in the hospital with a serious injury. His insurance company has no intention of settling, now or ever. This case is getting nasty, and both drivers believe they were wronged. They are being stubborn, and the injured driver's insurance company is certain it can place blame with "your" driver. About two years later, you are asked to go to a lawyer's office for what is known as a deposition.

People sometimes wonder why depositions are necessary. Can't we just talk to the lawyers on "our side" and then tell our story in court? But you saw what you saw, so you will tell it all again. On the appointed day, you show up right on time.

As the questioning begins, you are quite comfortable. You tell the story just as you did from the first day. Well, you changed it a little bit. You remember looking at your kitchen clock when you came back inside the house and it was closer to 8:00 P.M., later than originally thought. You had stopped to chat with a neighbor and had forgotten about that when you first talked to the investigator. The lawyer questioning you brings that out—there is nothing to hide, and time is not that important. The accident still happened and there was plenty of daylight. At least this is what you think. The lawyer for the other side begins to pin you down on the time of the accident and how much daylight there actually was.

So, what happens next? The attorney you have been dealing with suddenly drops out of sight. You wonder when the trial is going to start because you are planning a vacation and you do not want any scheduling conflicts. When the lawyer returns your call, you learn that you will not be called to testify after all. It seems that there are a few problems with your testimony. For one thing, other witnesses have said that it was "late dusk" at the time of the accident, and the National Meteorological Agency confirmed that. Furthermore, the exact spot where you were standing blocks the view of the side of the intersection where the other car was. Besides, it is an uphill drive to the stop sign and you could not even see a car approach it. Photographs have confirmed the presence of foliage, the grade of the hill, and so on. So, it appears that you did not see what you thought you saw, at least according to the lawyer. So long—and thanks for your cooperation.

Over the next few days, you keep thinking about that night. How could you have been so wrong? Or were you so wrong? You saw the other car stop. You are sure of that. And now it turns out your testimony is not valuable at all. You are thoroughly confused, but like most people, you become stubborn, too.

In case after case, lawyers and investigators pin down certain facts that may contradict what witnesses say. In essence, stubborn though you may be, you did not have a full grasp of the story as the other driver told it. Behind the scenes, investigators measured the grade of the road and consulted with relevant government agencies to learn the exact time of sunset on that evening. Another witness happened to check the time just before the accident occurred and she had to use the light on her watch. It was nearly dark—as you probably now realize. Funny how your initial memory did not include that fact.

The lawyers on both sides of the case were well prepared. They had to construct a version of their story based on the people and reports available to them. They took depositions, and as a result, you were not seen as a credible witness, which may insult you or make you angry. Some people begin to doubt themselves. They begin to believe that losing credibility as a witness is tantamount to not being a credible person. But in the nitty-gritty of court cases, the only important issue is that the other side could poke too many holes in your testimony. When you think about it, the deposition was not an unimportant event. Turned out it was better for "your" side that you did not testify.

If You Find Yourself…

Unfortunately, not all lawyers thoroughly prepare witnesses, and equally important, most of us think that becoming involved in a criminal investigation or civil case is something that happens to *other* people. I offer some advice you can use should you ever be called upon to testify, either in a case involving you directly as a party, or one in which you have no material interest, but may be in the position of a witness to an event.

1. *Say what you have to say in as few words as possible. Brevity is usually the wisest path.*

If you saw an accident or crime, then by all means, step forward and talk about what you witnessed. We need individuals to put themselves on the line and come forward. As we have seen, whistle blowers in corporations are as valuable to the legal system as eyewitnesses are to solving a murder. Would the fiscal messes created by Enron or WorldCom ever have come to public attention but for the courage of those few individuals who saw improper conduct and refused to sit back and do nothing about it?

On more than one occasion I have given my card to a flight attendant who has had to deal with an unruly passenger. Sometimes these people sue the airlines, and the flight attendant may need a good witness. I am not afraid to get involved if it means protecting someone who is trying to do her job, especially protecting others from an unruly person's behavior. However, if questioned, I still believe in using as few words as possible, because the more you say, the more opportunity you give to a cross-examiner to come after you. When this happens, it looks like another case of "no good deed goes unpunished."

A lawyer's case is based on the totality of the evidence collected. This is of obvious importance if you are a person accused of a crime. The same advice applies. You absolutely know you are innocent. Good. Call your lawyer before you start defending yourself to police and the press and anyone else who happens to be around. Tell your children to stay quiet, too. Minors should not be questioned without a parent present—and parents should call a lawyer. I recently dealt with a teenager who was stopped as she left a store, setting off the theft detectors. Pulled back into the store and asked to empty her purse, she removed a pair of sunglasses. When an officer called to the scene used a wand around the purse and found the sensor tag, which was now sitting loose in her purse, the girl said, "They must have fallen in my purse." Before she got herself in any deeper, I encouraged her to remain quiet. Even I did not believe what she was saying. The department store decided not to press charges because the girl had no previous record.

In another incident, some children of varying ages were gathered on the back porch of a second-floor apartment. Two boys, ages eleven and twelve, and the sister of another boy who was part of the group leaned against the porch railing, which suddenly gave way and the three children fell off the porch. The two boys did the equivalent of back flips in the air and landed on their feet, miraculously unharmed. The young girl was not so lucky, and the children immediately called 911. The girl was hospitalized with what turned out to be a fairly mild concussion and a couple of broken bones. An investigator hired by the parents' attorney questioned the boys as part of their initial preparation for a lawsuit.

Even in this situation, all the children on the porch needed the protection of at least their parents, if not a lawyer. The landlord's insurance company had its own investigators asking the kinds of questions that could imply that the children had done something to deliberately damage the porch railing. Kids being kids, they might have said more than was necessary, misstated how many times they had been on the porch, and so forth.

The case settled quickly because a number of people in the building had warned the landlord about the rotting wood on several railings, including the one that gave way. The landlord did not stand a chance when nearly all his tenants were prepared to testify about the condition of the porch, not to mention bring in pieces of rotting wood for the jury to examine. Still, the parents' lawyer, even knowing that the case was likely to settle, was laying the groundwork for an actual trial in which a couple of boys might be called on to describe their dramatic back flips and the 911 call that followed. That is why it was important for the children to understand the importance of just sticking to the facts. This is why I advise parents to teach their kids some "legal smarts," along with "street smarts."

2. *Tell the truth as you see it, and accept the fact that your truth will be different from someone else's truth.*

If you understand basic concepts of human perception and communication, you will tend to become less invested in all those initial details you reported. You believe the person who broke a contract with you is always difficult to work with, and you tell your lawyer about his antics. During the discovery phase of your case, depositions are taken that show that you have a history of demanding more than a contract states. Other people perceive you as difficult, and your opponent's lawyer has some witnesses lined up to say so.

It may turn out that the person did indeed break the contract and you are in the right in this situation, but I can assure you that your attorney is going to build a different version of the story during trial. This is one of the advantages of the deposition process. When I work with lawyers, I always advise them to take special care with the deposition phase of a case, precisely because what emerges may significantly alter the story they tell.

By the way, some people believe lawyers actually create the statements, literally put words in their clients' mouths. That should not happen and likely does not ever happen. In actuality, the witness is the best person to find the right words to clarify the testimony. I recall working with a plaintiff in a case who was being humble as she talked about the pain she felt. Her lawyer told her that this was not the time to be humble, not the time to keep jurors from understanding the severity of the pain. I looked to the middle-aged woman and said,

"Look, we weren't there and can't relate to your pain. What was it like? What is the best way you can describe it so we understand what you felt?" She thought for a few moments and then she spoke. "It was like going through surgery without anesthetic...." Ouch. We felt the pain. Our advice enabled her to find her own best way to clarify what she was feeling and relate this to the jury most effectively because she used her own words.

3. *Do not be afraid to change your account and modify your story if you realize your previous story was wrong. It is to everyone's advantage in the end.*

I recall one plaintiff who gave his lawyer (my client) a list of dates and times that he took the medication strictly as prescribed and that it made him very ill. He knew this information was not true, but he figured if he lied to his own lawyer and his lawyer believed it, he was somehow safe in his lie. He never corrected the information and it came back to haunt him at trial. Other witnesses contradicted his story because the defense found individuals who saw the plaintiff pull out the prescription bottle during various meals in restaurants and other times as well. In a material sense, this component of the testimony was not crucial to the underlying matter, but the plaintiff's credibility was severely challenged in the eyes of the jury.

If you thought four people attacked you and stole your briefcase, and then later you realize there were five, then call the detective and give him or her that information. Of course the detective will want to know what made you change your mind, but perhaps a few days later, when you were going over the crime once again, the images were clearer.

It may be that if the case ever goes to trial, you as the victim will be asked why you changed your story. You can simply explain that the presence of the fifth person came back to you later when the incident, which was understandably traumatic, became clearer. The lawyer who challenges you is doing his or her job. This does not mean that anyone will assume you have lied or are not credible.

4. *Be open about factors that could taint your credibility.*

You might think you are credible and completely impartial, but you failed to mention that you used to date the president of the company that is accused of making an unsafe product. He left you for another person and now you are testifying against him. You did not tell your lawyer this bit of personal information, and now the defendant's attorneys depose you. Oops—the whole tawdry tale comes out. You threw that glass at him and told him you would get even one day. "Well," say these lawyers, "we think this is exactly what you had in mind. What better way to get even than by testifying against him?" These things really do happen, which is why they make good television drama. Legal cases are filled with contradictory motivations and individual histories.

You insist you are telling the truth about being harmed by the product. Well, I believe you. But, the point, is, will the jury? You are a risky witness, and if I have others who will serve the same purpose, I may drop you from my witness list. This glitch could have been avoided. (Lawyers are supposed to ask these questions and get the information from you, but some lawyers are not as careful as they should be.)

On the other hand, if you tell me about the relationship, I may learn that you threw the glass after your lover (the defendant) threw your coat at you and shoved you toward the door. You had to put up a fight just to get a box of your belongings. You threw that glass in self-defense—to keep him away. The defendant may not be such an upstanding citizen after all. A trial is series of decisions, based on information we accumulate. During the deposition I might ask you about your personal relationship myself, just so we get it on the table. No longer is it a weapon the other side can use as a surprise.

When I discussed the storytelling model, I talked about Brian, the plaintiff who was injured by the allegedly unsafe saw. If there had been damaging facts in that case, such as the fact that Brian had not read the instructions about how to use the saw, we would have integrated our explanation into the opening and confirmed it through the questions on direct examination. An effective lawyer never waits for the other side to catch you in your weak facts. They strike first!

A few years ago, two police officers were accused of killing a man they were going to take into custody. The prosecution had a difficult task. They had to convince a jury that this drug dealer's death was caused by police actions. The drug dealer was not a model citizen and had a long criminal record. Unfortunately, the witnesses were prostitutes, convicted drug users, and pimps. What the prosecution did was bring all the unsavory information out, thereby taking the punch out of the cross-examination. These prosecutors won the case and the two police officers were sent to prison. The prosecution was seen as credible because they were not attempting to hide anything, not even the sordid history of their witnesses. When one side admits to some tawdry facts, it is much more difficult for the other side to get much mileage out of questions about them.

5. *Answer only the question that was asked of you, nothing more or less.*

This piece of advice is hard for many people, particularly for those who tend to be verbal and perhaps even articulate. I have prepared witnesses who answer questions in great detail. In one case, the witness said the stranger she saw was wearing a midnight blue suit with buttons that glittered. She was asked only to confirm that the suit was blue. A simple "yes" will do. All the other side needed to do to refute this witness was bring in the alleged suit and show the jury its dull white buttons. As ludicrous as it sounds, if the blue suit was critical to our case, we might have been forced to bring in a weather expert to explain the angle of the sun and the placement of the windows. Of course the buttons glittered when the sun hit them. This is precisely why it is important to prepare witnesses.

The way some individuals answer questions, you would think they are seizing the opportunity to give themselves a public-relations boost. One witness expected to go on and on about the big corporate groups he booked at his health resort. Occasionally a witness will do this and ends up sounding arrogant and unlikable. Besides, as a lawyer would say, all this embellishment is immaterial. The man was a witness in a hit-and-run accident, not a corporate takeover. He was not going to be more credible because of his self-importance.

If you are a party in your own case, then presumably your lawyer will prepare you for both direct testimony and cross-examination. All witnesses should be prepared for cross-examination, of course. Cross-examination is the opponent's chance to bring out information that supports another version of the "facts." Equally important, it is the other side's chance to tarnish your credibility and, frankly, make you look bad. Even in much scientific testimony, the truth is seldom absolute. This is why we caution witnesses not to elaborate every answer. The more they talk, the more ammunition they hand the other side.

6. *Don't let lawyers intimidate you during examination; it's not personal. They're just doing their job, and you have your job to do as an effective witness.*

"No, it didn't *seem* like a dark night. It *was* a dark night," you say. You wonder why the other lawyer is using words like "appears" or "seems" or "surmise." This appears or seems to weaken your testimony—at least that's what you surmise.

The lawyer is doing what is necessary to cast some doubt, not on you as a person, but on what you are saying. The dress was as blue as could be, but the other lawyer will say that it *appeared* blue in the dim room. The car *seemed* to stop at the red light; you simply say it *did* stop. But other witnesses say it did not, so these qualifying words help add to the doubt that already exists. These words are not meant to insult you, but simply set the stage to bring out a different version of the story in question.

One reason witnesses may dread testimony involves their fear of being tricked. For this reason, it is critical to be prepared. Unfortunately, witnesses end up feeling tricked because the lawyers have dropped the ball and have not prepared the witness for cross-examination. If you do not believe you are being prepared for all eventualities on the witness stand, then by all means raise this issue with your lawyer. One of the valuable outgrowths of having legal analysts on television is that they help average people better understand legal issues—and strategies and tactics. So, use what you know to evaluate what is going on in any legal case in which you are involved.

7. *Stay away from the media—far, far away.*

This is a serious rule, made more serious every day. You might think that the case you are involved in would never garner publicity. Think again. Today, we never know when something will be publicized. The smallest twist can make reporters come hunting. It is their job, so I am not faulting them. It is your duty as a witness, however minor you might think your role is, to do your job. Anything you say to a reporter can be used publicly, unless there is some prior agreement, and "off the record" can mean different things to different people.

I watched closely during my reporting of the O.J. Simpson case for NBC News, getting to sit in the trailer and watch myriad reporters put their stories together. I watched with fascination as I observed the respected correspondent David Bloom (who recently passed away in Iraq while covering the war) put his stories together with an absolute focus, tremendous tenacity, competitive edge, and overall thorough, tough reporting. Watching David rehearse his words over and over again until he had them just right, getting his story down to the exact second needed for his report that would be coming up in literally minutes, was amazing. Being a part of those stories meant knowing that my statements would have to fit in just right and make a particular point. There was no "off the record" to David; just a dedication to getting the exclusive angle, the most powerful message. That success carried him through to the end.

Cases have been seriously compromised because key witnesses or parties begin dealing with various media. Their theory is along the lines that if they can get the media to support their side, then a jury would begin with a favorable leaning at the time trial begins. The reality is that when the media get involved, the case takes on a life of its own and the truth is more difficult to ascertain.

We do not know how our stories will come across once they are retold by a reporter, or even several reporters. In high-profile cases, such as the murder of JonBenet Ramsey, reporters were desperate for the parents to talk to them. After all, remember the powerful details of the case.

A six-year-old was found dead in the family basement the day after Christmas 1996. The media's attention immediately turned to the parents, John and Patsy Ramsey, as the suspects. The Ramseys were smart to hire a spokesperson to field questions from media outlets that dug in for twenty-four-hour coverage. You may remember that average citizens wondered why these parents did not come forward and tell the world that they did not murder their child, especially as they became prime suspects.

Being a family of means and smart enough to hire savvy lawyers, this couple stayed out of the limelight, which was the right thing to do.

During that period the many commentators questioned the silence and concluded: "They're hiding something. It's not proper behavior for parents whose daughter has been murdered." Then, when they did give an interview or make a statement, their behavior was viewed as suspicious. Why weren't they crying and pleading? I disagreed with the commentators. Nonverbal behavior means something, but we do not know just what it indicates. One person cries and screams when their child is killed, and another acts like the Ramseys. It is hard to anticipate how any of us would act in such a situation unless we have been there. No single set of proper behaviors exists when it comes to grief and tragedy.

Susan Smith was an exemplary case. She is the mother who claimed her two young children were kidnapped, and she appeared on the morning talk shows crying and pleading for their return. Only within a few days, she confessed to drowning the boys by sending her car into the lake with the children trapped inside. She did this so she could establish a stronger relationship with a new boyfriend who did not want kids. All her anguish was essentially a fraud.

This issue of proper behavior is taking on a new dimension in the post-9/11 era. It will take a long time to see all the implications, but two recent examples serve to illustrate the wisdom of remaining quiet and listening to a lawyer's advice. In a case that has made its way through our federal criminal courts, John Walker, a young American, was captured in Afghanistan, and early reports indicated the possibility that he was fighting with the Taliban, one of the named enemies in our current war against terrorism. Unfortunately, Walker's father began appearing on television. I am positive that viewers, many of whom have gained some legal savvy over the last few years of watching trials and listening to lawyers talk, were shouting at the television and urging this distressed father to get off the air. With every word, he was creating a huge public-relations disaster as he described his grown son as a potential victim, a "boy," and possibly even brainwashed.

Family members can help or harm a potential defendant, and in this case in particular, trying to explain the inexplicable was a no-win situation. For all kinds of reasons, a plea agreement resulted in a prison sentence and both sides preferred this conclusion to a lengthy trial. Not having learned his lesson, John Walker's father put his foot square in his mouth again when he compared his son's incarceration to that of Nelson Mandela. Another big no-win situation.

No matter how insignificant your legal case or involvement in a case seems, refuse lengthy media appearances and interviews and ignore the journalists who are camped out in front of your house—or call you late at night. John Walker himself should have taken this advice, but he talked to reporters from news magazines. A family in this kind of crisis needs a strong voice to step in and give them advice that will help them in the long run. Too often, families and friends believe that a few words will clear up a "misunderstanding," but the best way to do that is to develop patience and refuse comment.

In a similar situation, the family of Richard Reid (the name that appeared on his passport), the man who boarded the American Airlines plane from Paris to Miami with the seeming intention of detonating explosives in his shoes, made some public statements. Their words attempted to explain the actions of Reid, or, in other words, provide an interpretation to the world that Reid was a victim of brainwashing. Family members, shaken with disbelief, report that Reid was lonely and found solace with Muslim brothers who became his family. He was not a good student and had few friends in his teen years. He became a petty criminal and engaged in some shoplifting, but later moved on to committing a vicious mugging, which landed him in jail. This was somehow supposed to trigger sympathy, but of course it had the opposite effect. Nowadays, sympathy for anyone engaged in violent acts is in short supply.

I resist the temptation to talk with the press about cases I work on. I am being very careful in this book to protect the matters I have worked on, as many clients do not give permission to provide actual details. In many cases, if the results of our research were released, the media would have a field day and the rights of clients would be severely jeopardized. The attorney-client privilege arguably extends to the work of trial consultants because we are an arm of the lawyer and certainly a member of the trial team. Therefore, I consider the privilege to last with my lawyer-client as long as the lawyer's privilege lasts with his or her client, and that's for life and beyond. Absent a client's permission to disclose protected information, for the most part, that information will never be released. This is not to say I have not had some tough moments with the media in my own work.

Lawyers are best advised to monitor their own comments to the media. I know this because my words have been misquoted numerous times. In one case, I asked to be quoted as an anonymous source and was named in the article. Another time, my words were so twisted that I was astounded. How could anyone have misinterpreted my few simple sentences about a prominent educational program that was undergoing some challenges from other programs? I got in a bit of hot water with my client, and even though I didn't say much and the few skimpy details I gave were "off the record," I learned my lesson. There is *no* off the record. Everything is *on* the record. So, if you see a reporter coming toward you, run the other way.

When We Don't Know What We Think We Know

Direct examination has many purposes, including a chance to present a clear and credible version of a continuous account—one chapter in the ongoing story that has a theme and a sequence. Each witness is on the stand to testify about a particular piece of the event or about the individuals involved in the event. Lawyers sometimes tell the jury that each witness provides a piece to the puzzle—the big picture. This is why direct examination should be memorable and add meaning to the case. For the opponent, direct examination is a search for contradiction, the time to anticipate the areas to focus on during cross-examination. This is why lawyers subject their own witnesses to a rigorous cross-examination preparation.

Few lawyers would ever walk into trial with less than complete control over the facts and law. Well, at least they are not supposed to. But we all make mistakes, and I sure made one in a trial of mine in my early days in practice. I represented the defendant in a case that alleged breach of contract against my client for automobile repairs and other related work. I had a star witness, the car mechanic, who told me that he believed the plaintiff (a young, attractive female, by the way…and this *is* relevant to the story) was lying and he was standing behind the defendant all the way. As the case progressed through discovery, the mechanic was never deposed and no statement was taken. He was solidly in the defendant's corner, or so we thought.

The plaintiff called him to the stand and I sat with a smirk on my face as I waited for his attack on the plaintiff to begin. Then, the mechanic snowed us all. He was a plaintiff's witness to the max. He took the stand and ended up encouraging the jury to award everything the plaintiff asked for—even more. I was stunned. The strategy had broken down and we were caught with our proverbial pants down. "No more questions, your honor," said my opponent.

"Any cross-examination, counsel?" the judge asked as he looked at my shocked face.

"Yes, your honor, I do have questions. Yes, I do," I said blankly, without a clue about what I was going to ask this turncoat. I stood up and paced for a bit as I pondered what question I would ask, knowing that I was about to violate a cardinal rule of cross-examination. You *never* ask a question to which you do not know the answer. Why? Because on cross-examination, in theory, you are challenging the other side's witness. They are not your friends. So you have to move carefully and strategically.

All of this went through my mind along with the thought, "Eventually, I will be home. I will get out of here. But for now, I am being watched closely by the jury and this witness who is smiling at me because he caught me off-guard. I must do something." And I violated the cardinal rule, because I think there is one time you can ask the question when you do not know the answer, and that is when it just doesn't matter. I figured I had lost the case, so what the heck.

"You know the plaintiff, don't you?" I asked.

I was thrilled to see that I had caught the witness off-guard. "Well, yeah, I do," he said.

"You have a personal relationship, don't you?"

"Yes, we do," he said, and at that exact moment, I saw a look of panic come across his face. He began to squirm in his chair and it was clear to me that I had struck a nerve. I was on a roll. I went on to get him to admit that the plaintiff and this "star" witness were dating at the time. He was her boyfriend all along and we had not caught it. So, as I said, you never walk into the courtroom without all the law and facts well under the belt. That one almost cost me greatly.

There is a classic case we hear about in law school of a lawyer asking one question too many, that one question to which he did not know the answer. In that case, the defendant was accused of biting off the plaintiff's nose. The key eyewitness was on the stand and confirmed that the defendant did, in fact, bite off the plaintiff's nose. Yet, on cross-examination, the lawyer carefully and strategically confirmed that the eyewitness was in no position to see the defendant bite off the nose. His view was blocked; he could not see the players, and ultimately the lawyer extracted an admission that the witness did *not* see the defendant bite off the nose. Now, that is where the excellent trial lawyer stops.

But when you ask that one question too many, you regret it. The cross-examiner went on to hammer home his point as he filled the room with his confident voice: "Well, then, if you didn't see the defendant bite off his nose…and it is clear that you did not, Mr. Witness, then how do you know he bit off the nose?"

The eyewitnesses said, "Well, I saw the defendant spit his nose out on the ground." That was that.

Sometimes one side gets in trouble because they do not have money and resources to do the research and the other side does. So one side has juror profiles and has worked with their own witnesses on both direct and cross-examination. This situation highlights the disparity in our system, and the unfairness shows. This is why in many criminal matters, jury consultants are willing to work without fee, or at very reduced fees. We need to balance the playing field. That is also why when a judge sleeps through the evidence, or in one case, where the trial lawyer kept falling asleep during the trial, this is sufficient reason for an appeals court to step in and require the case to be retried. Lack of preparation is essentially malpractice, and we need these checks in the system to ensure a fair trial.

Minimizing the Weaknesses

Based on my observations, an attorney who would never dream of walking into court shaky on any point of fact or law is remarkably likely to walk into that same courtroom shaky indeed about the expected performance of one or more of the witnesses. All sorts of things can break down when witnesses take the stand and get confronted with a tough cross-examiner.

For example, ask any witness about time and distance, and you soon see proof that most of us are poor at making judgments on these issues. "How close was the other car to you?" Or, "How long did you have hold of her neck as you choked her?" Unprepared witnesses usually give an answer that makes sense to them, but in reality is probably far from the truth.

In one of my partner Richard Gabriel's cases, there was testimony that a defendant choked the victim for three minutes. Richard worked with the prosecution to help the jury understand—experience—that length of time. And so the prosecutor sat in front of the jury and held a stopwatch in his hand and clicked it to start. Then, the prosecutor sat still for a full three minutes at which time he stopped the clock. "That, ladies and gentlemen, is how long the defendant had his hands on the victim's throat. And all that time, he choked the life out of her."

Three minutes is a *very* long time. The likelihood is that the defendant had not actually choked the victim for a full three minutes, but with that as the testimony, the prosecution was within its right to "run the clock" and give the jury the sense of a long and brutal death. Most people are not very good at time estimates, but in the courtroom, the consequences can be terminal. If you like, you can test this concept of time yourself.

Videotape yourself doing something and then several weeks or months later, think back and estimate how long it took you to do that task. After all, that is what happens in a lawsuit. You are asked to recall time and distance many months after the event. Then go back and watch the videotape and see how mistaken your estimate was. Being wrong is natural and not a crime, but in a trial, these are the kind of mistakes that make the difference between winning and losing.

First Impressions

Trial lawyers also recognize the effect of their demeanor on judges and juries. These impressions precede a jury's eventual rationale for siding for or against them. Non-lawyers often ask, "What effect does the lawyer's actual belief in the case have on the jury or judge?" What these individuals are really asking is: if a lawyer does not really believe in the client or the client's innocence or cause, then how can he or she be perceived as sincere?

This is not the appropriate question. The lawyer's job, regardless of personal beliefs, involves holding a strong belief in clients' rights to zealous representation, and to a belief in the system of justice itself. One lawyer friend of mine who has represented many high-profile criminal defendants said:

> Everyone wants to know how I can represent a guilty person, or how I feel when I lose a case. Actually, I don't care what people think about my representing people who did the crime. And I feel fine if I lose a case when my client *is* guilty. My job is to make the system work and to test it and test it again; if my client is found guilty for a crime he did, then I can sleep at night because it means the system is working. It's when I lose and I know my client is innocent that I can't sleep. That means the system has malfunctioned and an innocent person is doing time. But my talents can't overcome a solid case; it's just the way it is.

Judges and juries constantly observe and react to the intensity and sincerity exhibited by the lawyer. Are they getting a performance in court? Or is the lawyer truly committed to the client's position? For the sake of the system, it better be the latter. The strength of advocacy can be seen through the confidence and comfort of witnesses, achieved through extensive preparation. Of course, some witnesses inspire more confidence than others, in lawyers as well as in judges and juries. But, as you would expect, witnesses display a range of strengths and weaknesses.

Words Are Just a Part of the Package

The famous playwright Eugene Ionesco said, "It is not the answer that enlightens, but the question." Lawyers often blame the witness for difficulties on the stand, whether on direct or cross. But it may be that the lawyer is directly or indirectly responsible for the less-than-optimal job. Lawyers have the job of introducing witnesses to the range and nature of the questions they can expect during direct and cross-examination. In addition, the lawyer needs to consider how the jurors will perceive the testimony and the witness. Since we cannot call "central casting" and hire good witnesses, although at times we would certainly like to, we can prepare the witnesses. Too bad, though, some do not take well to our help.

I recall a banker who was more interested in travelling to Africa than he was in preparing for his testimony. He showed up moments before having to take the witness stand, appearing disheveled, with his scraggly ponytail hanging behind him. He expected to persuade a jury; he didn't. Others are frankly unsavory or otherwise difficult characters, but we must work with who we have, not who we would like to have. I once worked with a plaintiff in a personal-injury case. I was brought in to the case because the plaintiff's injuries, compounded with abuse of drugs, led him to throw himself against the wall until he had brain damage so severe it prevented him from making much sense when he spoke. He was a great challenge, but we worked together until he learned to answer with brief answers and some uncontrollable grunts. You will not see this kind of witness on television, but you will in the real world.

In addition to helping the witness make sense on the stand, I do not believe it is wrong for a witness to understand how their testimony fits with the pieces of the puzzle offered by others who will testify. I say this because many of my lawyer clients do not think that their witnesses need to have a global understanding of the case. I think witnesses should know the lawyer's mileposts and understand where they stand on that road. The danger is that some verbose witnesses can take a little understanding and do more damage than they are worth because they try to outguess what the lawyers are after in their questions. Once again, it is about proper witness training and preparation.

I once worked with a witness who after every question would ask, "Why would they ask that? What are they after?" And with some explanation, he would nod with comprehension, but begin to go beyond my questions with his answers. The rule to answer only what you are asked was a tough one for this witness, but with repetition of the process of question and answer, he also came to understand how to be a good witness. It takes time, but most witnesses can learn the skills.

Why Do Lawyers Ask Questions in Such a Lawyerly Way?

Once witnesses come to understand cross-examination as little more than a speech by the cross-examiner, the process is quickly understood and is less troubling to witnesses. They also understand that the questions will be asked so that they sound like statements. "You *did read* the contract before signing it, didn't you?" turns the question into a commentary. The witness immediately feels somewhat irrelevant, but if well prepared, the witness can hold his own. We work with our lawyer-clients to make sure they do not sound hostile or sarcastic as they make these statement-questions. As everyone knows, when our spouse or partner asks questions in the form of statements, we fear we may be in for a long evening. We may even object to being "interrogated."

When we prepare a witness, we may ask questions in a particular style to help them get used to "lawyer" style. For example, a technique called the "Loop Back Question" includes the answer given in the prior question. "Now, you've said that the goods showed up on Thursday. On that date, did you then…" By "looping back," we recast the previous statement in a way we like. If you live with a schoolteacher, you may be familiar with this form—it can sound suspiciously like a lecture. But it is not just about question form; lawyers like to get into a rhythm of asking questions, trying to get the witness on cross-examination into the habit of answering as expected. For example:

"You were the supervisor, weren't you?"

"Yes."

"And you were responsible for staff hiring and termination, weren't you?"

"Yes."

"And you had the authority to hire and fire employees like Ms. Maldo?"

"Yes."

And on and on as the witness gets used to answering in the affirmative until we hope the questions give the cross-examiner what he or she is after. Simply put, if you say "yes" a lot, you may just continue to say "yes" even when you meant to say "no."

"Then you knew Ms. Maldo was not religious when you terminated her employment, didn't you?"

If the "yes roll," works, we may get the "yes" we're after, even if the witness did not intend to say "yes." Repetition gets comfortable, for the lawyer anyway.

Linguistic Gymnastics

It is virtually impossible for individuals to relate every detail and component of events they experience. Our minds naturally block out some details, highlight others, and overall create the distorted picture we call reality. During seminars on witness preparation, many lawyers ask, "Why can't my witnesses just give me the *proper* answers on direct examination? I always have to fight for what I need from them." It is always easier to blame the inexperienced non-lawyer, but more often than not, the lawyer holds the ability to shape the truthful testimony of their witnesses.

Using words like "it seems to you" or "it appears that" may work to have witnesses understand that their memory may not be accurate. I recall one client of mine who was a defendant in a lawsuit that dealt with business issues. One evening, seemingly by coincidence, my client was having dinner in a neighborhood restaurant when the plaintiff came in with a new girlfriend (or so it seemed, since this plaintiff had more girlfriends than most calculators can tabulate). As my client related, after dinner, he began to leave the restaurant and walked past the plaintiff without acknowledging him. It was the appropriate conduct. When parties in a lawsuit are represented by counsel, all communication should go through the lawyers.

The plaintiff, whose ego is notoriously large, assumed that because my client ignored him as he passed by, the defendant was in fact challenging him. On his way out, the defendant stopped in the restroom, soon to find himself confronted by the controlling and domineering plaintiff. "You don't have the decency to talk to me?" In relating the event to me, my client was convinced that the plaintiff had threatened him. Given the setting (the restroom), and the fact that the plaintiff was fairly big and strong (and not above throwing his weight around), the memory seemed accurate.

Still, I did not want my client to lose perspective, and I suggested, "It appeared to you that following you into the restroom was to threaten you....It seemed that way." Just posing the question led the defendant to realize that there might, in fact, be another explanation. "Perhaps the plaintiff was actually hurt that your relationship has soured. Isn't it also possible that he was just hurting?" My client realized that this alternative explanation could be true as well. He was ready to add a counterclaim to the lawsuit, but some time and a bit of linguistic gymnastics on my part calmed him down. My client most likely made more headway by ignoring the plaintiff than by taking any other steps he had available. For example, he could have asked me to send a letter of warning to the plaintiff through his lawyer. We could have asked that he keep his distance and avoid direct contact. Sometimes though, these issues are better ignored. This was one of those situations.

Why Didn't He Testify?
Or, He Must Be Guilty as Sin

A defendant in a criminal case does not have the duty to testify. Jurors are told they must not hold a defendant's failure to testify against him in any way—and that is not an option. The burden rests with the prosecution and not with the defense. Regardless of the admonition, jurors may expect to hear a defendant declare his innocence and, more often than not, criminal defendants want to take the stand. Either they are truly innocent and want to "tell the world," or they are guilty but think they can fool the lawyers and the jury.

In nearly all criminal cases, the defense lawyer keeps the defendant off the stand. In the criminal case, O.J. Simpson probably wanted to take the stand. His ego likely led him to believe he could withstand whatever cross-examining lawyers could throw at him. Johnnie Cochran and the legal team were smart enough not to let that happen. If you followed the civil case, you heard legal analysts describe how his testimony was filleted before his very eyes and the jury's as well.

Defendants in a civil case do not have the same rights as they do in a criminal case. In a criminal case, a defendant faces loss of freedom and, hence, a protection against self-incrimination. But in a civil case, the risk is money. So, the same protections do not apply. Simpson had no choice but to take the witness stand when called, and he found it very difficult to stand by his story in the face of a well-executed cross-examination by the meticulously prepared Daniel Petrocelli.

In cases where the crime is particularly heinous, as in the murder of a child, many trial watchers, including reporters, fall back on the emotional issues involved. They do not understand how an accused child molester and murderer does not want to make a statement of innocence for the whole world to hear. I can only imagine how difficult it must be for an innocent person *not* to testify. But lawyers usually know best, and the reason they keep their clients off the stand is not necessarily a question of guilt or innocence.

If a matter has gone to trial, then there are likely two very strong versions of the same event; there are facts, which in the telling may differ only with the perspective with which they are related. So, even the innocent defendant faces witnesses who saw him, clothing that matches, an alibi that cannot be proved, and on and on. Even innocent defendants can be made to look guilty if the other side's lawyer pounds away at them, or even chips away at inconsistencies in her version of the story.

A defendant can exercise the decision to avoid the witness stand in a criminal case, but in a civil case, he cannot. Since a civil case is about something other than freedom and liberty, our system will not get in the way of resolving the civil dispute by protecting a party. I have worked in many cases in which my client would have loved the chance to avoid putting his client on the stand. In one situation, the plaintiff was an elderly woman who, although she was claiming money damages in her lawsuit, found it nearly impossible to place any blame or responsibility when it came to taking the stand and testifying. "I know she didn't mean to hurt me," she said. "I'm not really in that much pain...." She may not have been in pain, but her lawyer sure was after she took the stand.

Here Come the Experts

Expert witnesses are a special case. Unlike untrained lay witnesses who have found themselves caught up in a lawsuit, experts are brought into a case because they have special knowledge—expertise. Experts are usually an interesting bunch, but, truthfully, they often give lawyers big headaches. Maybe it is their vast experience, or perhaps all those degrees behind their names, or maybe it is the aggressive and confident demeanor with which they can talk about some of the most complex (and often dreadfully dull) information. Whatever the reason, many lawyers are uncomfortable when faced with questioning expert witnesses.

Since many experts enhance their professional lives by testifying at trials, lawyers are faced with the challenge of "controlling" the expert in deposition and at trial. The expert may want to recite his or her entire résumé or list every scientific discovery for which they are solely responsible, but the lawyers have an interest in narrowing the scope. Lawyers use these expert witnesses to gain points for their case, that is, adding "authoritative" information for jurors to consider. Experts are often used in technical fields such as medicine, engineering, or other sciences, and in financial arenas such as accounting.

I believe lawyers should take comfort in the fact that they do not share the expert's background and specific training. Some of the worst examples of lawyer questioning are found in depositions or trial transcripts conducted by lawyers who do have the same academic degrees and experience as an engineer or a doctor. For example, I read a deposition transcript once where a lawyer with a medical degree deposed a defendant surgeon. I do not recall any words containing less than fifteen letters, and very few words were used that were not medical terminology. This document would have little value as an impeachment tool at trial without first engaging in educating the jury to lay the foundation for the long, dull slog through the expert's information, at least as put forth in the deposition.

In another case, the lawyer, who was also a civil engineer, loved to challenge engineering experts in every way he could. Transcripts of his depositions looked like a battlefield of insult and innuendo, with a wonderful patter that impresses other professionals, but not necessarily the jury in cases where that witness was unavailable and all the jury heard was the transcript read into the court record. Sometimes these dueling experts (including the expert who forgets he is working as a lawyer) turn the interchange into a forum for personal challenge.

Lawyers may learn the hard way that questioning experts can lead them down unexpected paths. Too many lawyers think the best way to go after an adversarial expert is to challenge the theories they present. But, as I tell lawyer groups in my lectures, it is unwise to attack an expert's theory. I once questioned a respected life-expectancy expert, who had built a successful career through research, writing, and testifying. She was not going to be caught off-guard by some general attack on her life's work. The only way to challenge her was to challenge the specific facts on which she based her theory. When confronted with facts that did not fit into her equation, she would brush them off with a "that isn't relevant or necessary to the calculation." But the confrontation was necessary because the very facts rejected by that witness became the critical facts of my expert witness's theory.

Sometimes experts and lawyers can work at cross-purposes. I had dinner one evening with my friend and noted forensic expert Dr. Michael Baden and his wife, television commentator and lawyer Linda Kenny. We talked about Ground Zero and the decision made that clearing the destruction as quickly as possible was given priority over recovering decedents' remains and physical evidence. "Normally at a mass disaster," Dr. Baden said, "the first priority is to search for any living victims, as was done at Ground Zero. But it was a crime scene and normally forensic scientists, who include pathologists, anthropologists, dentists, and crime scene investigators, then respond to the scene to identify and collect bodies, body parts, and physical evidence. That wasn't done at Ground Zero and that's why so many victims have not been identified—and why critical girders that were the first to give way have not been recovered."

Dr. Baden was concerned because identification of the bodies is necessary to help families bring some closure to their grief. Because he knew that experts would be called upon to study details, draw conclusions, and give opinions and testimony involving causes of death, pain and suffering, and the structural integrity of buildings and airplanes, every detail may become critical. As in any case, especially one of this magnitude, at the time of the event, people are not thinking about future potential litigation. They act from their heart and passion. Lawyers and experts think differently. For better or worse, for us, every event represents a possible lawsuit.

There are certain details the experts rely on and plug into their theories in order to produce whatever conclusions they come to. The best experts learn to resist the challenge by saying that whatever facts they have not incorporated into their work do not matter. But in fact, these unincorporated facts often do matter, so enter the other side's expert. In other words, experts rely on the facts provided to them by the lawyer who retained them. The accounting practice is ethical because…and on the other side, no, it is unethical because…. Each accounting practice has it champions, just as each DNA expert or time-of-death expert or back-injury expert has theories they apply to a set of facts. As such, almost every case has a series of facts that would invalidate or significantly modify the results produced on each side. When you watch trials, look for the line of questioning that challenges the factual foundation upon which the experts drew their conclusions. Know there is an expert on the other side waiting to challenge those facts and methods and offer an alternative method with nearly opposite, or at least contradictory, conclusions. But that is the expert game.

Show Me the Evidence, Don't Just Talk at Me

Sometimes, witnesses are silent. That is, they come in the form of evidence that is presented by charts, graphs, guns, a truck that exploded, or even the infamous glove. Like a metaphor, demonstrative evidence can be used to bring home a key point. Also, the world has changed with regard to the use of computers and graphics in the courtroom. Until the O.J. Simpson case, lawyers were hesitant (mostly in civil cases) to use computer graphics and high-tech evidence because they feared it would make them look too wealthy. What would juries think about parties who were asking for money and apparently had tremendous resources available? Did they really need more money? And, what would a jury think when a defendant used such resources? If they had the funds to do such impressive work, then certainly they could afford to pay a verdict rendered against it.

However, in terms of educating the public, the Simpson case exerted influence again. People watched their televisions every day and saw the most sophisticated techniques in use. There seemed no end to the technology and resources, and no one seemed put off by it. And so today, we see that jurors are not bothered by technology. In fact, they appreciate and expect that the parties take the steps necessary to make evidence clear. They would rather see evidence come in more quickly and effectively and do not seem concerned that such efforts are expensive. We continue to see increased use of computer animation (I have worked with engineers who animate bridge or building collapses to provide a 360-degree perspective on how a failure event occurred). We see all sorts of charts and graphs used daily in courtrooms around the country to the pleasure of jurors, who find it easier to do their job.

In one of one our firm's cases, we used computer animation to demonstrate the power of the impact of a collision; in another case, animation was used to present a collision from varying angles, providing the jury with the perspective that even a live film or videotape could not offer. In computer animation done of the World Trade Center collapse, the manner in which the steel melted after the aircraft's impact illustrated how and where pockets of life-saving space were created, and explained how and why these pillars of seeming perfection tumbled to the ground in a matter of hours.

One popular aid I often create with my clients is a timeline. It is too easy for a lawyer to confuse jurors with the order of events. In a case involving the passing and misuse of a municipal bond, I worked with my client to visually demonstrate the steps of passing a municipal bond and how the money needs to be spent. In another case involving allegations of poor home construction, we used a visual chart showing the steps of construction using pictures of machinery to illustrate the process, which was crucial for a jury to understand. When my client wishes to highlight particular language from a statement or deposition, we use a computer to highlight the key phrases and then we enlarge them before the jury's eyes.

You have heard the phrase that a picture is worth a thousand words, and that is certainly true in the courtroom. Nowadays, preparing visual aids is as important as preparing witnesses, so jury consultants work with clients to create these tools to match the case theme and the metaphor that brings the point alive. This is one of the most difficult lessons to teach my lawyer-clients.

Lawyers who live in a world of documents think that putting that document on a poster board is assisting the jury's understanding. This is often a mistake. In my case alleging religious discrimination, my client created a chart to show the standard organization of a corporation. This simple chart proved to have quite an impact when she was able to contrast this acceptable chart with the corporation's actual organizational chart, which placed God in the center. The message was clear for the jury.

Solving—or Resolving—the Puzzle

So now you have the pieces of the puzzle. Witness testimony, visual aids, and evidence help witnesses establish and explain their story. Together, they form the meat on the bones of the case theme and story. Along with the lawyers' arguments, the jury is given the task of putting it all together and figuring out what happened. But they do not get to do this freely. Their decisions are guided by instructions from the judge, legal instructions that the judge reads to the jury, most often at the conclusion of all the evidence. Some judges read the instructions to the jury at the beginning of the case so the jurors know what rules must guide their work.

The next chapter takes a look at how the jury is charged to do its work, and then explores the very complicated process of jury decision making. It is a world everyone likes to hazard guesses about, but few really understand. Let's step into that world.

chapter 8

It Ain't Over 'til the Last Juror Sings

We always come back to the exchange we associate most with our legal system:

"Ladies and gentlemen of the jury, have you reached a verdict?" the judge asks.

"We have, your honor," the foreperson says.

"What say you?"

"We find the defendant guilty of the charge of murder in the first degree." Or, "We, the jury, find for the defendant and against the plaintiff and award zero damages in this matter."

Regardless of the verdict (or the exact wording of the exchange between judge and foreperson), we can count on three things occurring. The first is the increasing tension that comes with anticipation. That short exchange can seem to take an eternity. Both sides probably experience hope mixed with fear, or confidence mixed with doubt. Almost no one copes with only a single emotion or sense about the verdict. "Trial junkies" sometimes say they experience the same thing, and they do not even have a stake in the outcome. Yet if they have listened and gone through the thought processes and formed impressions throughout the trial, then they feel the tension as the verdict is announced.

Both sides always have so much riding on their case that a courtroom on "verdict day" is one of the most emotionally charged settings you will ever see. Without fail, one side is victorious, often jubilant, and one side usually sits in dismay and even anguish. Lawyers sometimes comfort the defeated defendant or party in a civil case, so in that way, it is not unlike what you see during television dramas. Even when major networks do not cover the day-to-day testimony in a trial, they may consider the verdict sufficient to warrant "breaking news" status. Lawyers standing shoulder to shoulder with their clients are defining moments for everyone involved—and for our system itself.

In addition, one side or the other will believe what the jury did was wrong, but that is just an opinion. The only opinion that counts is the jury's verdict. This is why everyone involved is eager to find out what led to that decision. How did the jury reach its conclusions?

In addition to the three major reactions to a verdict—pleasure, disappointment, and curiosity—three theories exist about the function of a jury. The first is that jurors merely find the facts. This is a naïve approach because it assumes that the jury will accept the "rules of the game," as the judge instructs them. Second, we have the theory that jurors use legal reasoning in their deliberation. This more sophisticated approach says that the jury applies the facts to the legal rules presented by the judge. The third approach is what I call the realistic theory. I believe that juries, as a rule, would like to apply the law presented *if* they understand it. I think they will apply it and follow as best they can in most cases, but will either sidestep it, bastardize their interpretation of it, or downright ignore it when a set of facts strongly affects them. These situations may lead them to produce a verdict that contradicts what the law would have them do in that case. In other words, in many cases, the jurors determine which side they want to win the case and then force the facts to fit the law presented. Some will even ignore the law presented to them. Others will defiantly negate or nullify the law to do what they personally believe is right, regardless of what the law says. Given this third "truth," it is no wonder that controversy often surrounds our legal system.

Several cases stand out as examples of the way jurors can surprise everyone and "go independent." For example, in Chicago, the verdict in the Michael Ceriale ("cop killing") case I discussed earlier, illustrated that eleven jurors were completely convinced of the defendant's guilt, while one lone juror refused to give in, even after days of tense deliberation. A real-life *Twelve Angry Men*, this case highlights a situation in which a juror with a strong disposition cannot be persuaded away from deeply ingrained beliefs and values. This does not happen often, but when it does, everyone wants to know why. However, to jury consultants and trial watchers, every verdict is the object of curiosity.

Help Wanted: Psychics

We know one thing for sure: there is really no way to predict what a jury will ultimately do. I give no credence to the consultants who claim they can predict verdicts, even when they prove to be right. We would all love to have psychics reassure us that our side is going to win, no matter how long the jury deliberates.

I am often amused by lawyers' efforts to predict what's going on in the jury room based on how long the deliberation goes on, but I fall victim to these predictions myself, and sometimes it can be embarrassing. You may recall that the jury in the O.J. Simpson criminal case was out only three and one-half hours when they announced that they had a verdict. All network experts rushed to the news studios to put our predictions on the line. This is one feature of media legal analysis I do not like because I know predictions are guesswork. Some lawyers always say that a short deliberation in a criminal matter usually means acquittal. After all, the jurors realize quickly that the prosecution has not met its burden and they vote to acquit and are ready to go home. But then, some lawyers claim the opposite. A swift deliberation means that the evidence is clear, they say, so there is nothing more to consider, and a vote easily produces a guilty verdict.

Along with my other "talking head" colleagues, I was ready to go on the air throughout the evening before the morning the Simpson verdict would be announced. By the way, the timing of the Simpson verdict was as unusual as every other event in the case. It seems that only Judge Ito would hold a verdict overnight in order to give the networks a chance to gear up for their coverage. However, even Johnnie Cochran had left town shortly after the jury began deliberations because he did not expect the jury to return so quickly. Because it was West Coast time, the morning network programs had many hours to fill. Sharing the multi-head screen with other legal experts, Tom Brokaw went around the group and my three colleagues predicted acquittal. "A clear rejection of the prosecution's case," the mostly defense-oriented group stated. Now, as you know, television is usually all about sound bites. We have no time to give lengthy explanations, let alone provide real analysis, and producers do not like wishy-washy answers like "it depends." So, I had to pick a side. I chose to predict conviction.

Even putting attacks on the evidence aside, it was possible the jurors knew deep inside that the trial had overwhelming testimony that was tough to explain away. So, I concluded, their common sense and logic would prevail and the jurors would react to this overwhelming testimony. I stood out as the lone "personality" in that group who predicted conviction. I actually felt no more certain about it than I would have predicting an acquittal. The next morning as we all listened as the verdict was announced, I stood out among the experts assembled in our various studios as the one who wore the proverbial "egg on my face." Actually, I didn't seem to be alone. Some of the players in the courtroom, including Simpson friend Robert Kardashian, seemed to be in complete disbelief as the verdict was announced.

In truth, however, the verdict could not be explained by length of deliberation. In fact, had the jury deliberated for a period of several days, it is possible that the "all-O.J. all-the-time" television coverage would have filled the hours discussing how the jury was carefully reviewing the evidence. There may have been less criticism of the jurors had they either actually reviewed, or took the time to create the impression that they were carefully reviewing, the evidence that took months to present. The reality is that these jurors were tired, recognized that they did not believe the prosecution had met its burden, and were prepared to say so and go home. Had Judge Ito not sequestered the jurors for the months of the trial, he may also have had a group of people more willing to spend some time discussing the evidence.

In a more recent case, the David Westerfield case, the talking heads had many days to fill with speculation about what the jury was up to in their deliberations. He was accused of kidnapping and murdering Danielle van Dam, and to many of the commentators, the jury was taking too long, whatever that means. Some called the case a "slam dunk" for a guilty verdict, and as the days passed, they began to argue that the jury could be hung. Analysts also kept track of the number of hours the jury deliberated each day, which opened another area of banter—and criticism. On some shows, you would have thought the jury was on trial. In reality, all this on-air back-and-forth discussion is filling time with speculation about why the jury asked for this or that piece of evidence and so forth. It is the nature of today's legal coverage. I imagine the likes of Clarence Darrow would have been astonished by it. Since I did not serve as a legal analyst in that case, I was free to sit back and watch. When the jury came back, after nine days or so, with a guilty verdict, we all saw the same analysts defend the jury and quickly move their analysis to the sentencing phase of the trial. Would the jury impose the death penalty as the prosecution asked? That issue alone filled many hours of coverage.

Similarly in a civil case, a short deliberation can suggest a plaintiff's verdict because the overwhelming evidence suggests a swift award of money, perhaps even more than asked for by the plaintiff. Conversely, the defense lawyer would not be wrong to assume a short deliberation means that the jury believed the plaintiff did not meet its burden of proof and therefore comes to the rescue of the defense. So, lawyers will forever predict and make assumptions about what the length of deliberation means, but the fact is, we do not really know.

Who Is the Winner?

Ultimately, the success or failure of a verdict is often one of perception. I once worked on a case in which a professional in his early thirties was in his car and was hit by another vehicle whose driver has blown a stop sign. The plaintiff's passenger was killed. The plaintiff was rendered physically unable to move or speak, but had full mental awareness. This state is known as near locked-in syndrome. You may recall the case I mentioned where an individual was left in this state after a brutal physical attack in an elevator. Individuals in this condition are unable to move any part of the body except for the ability to blink their eyelids or maybe move a finger. In this case, the plaintiff could only blink, but his mind was functioning perfecting. Frankly, this young man wanted to die, and testimony came in that supported that state of mind. The experts for the plaintiff predicted a normal life expectancy, and all experts agreed there would never be an improved condition. Defense experts argued that the plaintiff was unlikely to live more than a few additional years.

The dollar amount I refer to here is almost twenty years old, but suffice it to say that the verdict in the case, $9.3 million, set records at the time. In a manner of speaking, this sounds like a true plaintiff's victory, but given the condition of the plaintiff, nothing short of a miraculous recovery would have seemed much like victory. Still, the money would take care of the young man for however long he lived. However, the success of a verdict is a matter of perception.

This case was all about damages, that is, the total dollars awarded. The defense admitted liability, and the defense lawyers told the jury that a verdict in the amount of $4 million to $5 million would be appropriate in the case. This was a counteroffer to the plaintiff's request that the jury award $33 million. So, who won? An offer to settle the case before trial, rejected by the plaintiff, was in the amount of $10 million! Nearly $100 million of insurance money was available to be paid out if required in the case.

That evening, news broadcasts featured the plaintiff's lawyer, who was congratulated for the fine record-setting verdict as reporters asked how he did it. This lawyer was wise to accept the congratulations and humbly discuss the importance of providing proper care for the plaintiff. But the real winner (again, to the extent that word even applies in such a tragic set of events) was the defense lawyer. Facing a verdict that could be counted in tens of millions, and already having offered $10 million, it is clear that the verdict was a success of heroic proportions. While that result served the defense firm well in the insurance industry, it did not do much to build a favorable image in the community at large. That is why analyzing verdicts is a study of perceptions.

Here, the jury appeared to see through a bit of the bravado of the plaintiff's lawyer. They noted that with the defense admitting liability, it added credibility to their case. That is, they noted that the plaintiff's lawyer appeared to attack the defense as if it was trying to avoid being found liable. They preferred the comforting tone of the defense lawyer who said, "Take care of this man. We want you to take care of him." While lawyer demeanor does not have the weight of the evidence the jurors must weigh, the compatibility of that demeanor with the message helps the jury accept that lawyer's position. Here, the defense lawyer who says, "We care and we are going to take care of this plaintiff," is much easier to assimilate in the deliberation than a screaming plaintiff's lawyer.

Is It Just a Game of Chance? Not Exactly

While one can never confidently predict a verdict, jury consultants can help take a bit of the surprise (and sometimes sting) out of verdicts. One of the most labor-intensive projects is having a mirror jury. This means that the consultant recruits individuals from the community to sit in the courtroom and watch (or "shadow") the trial every day. We try to find jurors who are much like the actual jurors in the case.

Each night, at the conclusion of the day's proceedings, the consultant meets with or telephones each of the mirror jurors to get their reactions to the testimony presented that day. The value of this project is that it helps the jury consultant provide daily insight to the lawyers about the actual jurors' perceptions of the evidence. As a result of what the mirror jurors tell us, we work with the lawyers to shift strategy midcourse if necessary. This is the consultant's way of staying on top of the progression of the planned case. It is a way we can test our case theme and the impact of the evidence and testimony as it comes in.

Where Did You Find This Bunch?

Running a mirror jury is a challenge because it is difficult to find people who are not only willing to listen to an entire trial but actually have the time to spend in a courtroom for many days. I recall a civil case that involved many complex issues including antitrust and patent violations. The plaintiffs hired us to assemble a mirror jury for a trial likely to go on for several months.

As you might guess, the prospects are people who are unemployed—not always by choice—retired, or do not have to work. We do pay them a daily fee, but somewhere between $150 and $200 a day is not enough to motivate most people to quit their jobs. A few people do see this service as a kind of a "career move" up, because they make more than they did when stuck flipping hamburgers or cleaning motel rooms. As you can imagine, we have found some real characters. Madge had been a waitress in a bar for her whole life. She said the word "lawyer" as "liar" but didn't mean anything by it. As a bar waitress she was a talker, and during her temporary "day" job she was the same way. So, while all mirror jurors were admonished not to discuss the proceedings with anyone, she constantly talked to anyone she could find who would listen to her. For the most part, she did not say anything relevant, but she could not shut up during the day-to-day grind of the trial.

Then we had Irwin, a fellow who thought he understood it all, including the use of (what he called) "despositions" at trial. You could try to tell him that these were *depositions*, but to Irwin, that was a distinction without a difference. He was also a bit paranoid and thought everyone was talking about him. He wanted to give interviews on his terms and on his timetable. To say he was moody is an understatement.

Marlene was an elderly woman who was thrilled to be remaining active in her later years. She awaited our nightly telephone calls and was always ready to give her reactions often based on her experiences with her family. "I have a cousin who is like that and I don't like him for it…and I didn't like this expert for what he said neither!"

You can get some problematic folks on the mirror jury as well. In this case we had a couple of men in their thirties, both had been unemployed and were very thankful for some income for awhile. One of the men, Ian, would constantly ask when he would be able to do this again. I guess a career as a professional mirror juror looked good to him. The other man, Tony, was a bit sleazy. We had reports from the other mirror jurors that Tony was not showing up in court, or came for a short while and left. (It's amazing how seriously the jurors took on a "policing" duty. They loved to let me know which of their colleagues were late, which talked during testimony, and who brought their lunch).

I would call Tony in the evening and he would try to create the impression that he was there. Specific questions, like, "Hey Tony, what was your reaction to the line of questioning about alternative manufacturing methods?" got a stumbling and rambling response that confirmed that Tony was either not there or not paying much attention. I fired Tony. And so it goes.

A mirror-jury project provided significant information in this antitrust trial. After each day of this very complex and complicated trial, our interviews indicated that the jurors were not impressed with the plaintiff's case. We were representing a group of plaintiffs in a related lawsuit whose case would be heard following this case. Even the expert testimony was confusing and weakly perceived by the mirror jurors. By the end of the plaintiff's case, our jurors were ready to vote for the defense.

We never did find out what the real jurors would do because the judge in the case granted a directed verdict for the defense. This meant that the judge determined that the plaintiff had not presented enough evidence to continue the case and hear the defense's response. The case was over. Our mirror jury was on track and saw the case much the way the judge did, even without legal instructions. Our clients never got to trial.

Lawyers and jury consultants engage in ongoing debate about the real value of these mirror juries as reflections of what the actual jurors are thinking. Some consultants swear by their usefulness, and others do not think much of them. They certainly are expensive to run, and while we attempt to find jurors who truly mirror the actual jurors, the reality is that finding close comparability is difficult. However, I believe in focus groups and collecting as much information as possible, which may include a mirror jury. These men and women provide immediate responses that help the lawyers adjust their approach on a daily basis. As a scientific tool, I remain a skeptic; but for providing feedback for lawyers, I think it is, at a minimum, a viable tool.

For example, when my mirror jurors report that they are "lost" in the technical testimony of an expert, I have my client meet with his expert that night and reconsider how they are walking through the testimony. The use of more graphs or charts, and an intentional effort to use more common terms and metaphors that people can understand, is often the remedy. In cases where the jurors report that they are simply not persuaded by a witness, I try to explore what is behind their evaluations. If they tell me something we can fix (like "I wish I knew more about her credentials") then we do so. When it is a matter of "I just don't trust her," we have a more difficult task ahead. If the witness completes his or her testimony before we get the feedback, then we work with the lawyer to confirm the needed testimony through other witnesses or through evidence that can serve to confirm the needed points when closing argument comes along.

The Juror's Tools

As they exercise their role as finders of fact, jurors integrate their interpretation and perception of evidence and testimony. The jurors are charged with determining what happened based on the conflicting accounts. Exercising this responsibility does not happen without guidance and structure. Some people do not realize it (and you rarely see much about this issue on television programs), but prior to the jury going off to deliberate, they are given legal instructions by the judge. By legal instructions, I mean a series of definitions, guidelines, and step-by-step expectations designed to guide the jurors along in the deliberation process. These instructions provide a key piece to understanding verdicts that sometimes go against your own common sense or seem to contradict what you expected from reading the newspaper accounts of the trial. Every "offense" has a specific legal definition, which then guides the jurors. But not all legal cases, either criminal or civil, appear to fit neatly into a box.

The point is that juries do not officially have free reign over their deliberation. The legal system places expectations on jurors that they will find the facts within the scope of the law provided to them by the court. The verdict is supposed to result from the law as presented and not from personal beliefs. Earlier I discussed the fact that a behavior or conduct does not have any legal meaning until it can be defined by a standard under the law. So, if A kills B, it is not murder under the law unless there are certain factors present, such as the willful intent to kill another person with malice and without justification or other legal excuse or purpose. So, for a jury to find a person guilty of a crime, or to award money for a wrongful act, the jury must be able to find that the facts they determine meet the definition of the crime or standard.

In addition, where the prosecutors in a criminal case are seeking a maximum penalty or punishment, they will want to charge what are called "special circumstances." These particulars are defined by statute and specify specific elements that, when present and proved in the current case to the jury's satisfaction, permit the imposition of the harshest sanction, such as death. They are like aggravating circumstances, facts that add to the heinous nature of the crime. For example, to get an instruction specific to multiple murders, the special circumstance of "intent" to kill more than one person would have to be proved. The special circumstance of felony murder requires that the murder be accompanied by, for example, the intentional crime of burglary or robbery.

Jury instructions define and clarify the burden of proof (that is, who has to prove the case and by how much). That is how a jury knows that a criminal case is guided by the standard of proof beyond a reasonable doubt while a civil case is determined by measuring the evidence by its preponderance. The different standards assuredly produce different results even from the very same evidence. This is how one can explain otherwise seemingly contradictory verdicts when the same case undergoes both a criminal and civil case. Again, the O.J. case immediately comes to mind. In the criminal case, the jury determined that the prosecution could not meet its burden of proof beyond a reasonable doubt. In the civil case, the jury found that for the most part, the same evidence did meet a lesser standard of "more likely than not" in evaluating the evidence. In other words, in the civil case, the jury found that it was more likely than not that Simpson committed the wrongful act.

This is why we can see one verdict in a state trial, for example, but then what appears to be a contrary verdict from a federal case that arises out of the same facts but addresses a different cause of action. For example, an action against police officers in the state court might address allegations of abuse or battery, but on the federal level, charges of civil rights violations can be addressed. Each of these different counts or theories brings with it its own verdict and consequences.

In the LAPD/Rodney King cases, my former jury consultant colleague, Jo-Ellan Dimitrius, worked in both the Simi Valley case and in the federal trial. You may recall that the jury found all the police defendants not guilty in the state trial, but found some of the defendants guilty in the subsequent federal criminal trial. Different instructions produced different verdicts.

The instructions are selected by the lawyers and then presented to the judge, who selects those that ultimately are read to the jury. Where all lawyers agree on some of the instructions (such as standard instructions on burden of proof and how to weigh evidence), the judge will generally include the suggested instructions without further discussion. Strategy enters the picture when the parties disagree on whether a particular instruction should be given, or over what version of an instruction should be included. Here, the lawyers argue to the judge, who then decides which instruction is given. Because these instructions are the law that form the framework within which the deliberation must occur, the decisions on which contested instructions will ultimately be given can determine what a jury will do and which way the case will go. I have worked in many cases where the lawyers do significant battling over the wording of an instruction, or the inclusion or exclusion of a specific instruction. These are legal battles to be sure, but these are the rules of the game, rules that may determine the game.

Good Reasons for Different Burdens of Proof

In a criminal case, the consequences facing the defendant are loss of freedom through imprisonment and even death. As Americans, we should expect the highest standard of proof in criminal cases as part of our effort to ensure that only a guilty person can be found guilty. Juries can still make a mistake under such a tough standard, but imagine the degree of concern that would occur if the standard were any lower than beyond a reasonable doubt. One can only imagine the crowded prisons.

In a civil case, we are usually presented with a dispute between two people or entities. Here, the system's goal is to resolve the issue and determine whether one side or the other should prevail. With a more difficult standard than "more likely than not," a jury would be doing more than just resolving a dispute. It would be the system suggesting that a person who sues should have a higher standard than the person who is being sued, and this would not make much sense in most civil cases. The existence of our civil-dispute system is to encourage people to resolve their disputes peacefully and among peers, without having to resort to violence and the duels of olden days.

It is true that the difference of proof standards means that one set of facts can produce dissatisfaction in one court, but resolution in the other. I worked in a case in which the parties got into an old-fashioned bar-room brawl. Charges were filed against the alleged aggressor, Ron, but ultimately the case was resolved before trial. The prosecutor did not believe she had sufficient evidence to get a verdict for assault and battery, and got Ron to agree to probation for one year. But this verdict did not stop the plaintiff, Angela, from filing a civil complaint against Ron. She alleged that Ron hit her in the bar and started the fight; he denied all allegations. In the civil case, the jury had to decide which party's story was more likely true than not true.

I will never forget the courtroom demonstration as my client, the plaintiff's lawyer, had his client, petite and feminine appearing (at least in court) Angela, stand there while the large and imposing Ron stood above her to demonstrate how he may have made contact with her face. The judge permitted this display, and the jury was glued to the action. My client also had Angela show the jury the scars that were supposedly visible in her mouth that resulted from the fight. (I couldn't see anything and believe whatever damage that may have been there before was now healed, but after the courtroom display, the jury may well have thought they saw some scars; remember, if you show people a picture of Bugs Bunny in front of Disneyland, they will report that they too saw Bugs there.) Again, different standards, different instructions, and different verdicts. Of course, ultimately, while Ron paid money for what was proven to be more likely than not, he did not serve jail time because the state did not think it could prove its case beyond a reasonable doubt.

Where Did This Verdict Come From?

So, given the jury instructions, one would expect correct verdicts; that is, verdicts determined solely on the law guiding deliberations. But sometimes this does not occur, and the reason for it is quite simple, if odd. As a rule, jurors do not understand the legal instructions the judge gives them. How do we know this? And further, how can we make instructions more effective without rendering them ambiguous in the process? To take the issue one step further, what do we do about jurors who choose not to follow the instructions and, in fact, willfully act to contradict the instructions?

Jurors are instructed at every step of the trial. Throughout the trial, the judge tells the jury to disregard a piece of evidence or testimony, or tells them for what purpose they may listen to a certain answer. Most of us know that it is difficult to disregard a statement, even if a judge were to tell us to put it out of our minds. It is like telling the jurors to ignore the elephant in the courtroom. Even when we hear that "disregard the last statement" line in a movie, we know that what is supposed to be disregarded almost always get discussed in the jury's decision. We can never take back what has been said out loud.

Unfortunately, instructions to the jury can become further complicated because the judge, in an effort to avoid ambiguity, speaks in "legalese." The problem is that the effort to be clear is simply made more convoluted. For example, consider the jury instruction: "A plaintiff who was not contributorily negligent and who did not assume the risk of harm and who was injured as a proximate result of some negligent conduct on the part of a defendant is entitled to recover compensation for such injury from that defendant." Most jurors have likely tuned out after the word "contributorily." And, the instruction actually goes on to present a series of elements to be proven, if anyone is still listening.

Not only is the language in instructions difficult to comprehend, but usually a large number of instructions (often a minimum of fifteen) must be considered. Most jurors have good intentions and want to do the right thing, but they are not necessarily equipped with the ability to properly interpret and apply the instructions.

I remember the words of Mary Timothy, the foreperson in the Angela Davis case back in the early 1970s. You may recall Angela Davis, the militant African-American activist who gained international recognition during her imprisonment and trial for conspiracy in 1970–72. Davis had been a doctoral candidate at the University of California in San Diego. Because of her political and social leanings, and despite an excellent record as a teacher, her appointment as a lecturer in the philosophy department was not renewed. Davis soon became a champion for black prisoners. After becoming involved with revolutionaries, she was suspected of complicity in an event in which Jonathan Jackson, the younger brother of revolutionary George Jackson (one of the Soledad Brothers), was killed in an escape and kidnapping attempt from a California courthouse.

Davis was eventually arrested having been one of the FBI's "most wanted criminals," facing charges of kidnapping, murder, and conspiracy. In an interesting twist, an all-white jury eventually acquitted her of all charges. Ms. Timothy wrote: "The judge read well, clearly, and with ease. He tried to make the formal wording of the legal writing interesting and understandable to a group of twelve average citizens. But speaking strictly for myself, it was a losing battle."

Perhaps the entire problem of creating understandable jury instructions was summed up best by Sandra, a juror in a complex commercial trial who said to me, "I'd be lying if I told you I understood all that legal mumbo jumbo the judge read to us. To be honest, I believed that [plaintiff] was screwed by the [defendant] and that's what we set out to do…fix it!"

The Battle to Find Solutions

Many legal scholars have studied and continue to study ways to more effectively charge the jury, which is the formal name for giving instructions. Some have suggested that the charge be skipped altogether. After all, why confuse the jurors? Let them review the evidence and find the facts, which is their job. This is not a good solution because along with finding the facts, the jurors' decisions about guilt or liability are determined by how the facts presented are viewed within the framework of the laws that apply. It bears repeating that no one is guilty of anything until the behaviors at issue are seen in light of the parameters of the legal definitions and standards. Perhaps the better road involves greater efforts to make jury instructions clear enough so that average people can understand them. But as soon as you try to clarify and simplify legal issues, ambiguity invariably results and soon the instructions can be interpreted several different ways.

This has been a difficult battle for many years. I believe the instructions should be given at the beginning of the case, which then allows jurors to understand the framework within which the evidence should be viewed. They should be repeated at the conclusion of the case, which stresses their importance, and written, or hard copies of the instructions should be given to each juror for their review throughout the deliberation. Some judges follow this procedure.

The lawyers, who are the ones who have submitted the instructions to the judge, then have the right and duty to craft their closing arguments in a way that emphasizes the instructions. This is about the best we can do. In the end, we can only hope that the jurors will do their job, as we have the right to expect.

Gathering around the Big Table

In many ways, a jury is much like any small random group. They are men and women brought together for face-to-face interaction, with an opportunity to exert influence on each other. They operate with a degree of interdependence and with a common goal to resolve and decide the case before them. Every group goes through stages of development, so to speak, and a jury is no different—we see the same process occur again and again. As they enter their deliberations, they first go through an orientation stage, which we might call a "social" phase, during which they exchange some personal small talk or sharing. Of course, this is much like the chitchat they have had amongst themselves during the course of the trial.

Since the judge forbids the jurors from talking about the case itself, the conversations are much more likely to address the issue of who is walking the family dog, how many kids the jurors have, and who went where on vacation. But in settling into the deliberations, they now seek to establish their role in relation to one another. As deliberation continues, the jurors enter into a role and conflict development stage. Here, the jurors develop into their roles on the jury. I do not mean only the elected or selected foreperson, but the series of functions that jurors must step into as needs arise. Some jurors initiate action, and may help organize or synthesize evidence. Anytime a lawyer sits on a jury, you can be sure the other jurors look to her for guidance and direction. In my experience, most lawyers are pleased to grab on to that role. Other jurors provide social support and help ease tensions when they arise. We might say these are the peacemakers; they may promote compromise and attempt to restore harmony.

Functional roles are needed because other jurors may well step into dysfunctional roles. We have the blocker, one who seemingly has nothing to do but complain and is hostile to the process. I once saw the classic blocker in Gary, who wanted nothing more to get out and get home. Unfortunately, the "Garys" sabotage themselves because they prevent others from moving the process along. We also find the self-interest pleader, individuals who want everyone else to feel sorry for them and thus lean their way. I have seen jurors who want to get home to take care of their kids or to care for an elderly parent, for example, step quickly into this role.

Perhaps the most important role in the deliberation process is that of the leader. I do not necessarily mean the foreperson who has been elected, selected, or perhaps volunteered for the role. The foreperson is the designated leader, but it is fascinating to see another leader emerge, usually a person with positive influence on the group. The foreperson usually stays in that role throughout the trial, but the role of leader may shift from person to person as the proceedings progress. Some leaders are autocratic; they dictate policy and procedure. Other leaders are more democratic in that they encourage the group to participate in deciding the direction the group is taking.

In one of our mock juries, an elderly woman, Edith, emerged as a leader. It was clear where she wanted the group to go, but she always checked with everyone before summarizing the consensus that appeared to being forming. She was meticulous in making sure everyone was on board. It was not uncommon to hear Edith say, "Now, you've talked enough. Let's let Lucille put her two cents in," or, "Bob, would you stop commenting on what other people say. We listened to you, now you need to give the courtesy to others!" She was colorful and delightful. Few found it difficult to like her and no one could go against her instructions.

If deliberation goes on for a while, coalitions or subgroups may develop, which can lead to conflict among the jurors. We tend to think of conflict as a problem, but guided by an effective leader, conflict can be a positive development. With differences on the table, the jury can work through the issues and seek compromise and resolution. For example, in the federal case alleging police misconduct against Rodney King, the prosecutors asked the jurors to convict all four LAPD officers; the defense sought to get all four found not guilty. The jurors had a difficult dilemma because Los Angeles had already experienced a series of riots following the state trial in which the officers were acquitted. An acquittal in the federal trial could cause L.A. to erupt again; on the other hand, convicting all four could leave the city facing a "blue flu."

Given all these circumstances, the jurors negotiated and found their own road to resolution of the conflict. They convicted two of the officers who were clearly the instigators of the conduct against Rodney King and they acquitted the other two defendants who were seemingly subordinates who got pulled into the situation. I recall that the jurors reported that when they came up with their resolution they gave each other a "high five" because they knew they had found both a just verdict and one that led to peace in the community. In fact, most people do not even recall this verdict because it sat well with the community.

Conflict can be good because it prevents "groupthink." This term refers to situations in which a group of people who have a decision to make spend a lot of time together and develop a strong rapport. This can lead to a situation where a desire for group consensus outweighs critical thinking—and no one is tossing out challenges.

When stakes are high, the need for careful analysis and challenge is great. Among jurors, skepticism is healthy and desired. We need jurors to raise questions and challenge positions. Those who are "playing around" or who are impatient with the process do not welcome skepticism or healthy challenges that require rethinking assumptions.

Playing by the Rules—Or Not

It is troublesome to think that a jury will sidestep the law presented to them and render a verdict that even they would admit is contrary to the law. You cannot play the game fairly when you do not play by the rules. Of course, if one believes the rules are unfair or produce the "wrong result," then what do you do? There is much evidence about what is known as jury nullification. Sometimes it is clear that the jury has set the law aside; other times, it only appears that way to a party who is stunned by a verdict.

Some accused the jury in the O.J. Simpson case of not applying the law because the evidence appeared overwhelming. However, jury instructions do not tell jurors to assume someone is guilty until proven innocent; the prosecution has the entire burden of persuasion. In addition, nothing is to be inferred by the defendant's choice not to testify. When you look at the questions of doubt raised by the defense (i.e., no positive identification of Simpson at the scene, a glove that did not fit, some question about the timeline and so on), it did not require a great leap for the jurors to conclude that the prosecution did not meet its burden.

Added to everything else, for many jurors, life experience included knowledge—or at least deep suspicion—that police have been known to plant evidence. The verdict had nothing to do with whether Simpson actually committed the crime; the jury followed its instructions and had to determine whether or not the prosecution met its burden of proof.

In another case, a dear friend of mine, Kaye Ballard, an actress and comedienne, sued the City of Chicago some years ago following a fall on what was alleged to be a hazardous street. Kaye figured she was in trouble when one juror was asked on jury selection how far she went in school. The juror's response? "Three blocks." Yet Kaye, based on her lawyer's analysis, rejected a settlement offer because the liability appeared clear. But the evidence presented included the fact that Kaye had just completed a very successful year of theatrical appearances. Although she wore a brace to work and was in constant pain, it appeared that the jury in her case could not get beyond a seeming failure to prove damages. Apparently, little sympathy could be mustered for a "star" who came from the West Coast and who continued to work. The verdict was zero dollars.

Many years later, Kaye remains angry, but with her sense of humor intact, she believes that the jury did not follow the instructions given to them. She is convinced that Chicago jurors take care of their own, but she was not one of them. Nullification, or failure to meet the burden of proof? Unless jury consultants or lawyers interview jurors, we—and Kaye—are left to wonder.

The concept and practice of jury nullification is not new; in fact, it dates back to at least early English common law and our colonial era. One very famous U.S. case of nullification involved John Peter Zenger, the publisher of the *New York Weekly Journal* who was acquitted of criminal libel in the eighteenth century. In late 1733, Zenger began publishing a newspaper in New York that consistently published articles critical of the colony's newly appointed governor, William Cosby. In 1734, Cosby had Zenger arrested and charged with libel. After spending many months in jail, Zenger was tried and defended by a famous Philadelphia lawyer, Andrew Hamilton.

The public closely watched the case, and when it became clear that the court seemed to be guiding the verdict toward conviction, Hamilton decided to argue his case directly to the jury. They returned after a short deliberation with a verdict of *not* guilty. The governor was none too pleased, but the people had taken matters into their own hands. In that situation, the "revolutionary" spirit prevailed.

Situational Approval

The problem with jury-nullification issues is that most of us tend to be against it in a general theoretical way, but like it a lot in a select few cases near and dear to our hearts. Let's look back 150 years or so and see how it is easy to applaud the juries who refused to convict individuals who had helped runaway slaves. These jurors were in essence making a public-policy statement, or to put it another way, they were making a statement about fundamental rights and wrongs within an institution that was still legal at that time. On the other hand, we are likely to express disgust with the all-white juries in several Southern states, that, after the Civil War, refused to convict white individuals for crimes committed against African-Americans.

In both instances, juries essentially refused to follow the law. In the first case, nullification was a way for jurors to express their beliefs that the laws the accused broke were unjust in the first place. This has happened numerous times over the course of this country's history, and it will likely continue to be one method to bring about social change. Over time, the law expanded rights and protections, and juror actions no doubt contributed to the change. In the second instance, juries were protesting social change they did not agree with, but eventually their actions led to *greater* sensitivity to racial composition of juries. It was not their intention, but it was better for society. For example, we have seen "conviction by race," so to speak, lessen in our society.

In addition, given some verdicts, such as in the Angela Davis case mentioned earlier, the issue may not be the case of jurors not following the law as much as a case of not understanding it. This comes back to judges' instructions. Jury consultants are important here, too, because we can attempt to monitor how our shadow jurors are interpreting the facts as applied to specific law. Whether we approve or not, nullification based on knowledge of the law has intention behind it; incongruous verdicts that result from confusion about the law undermine the intent of our system.

To Nullify or Not to Nullify

Although for obvious reasons jury nullification is not generally popular with lawyers and judges, I must admit that I like the power embedded in the concept of jurors as "legislators." In other words, these men and women have a chance to adjust the law when as a united body they believe it is unjust. Nullification is part of our system of checks and balances. Some laws defy common sense or no longer "match" evolving social issues, so during the course of our history, juries have called our attention to these laws. Challenges to sodomy laws, for example, will continue to take place as long as states have such statutes on their books. Through time, we can expect changes in the laws that limit or cap damages in some instances like medical-malpractice matters, or we will change the way experts and their testimony are handled.

My only caveat on the nullification issue is that it is important that jurors "legislate" with a knowing nullification rather than because they did not understand the jury instructions. Certainly, we want jurors who apply the law to case facts consistently. We expect this consistency because this is the way our system functions over time, and stability within the system is necessary to keep it functioning. In other words, we want to avoid the necessity of doing extensive overhauls of the system every few decades because of jury behavior. Special verdict forms, which guide the juror deliberations through specific fact-finding questions, are one means of achieving this consistency, although they may restrain free-flowing dialogue.

Discouraging Nullification

I have interviewed jurors who made it clear that they were going to "take care of" an injured plaintiff when there were substantial defendants (such as a corporation) or presumed resources such as insurance available.

As you might guess, the "system's" response to nullification arguments is to discourage it. In short, while juries have the power to nullify, they have no legal right to do so. We can legitimately argue that jury nullification violates the promise the jurors have made to find facts and apply the law as given to them by the court. Practiced regularly, nullification poses the risk that we will chip away at the very foundation of our legal system. This is why lawyers and legal analysts continue to argue about the issue.

Lawyers try to avoid jury nullification by giving jurors what is called a "special verdict form." This is a verdict form that goes beyond the general statement: "We the jury find for the defendant and against the plaintiff." These verdict forms provide a series of questions the jurors must answer. The questions are designed to guide the deliberation. One lawyer-client of mine said he thinks these special verdict forms were created to "keep the damn jury on track and not let them go off on some damn tangent in space!" The reality of these forms is that they do help guide the discussion and point the jurors to the exact issues they must address and resolve. For example, in one case the question on the form read:

> Do you find that the supervisor had the responsibility of reading the contract and forwarding it on to the vice president? If your answer is yes, proceed to the next question. If your answer is no, then you must return with a verdict of no liability and your deliberations are completed.

By walking the jurors through each factual step, they remind the jurors both how to follow the law as well as direct them to follow the law. But most lawyers will tell you that even with special verdict forms in both criminal and civil cases, jury nullification continues to occur. Even with a verdict form to walk them through a series of questions to guide their deliberation, jurors still are not prevented from reaching the verdict that their gut, head, and heart tell them to reach.

In an interesting twist in the questions raised about jury nullification, the California Supreme Court held in *People v. Williams*, a 2001 case, that a trial court may dismiss a juror who discloses an intent to nullify a verdict. The court was not taking a stand against nullification. It also acknowledged a jury's ability to set aside and disregard jury instructions. So, the court simply continued the question of what it can do to prevent or fight nullification.

In *People v. Williams*, the defendant was charged with, among other crimes, statutory rape of his sixteen-year-old girlfriend. During deliberation, one of the jurors said that he was philosophically opposed to the law on statutory rape and refused to convict the defendant regardless of what anyone said. For that juror, the case was closed. The foreperson informed the judge who, after conferring with the juror, dismissed him.

How can the California Supreme Court affirm the dismissal of a juror for declaring that he would not follow the law and at the same time acknowledge that jurors have the right (or at least the ability) not to follow the law? The court answers this question by stating that while jurors can disregard particular instructions given to them, they still have a concurrent responsibility to find the facts and deliver a verdict based on the law given to them. If a juror announces that he will ignore this obligation, then he can be dismissed.

In *Williams*, the judge heard about the nullification because the one juror involved was likely upsetting the other jurors. It is more common for a jury as a whole to determine that it will set aside the law and not follow it. In that situation, who will speak up and complain? And so the nullification occurs without challenge. I suppose that a jury that agrees *en toto* with a decision and chooses not to discuss their deliberations or verdict will succeed in nullification because they are not publicly accountable. We saw in the Heidi Fleiss case that jurors willing to talk about the process, especially because they are not pleased with the outcome, put their very verdict in jeopardy.

Tell It to the Judge

Given jury-nullification issues (along with the belief juries do not understand instructions), some within the legal system think we should eliminate juries and allow judges to decide cases. Would this improve the system? In my "lawyerly" opinion, it depends. When the individual (such as a judge) is an expert in the topic, that one person may likely produce a better result than a jury comprised of nonexperts. Wouldn't an accountant be in the best position to judge whether the alleged abuses of another accountant's practice met professional standards?

In the *Crawford v. State* case discussed much earlier in the book, a judge rather than a jury tried Crawford (who was charged with murder for killing a home intruder). His lawyers gambled that a judge would have the sophistication to see beyond the fact that Crawford had likely committed each of the elements charged but see the excuse of self-defense as crucial. A jury may not have been able to see and accept that excuse. In these instances, the lawyers assume that a group of jurors would reduce, or "nullify" the effectiveness of the more expert judge. However, even judges and experts possess bias that interferes with their evaluation of the evidence. So, the group of jurors provides some assurance that a lively exchange of ideas and thoughts would ultimately produce the "correct" verdict. Either way, someone is not going to be happy when the verdict is rendered, either by judge or jury.

We Lost, What Now?

The first thing every losing lawyer does is ask the judge to reverse the verdict. This is a standard motion, called a motion for a judgment *non obstante veredicto*, which translates to "a judgment not withstanding the verdict." This would occur in a case where what the jury did was so contrary to the weight of the evidence and testimony that the judge finds that he or she cannot and will not let the verdict stand as a matter of law. In most cases, the judge does not want to interfere with what the jury does, and he or she will deny the motion. But it happens. Recall my mention of the San Francisco dog-mauling case in which the judge set aside the jury's finding of guilty on a charge of second-degree murder. If the verdict appears to be out of line with the evidence, the court will step in as a matter of law and do something about it. Most commonly, judges will reduce the amount of damages that a jury has awarded a plaintiff citing heightened emotions and recognizing that the verdict is out of line.

The losing lawyer's next step is to appeal. In a civil case, a defense lawyer who gets hit with a significant verdict can also ask the judge to lower the amount awarded, in what is called a motion for *remittitur*, while the plaintiff may counter with a request for more money in a motion for *additur*. At any phase of the trial and post-trial, the lawyers may continue to discuss settlement of the case in order to achieve certainty of result and avoid the uncertainty of the appellate process. Given all the possible motions and appeals, it is no wonder that many judicial watchers continue to point out that the wheels of justice grind slowly.

Of course, there are strategic reasons that certain cases take time to work their way through the system. This certainly occurs when the media are focused on a case. The same is true in every community where a high-profile case is taking place. The lawyers need time to let more reasonable minds prevail. I am working in one murder case that was front-page news for weeks because it involved the arrests of people in a long-unsolved murder. Allowing many months to pass does not erase the case from public conscience, but it allows community attention to go on to other matters as the lawyers work up their case.

It Really Isn't Over, Is It?

The jury may spend considerable time reaching a verdict, but in death-penalty matters, their work is not complete because they must then enter the "penalty phase." For example, after the jury found David Westerfield guilty of the kidnapping and murder of Danielle van Dam, they had to reconvene a few days later to hear the two sides argue for and against applying the death penalty. This is not as simple as it may sound. One could argue that individuals chosen for the jury were "death-penalty qualified," meaning that they believed that under certain conditions, they could vote to recommend a sentence of death to the judge. Once the prosecution states it will seek the death penalty, then, quite logically, the prosecution is entitled to eliminate any juror who is philosophically against the death penalty in all situations for any reason, including the view that execution is contrary to their religious beliefs. Prosecutors want men and women who will apply the death penalty more often than not for particularly heinous crimes. The best the defense can do is look for individuals who express more ambivalence and are willing to consider the question on a case-by-case basis.

When Court TV compiled juror profiles and posted them on their website, the legal analysts went through the lists and looked at the information they gathered from verbal exchanges in the courtroom during *voir dire*. These were not "official" profiles; the written juror questionnaires were put under seal; neither had the jury consultants created these profiles. The Court TV profiles, which included information about age, sex, occupation, and so forth, were based only on what was public information in the first place. In fact, much to a producer's chagrin, I turned down network requests to comment following the verdict because, without detailed and actual juror profiles, anything I had to say would be little more than conjecture. Within the brief profile information that was known, it did appear that a few jurors held qualified support of the death penalty. In addition, their philosophical support may have had different grounds (i.e., as a deterrent or because it fulfills the "eye for an eye" concept).

Prosecutors know that a jury finding a defendant guilty in the guilt phase of a trial does not ensure that those same jurors will ultimately recommend the imposition of death in the next phase of the trial. Each side presents its arguments: the prosecution typically reinforces the heinous nature of the crime, emphasizes the aggravating circumstances (often prescribed by statute) such as the commission of other acts in addition to the murder, and also presents victim impact statements— almost nothing is more dramatic than presenting the emotional consequences of a murdered small child. The defense offers mitigating circumstances or other factors in an attempt to convince the jury that the defendant does not deserve to die for the crime. In some situations, the arguments are fairly clear-cut. For example, Susan Smith and Andrea Yates both admitted responsibility for killing their children. In both cases, the jury heard arguments about the women's mental conditions, and in Ms. Yates's case, evidence of severe mental illness. The juries that convicted each woman of murder chose not to apply the death penalty. In other situations, the defense may talk about the defendant's youth or diminished mental capacity because of low intelligence. Although in one recent case in which I offered some minor consult, a mentally retarded defendant was convicted of abusing and killing his mentally retarded daughter. The thought was that a focus on the defendant's inability to recognize what he was doing could be sufficient to preclude the death penalty; the jury and judge had little hesitation in imposing a death sentence under circumstances it obviously considered to be inexcusable.

Westerfield's situation, however, presented a different challenge for the defense because he never wavered from maintaining his innocence. Yet, once he was found guilty, Westerfield's lawyers could no longer argue innocence in the death-penalty phase. It's a strange shift, but the lawyers essentially now say, "Well, OK, he did it. But you shouldn't put him to death." Here, the value of jury consultants who know the details of the jurors' lives can help craft logical and emotional appeals to get the jurors to send the defendant to prison for life. The arguments often take on global scope. "Who are we to play God? To be kept in a tiny cell for the rest of one's life is a punishment worse than a swift death by injection, so doesn't it make sense to let the defendant spend every day of his life having to think about what he did? Maybe, just maybe, some good can come out of this by having this defendant teach others the errors of his ways so that when others get out, they will never consider taking another misstep in society."

After a long deliberation, the jury came back with a recommendation of the death penalty for Westerfield. Nothing in Westerfield's character or background, nor anything argued by his counsel, led the jury to justify sparing him. As observers, the public likely had little doubt as to what the jury would do. But for those jurors, who were faced with making one of the most difficult decisions of their lives, namely suggesting to the judge that he order a man put to death, it is not a decision that can ever be made lightly, and without psychological second-guessing.

When Unanimity Isn't Necessary

As you might assume, jurors must reach unanimity in a criminal trial. It makes perfect sense. If we were to allow a jury to convict someone on a verdict of eleven to one, then we can never be sure we have met the burden of proof. We must be certain beyond a reasonable doubt that the defendant is guilty. If one juror votes against guilty and has very strong doubts, well above and beyond what others would consider reasonable, then it wouldn't make sense to convict someone even if the other eleven were absolutely certain of guilty without doubt. It is one and all who must agree.

But in the world of civil cases, remember that the mission is mostly to resolve a dispute between arguing parties. Therefore, the Supreme Court permits juries to make their decisions with less than a unanimous verdict. In fact, the Supreme Court has gone as far as to permit a decision that is nine jurors to three to be sufficient for an acceptable verdict. This means that lawyers and their consultants can focus their efforts on reaching and convincing particular jurors to go their way. They can, in effect, give up on one or two and know that they can still win the verdict. I remember one such case where my clients were convinced that they were in fine shape with all but one juror. I warned them during the trial that the one adverse juror appeared to be of strong will. I was concerned that he would become the jury foreperson, which he did. Fortunately, he was unable to convince anyone else to see things his way. Although those deliberations, in a relatively simple personal-injury case, appeared to drag on for two days, he ultimately gave up and the jury returned with his lone contrary vote.

The fact that a civil jury does not have to reach a unanimous verdict raises another concern. Will a jury stop deliberating once it reaches an acceptable split? After all, unanimity means that the jury must keep going until they agree or deadlock; in most civil matters, the pain can be short-circuited. Judges are ordinarily quite strong in directing jurors to carry on a full and complete review of and debate over the evidence.

The Jury Consultant Is Busy Again

The jury consultant helps the lawyer even after the verdict is rendered. This last phase of the consultant's work is known as the post-trial juror interviews. We talk with the jurors to find out what went right and what went wrong. The lawyers could conduct the interviews themselves, and often do, but generally, jurors are more likely to open up and be honest with the consultants because they are not worried about sparing anyone's feelings. After all, many of us find it easy to say what we think about another person to people other than the person himself or herself. The interviews must be conducted with the permission of the court, and the jurors are free to participate or not.

Judges protect jurors who do not wish to be bothered with post-trial interviews. For example, *Rodriguez v. Bridgestone/Firestone, Inc.*, was the first case to be tried against the tire maker since the massive recall of tires in 2000, resulting from tire blowouts and subsequent vehicle rollovers. In this case, one of the plaintiffs, Marisa Rodriguez, suffered brain damage and was confined to a wheelchair. The case settled in August during jury deliberations for a reported $7.5 million. Reporters for *The National Law Journal* in October 2001 and others who followed this case wanted to talk with the jurors to see what was going on inside the deliberation room. The judge in this Texas case wanted to be sure the jurors were not bothered, and he issued an order that prohibited the press from contacting jurors without first obtaining the permission of the judge. This order was upheld on appeal. Some considered the judge's order out of line and cited free-speech rights and the press's right and duty to gather and report news in a free society.

The court's point of view deserves consideration, too. This case was the first to go to trial in a group of pending cases that potentially numbered in the hundreds. What unfair influence would be gained by interviewing the jurors? How would future jury pools be contaminated as a result of what they read about this case, even though it settled? Perhaps general support for the judge's order existed because the media had inappropriately contacted jurors by finding their names and addresses in court papers, and did so without permission. Moreover, the jurors seemingly made it clear that they did not want to be contacted. There will always be a battle between the court system's desire to protect those who give of their time as jurors and various media efforts to hunt them down and get an interview for the sake of journalism. As long as there are high-profile cases, jurors will be sought out to be media stars, at least for their proverbial fifteen minutes of fame.

The Unwelcome Reality

No lawyer tries a case to verdict with an expectation that it will eventually see an appeal, but many times, that is the reality. So, lawyers do not underestimate the value and wealth of information gained through interviewing jurors after a verdict. W. Edwards Deming, the father of quality management, once described a strictly numerical evaluation of performance as a force of destruction that sucks the joy from work tasks. If an attorney does not attempt to follow up with jurors about their impressions, then the verdict, the "numbers," are all they have.

Besides, speculation about what worked at trial and what did not is often the trial lawyer's favorite indoor sport.

If the lawyers plan to appeal, or even just learn the reasons for the verdict, the jury interview is the logical starting point. Lawyers want to know who (or sometimes what) made the strongest impression on the jurors, and when and how these impressions were formed and then justified through the deliberation. Although this seems straightforward, lawyers are really probing the jurors' memories of the case. Can they recount the gist of the issues involved? I like to ask if the theme worked, and what they remember about the witnesses, the attorneys, and even the judge. This is much like the "post-trial" discussions that take place during our focus groups, only this is a one-on-one process. This is a subjective process; there are no right answers. I just want to understand the jurors' reality so we can better dissect what happened in the case.

My partner, Richard Gabriel, has developed a protocol we use when conducting post-trial interviews. It is quite detailed and usually asks jurors for impressions of all the witnesses and arguments. Because it is so detailed, we try to set an appointment ahead of time so we do not inconvenience a juror willing to spend time with us. They have absolutely no obligation to talk to anyone, so we know they are doing us a courtesy to allow us to probe their ideas about the case, down to the day-to-day atmosphere in the courtroom and personalities of the lawyers and the judge. In essence, we want to know what grabs jurors' attention and what leaves them cold. If possible, we record the interviews and use videotape if the juror permits us to and we are meeting in person. Being students of human behavior, jury consultants watch for body language, and we try to spot which bit of evidence has the most emotional charge and which of the many "players" made the most lasting impression. We do not always like what we hear, but these men and women are valuable contributors to our work.

I recall a case where my client was the lawyer of a defendant who got hit with a sizable verdict. As I spoke with individual jurors, there was a common theme in their comments. As I compiled the various interviews, I got the following composite picture of the case:

The defendants didn't seem to care about their employees. They talked about their rules and following corporate procedures, but there was no recognition of the specific needs of their employees or their families. They were mean, cold. I really think they don't like blacks! I just believed the various plaintiffs and believed that the incidents of discrimination they talked about actually happened. This kind of behavior just has to stop.

In that case, my clients had done very little research and relied on a strategy of pointing their finger at "ungrateful" employees. I wished I had been called in earlier in the case because the problem was a much larger one. Overall image and lack of credibility were working against the defendant before the case even got underway.

Smart lawyers want to hear what our post-trial interviews produced. But even when they go in with an open mind, they are human, too, and few of us take kindly to being told we have done a bad job, our information was weak, or the jurors thought we were arrogant grandstanders. One lawyer we work with regularly opens these sessions with us by saying the tongue-in-cheek remark: "So, how did I screw up this time?"

Lawyers may think jurors are wrong, but in the end the jurors' opinions are the only ones that count. Armed with post-trial information, whether headed for a new trial or pursuing the case on appeal, the lawyer will have a much clearer sense of which case components (as packaged and presented) accomplished their aim for the majority of jurors. This kind of information cannot be overvalued. It becomes a compass for lawyers in their future trials.

And so our path comes full circle, from the consultant's assisting the lawyer with evaluating the case at the beginning of the representation all the way through the verdict and into appeal. We are left with one final question: what does the future hold? Our world continues to unfold, our system survives, and new kinds of cases arise every day. The final chapter takes out the crystal ball to look at what the role of the trial consultant may be like in the future…and some personal thoughts and concerns to ensure that the safeguards of our legal system are both monitored and preserved.

chapter 9

Fair, But Partial: As Good as It Gets

In some respects, we end where we begin, with the knowledge that we start each new legal interaction, from a criminal trial to a complex corporate civil suit, by understanding that objective truth does not exist. No single set of facts becomes so clear that no one in his or her right mind could reach any verdict other than the one being sought by a particular lawyer. In a world where no absolutes exist, we are left with only positions and arguments. We do have the next best thing—a very close second—to no right answers. We have advocates, the lawyers, who represent positions to juries, the men and women who ultimately determine what reality prevails within the confines of the law that governs a particular case.

Lawyers are trained to find, craft, and deliver the strongest and best arguments they can for their client. Even when we accept the idea that lawyers have the specific duty to be strong advocates for their clients, most people still grumble from time to time because they find themselves certain of someone's guilt or innocence. All the legal maneuverings in that situation may seem superfluous at best, and out-and-out wrong in others. Grumbling goes with the territory of our advocacy system, and it has worked well for more than two hundred years, with added refinements resulting from expanded civil rights and our increased knowledge of human behavior.

Moving Forward

Through extensive research taking place over recent decades, psychologists and social scientists have confirmed what most of us have intuitively known all along: different people will hear the very same evidence but perceive it differently. As obvious as this may seem, I still encounter lawyers who stubbornly insist that their brilliantly crafted arguments will carry the day. They hang on to the notion that anyone with an ounce of sense could see the truth in what they say. But in our era, lawyers adopt that attitude at their own peril. Equally important, clients *hire* lawyers with this attitude at their own peril.

Given what you now understand, I can guess that you would not like to be a party in a lawsuit or in a fight for your freedom in a criminal trial led by a lawyer who operated only with old methods. If that should happen, however, and the case does not go your way, is the system broken or was your lawyer not the most effective advocate for you? Most likely, you would always wonder if you misread, or just plain missed, the jurors.

New information about human behavior and communication is the fundamental reason that the tools of the trial consultant should now be seen as integral to the modern advocacy process. As in every other field, we are updating the tools to meet new demands. Today's jurors are asked to perform increasingly complex tasks, which are becoming even more so as scientific information becomes increasingly challenging and the types of crimes and potential liability have twists and turns never anticipated even twenty-five years ago.

Certainly, two hundred years ago no one could have imagined a phenomenon like Internet crime, for example, not to mention the series of crimes involved in horrendous terrorist acts. The threat of terrorism brings in issues involving who can enter our country and how long they can stay, what kind of searches of person and property are legitimate, and on and on. A single case might require knowledge of many areas of the law, all of which must be explained to a jury. Increasing complexity of legal issues has converged with expanded knowledge of human behavior, and the result is the concern about maintaining what we simply call justice, as if it were that simple.

Consider the evolution of the law to increasingly place legal (and punishable) responsibility on parents or others for not acting where the system thinks they should, or not being aware where the system thinks they should. For example, as I write this, law enforcement agents are considering bringing charges against the parents of an eighteen-year-old who died of an overdose of heroin in their home. The parents did not supply the drugs, nor did they know that he had them. However, we may be seeing an evolving trend, where we outline expected behavior on the part of those who are or should be in a position to keep others from getting into trouble. From the jury consultant's perspective, I want to know how prospective jurors view the responsibilities of those who did *not* prevent a crime or wrongdoing from happening.

Are We Due for a Change—Or Even an Overhaul?

A few legal professionals propose drastic action, such as eliminating the jury system, and other slightly less radical men and women claim it is due for an overhaul. Some of us do not come down on either side, even though we do not contend that the system works without error or flaw. We know a plethora of problems exist because we deal with them every day. Despite this, many of my colleagues and I maintain that juries are still overall better finders of fact than a judge acting alone. Some of the perceived weaknesses of juries are also their strengths. In debates about the jury system, I find myself reluctant to tinker too much with the bedrock of the justice system. The same elements that made it revolutionary more than two centuries ago make it too good to throw over now.

The fact that juries are comprised of varying personalities and often come from all strata of society generally means that the jury as a group is better able to judge motives than one individual. In addition, a group of jurors can remember more information and evidence than one person can, even a judge. Frankly, in some situations, a jury provides an escape route from an incompetent trial judge. Most people tend to idealize judges, but they are only human and can be inept, not to mention rigid or unfair. Unfortunately, a judge may dislike one of the lawyers or another participant, so the parties have a better chance of a fair hearing with a jury.

Finally, I really like the notion that an average citizen can be pulled in off the street to resolve most legal matters, from a simple shoplifting case to one involving scientific evidence and far-reaching issues. If a jury does something so off the mark that it is clearly wrong, then the appellate process can step in to rectify or otherwise change the outcome or direction of the proceedings. Yes, glitches occur in the appeal process, too, but overall, it provides a critical safeguard in our system.

If we removed jury trials from our system, think how distant most citizens would feel about fundamental legal processes. Jury duty, like casting a vote, is one of the important civic responsibilities that keep us engaged in our place in the community and our country. Even if you have never been called for jury duty, or you have received a notice and attempted to escape that fate, you probably still think of jury duty as a synonym for "citizen duty." In some ways, the idea of a trial by jury and your willingness to participate represent a basic component of the social contract we enter into just by being citizens.

Years ago, Harry Kalven and Hans Zeisel conducted a research project, which found that even judges strongly believe that, overall, the jury system is thoroughly satisfactory, even with its problems. As we look to the future, however, it is difficult to predict the exact direction in which the attitudes and values of upcoming generations will evolve. And just when the trends begin to solidify, some event comes along to "mess up" our understanding and predictions. Some experiences are nothing short of life-altering, and they mold and shape us as individuals and change our society. September 11, 2001, is one of those events, but other events may result in even more change, even if less dramatic.

The increasing number of corporate-accounting debacles, such as seen with Enron and WorldCom, or the wave of child kidnapping and murder occurrences, while very different in impact from the 9/11 attack, will also be factors in an ever-changing national attitude. Cases involving the Catholic Church or other religious institutions will for a significant period of time be affected by the priest abuse cases. So, in the end, all we can be sure of is that we will face life-changing and attitude-changing events in the future, just as we have in the past. It will be the jury psychologist who will be the key to understanding the changes as they impact whatever the case at bar is at that time.

Making predictions about catastrophic events such as the World Trade Center terrorist attack becomes even more challenging because long-term effects may not be permitted to solidify. By that I mean that events have not settled into one discrete experience we can easily analyze. For example, not a week goes by that the government does not issue a warning to our population. Sometimes these warnings are general, but sometimes they may be specific. We have no way to predict what might be next, just as no one predicted a spate of "diseased" mail.

Why does "living on the edge" make it more difficult to predict long-term changes in juror behavior? Well, each time big events occur, the long-term development of our thinking and behavior is suspended in time, and then we begin again. However, with each beginning, we become more deeply affected. As Americans, we are predisposed to expressing our outrage and then moving on. Indeed, in terms of the terrorism issues, we still are encouraged to keep living normally (usually shopping and travel are mentioned as primary "normal" activities we are encouraged to continue) while at the same time we are told to be vigilant and alert. This natural confusion about how to live day to day extends the time it will take for lasting attitude changes to evolve.

When we start looking for lasting changes in attitudes, we need perspective. Prior to September 11, we heard a story about a father who beat another father to death over how their children behaved and were treated on the ice rink (leaving the actions of body checking in hockey for another day). One man banged the other's head on the ground until he became unconscious; he subsequently died.

As I watched the case, I asked several questions in order to predict juror reactions. First, what possible excuse does a jury *need* to hear that justifies such violence over children's sports? Second, in this age when the effects of terrorism are so sensitive and raw, would jurors hold citizens to a standard of civility and tolerance higher than they otherwise might? Or, would the trial be kept out of the context of world events and evaluated only within the facts presented? Of course, this is the way the case should be heard. Given the result, a conviction on manslaughter, it appears that the jurors looked at the facts of the "sports" case and were able to keep reactions to a dramatic national event out of their deliberation. Among the tasks and goals of the lawyers, of course, is to get jurors to concentrate on the task at hand and focus on the evidence presented.

Reform around the Edges

As the legal and political realms continue to interact, there will be many struggles back and forth, and not all flaws in the system rise to a level that attract ongoing media attention. For example, earlier I discussed the case of the female forest preserve officer who had her $3 million verdict in her discrimination case remitted to $300,000 by the court. However, the way the tax laws are written, she could end up paying about $400,000 in taxes. This kind of thing happens because of flaws in the tax code. The plaintiff was not only awarded $300,000, but the defendant was also ordered to pay her attorneys' fees, which had reached a few hundred thousand dollars. The way the current tax laws are written, the money paid to cover attorneys' fees (ordered by the court) is considered as income to the plaintiff. This means that the plaintiff also has to pay taxes on the money paid to her lawyers. So, when all is "paid and done," the forest-preserve officer may have to pay more in taxes than she won through the reduced verdict amount. Clearly, something is wrong with that system and challenges will continue, although you may never hear about them on the evening news.

The Thing That's Certain in Life...Is Death

At times, "system watchers" wonder if increased consciousness about certain kinds of crimes will make juries more, for lack of a better term, "bloodthirsty." A jury issued life sentences without parole rather than recommending the death penalty to four disciples of Osama bin Laden for the 1998 bombings of the two U.S. embassies, one in Dar es Salaam, Tanzania, and the other in Nairobi, Kenya, which killed 231 people, including twelve Americans.

These men were the first to be convicted by a U.S. jury for carrying out bin Laden's 1998 edict to kill Americans, and these defendants received the maximum sentence. This sentence came down on October 18, 2001, a little more than a month after the attack on the World Trade Center. However, the trial had already been going on for about five months, and prosecution evidence was based on the theory that bin Laden and his group directed the bombings, using a satellite telephone from Afghanistan and messengers to communicate with others. Two of the defendants, Khalfan Khamis Mohamed, convicted for helping to grind TNT and load the bomb that struck the Tanzanian embassy, and Mohamed Al-'Owhali, who rode the bomb vehicle up to the Nairobi embassy and tossed grenades, could have been given death sentences. The jury had the power to do that. But they consciously chose not to do so in order to prevent these men from being viewed as and labeled martyrs, or so said the jurors. So, bloodthirsty or not, jurors may have other, stronger motives for their decisions.

A different jury might have put aside the "martyr" issue and sentenced the two men to death. Could it be that the jurors considered that a death sentence would involve years of appeals that would drag out the situation? After all, these defendants would have been entitled to the appeals process, which might produce years of additional publicity for the defendants. These life sentences avoided that, and these two will stay locked up in relative obscurity.

Did the jurors consider such things? Should they consider such things? The jury consultant looking back on this might find the answer in statistics. The Justice Department has reported that U.S. juries sentenced fewer convicts to death in the year 2000 than in any year since 1980. In addition, the number of people actually executed has dropped as well, even though executions receive extensive media coverage and average viewers may believe they take place with great frequency.

When it comes to the death penalty, science may influence jury behavior. Almost every week we hear reports about wrongly convicted defendants who are freed as a result of modern DNA tests. The consciousness of DNA may result in greater conviction percentages, but in cases where evidence could be explained or viewed in another way, it is likely jurors may be reluctant to apply the death penalty on the chance, regardless of how slight, that the defendant is innocent.

In other words, right now, we have two opposing pulls on jury behavior. Whatever patterns we see—or think we see—may take us down a new road even in the presence of fear (i.e., terrorism) and science (i.e., DNA). Polls consistently show that while a majority of Americans continue to support the death penalty, the percentage of that support continues to drop as time goes on. This means that as long as human beings experience the intense emotions tied with the commission of serious crimes like murder, there will always be an emotional desire for revenge present in our society, although our collective sense of rationality remains and continues to grow in us over time.

Like many people, I supported the death penalty for many years. It felt like the right thing to do when a person has committed a particularly heinous act. However, after years of working in the system, seeing errors made at every level within the system, and knowing that many an innocent person has served time on death row for crimes they did not commit, it has become clear to me that humans are not infallible. We need to make every effort to protect the safeguards that insure that the system works properly, and that includes giving defendants every available resource to insure that the system works as it should. In addition, if we collectively can come to believe that a life in prison without parole is a sufficient penalty for even the worst offenders, then we can rest easy that the one irreversible punishment, death, is not administered in error.

Setting Standards

As time marches on and events shape our lives, lawyers and their clients will continue to seek the services of trial consultants. We can consider this group of professionals as a new institution within our system, and it is here to stay. The growing number of trial consultants will work within a code of professional standards. During my term as president of the American Society of Trial Consultants, it was my first order of business to call for the creation of such a code. (I have provided the current code in its entirety as an appendix in this book). In the years since the formation of the code, it continues to evolve in order to remain relevant and meaningful. I am proud of that accomplishment.

Uniformity of standards is important because one of the most important elements of a lawyer's relationship with a client is the attorney-client privilege. When the lawyer hires the consultant, we can argue that the trial consultant's work in connection with the trial also should enjoy the protections of the attorney-client privilege. However, if a litigant hires the trial consultant, no such protection exists because the link between the attorney and the consultant is broken.

As an aside, trial consultants do not have a win-loss record. We neither win nor lose cases. Rather, we are part of the trial team. The ultimate win or loss belongs to the lawyer who tries the case. I am troubled when I come across advertising or statements in which a consultant claims he or she has won a certain case or percentage of cases. How can that be? What we do is provide information to the lawyers who then accept or reject it. If a lawyer accepts our advice, that does not mean the consultant won the trial, any more than rejecting our advice means the consultant loses a case.

Trial consultants are not Merlin either, although some may elevate themselves to that level. The best consultants are the ones who can clearly and concisely present their findings to their client and who can effectively prepare witnesses and undertake the tasks assigned to them by their lawyer-clients. We may like to think of ourselves as more important than that, but it is where we fall in the scheme of things.

The Road Less Traveled

More than 90 percent of civil cases settle before trial, so it is clear that lawyers recognize that trials are not necessarily the best road to resolution. In the future, consultants will likely play a larger role in other settings, such as alternative dispute resolution. Mediation is one example. I have served as a mediator for the blue-ribbon panel of mediators who work for the court system in Cook County, specifically in Chicago, and I know that cases are not always about money.

I will never forget one case in which I served as mediator. The defendant, an elderly man in his eighties, was being sued for the wrongful death of a young woman, which occurred as a result of a car accident. The insurance company representing the defendant offered as a settlement to the case the full amount of proceeds of the insurance policy that the insurer held for its insured, the elderly driver. They made the offer shortly after the plaintiffs (the family of the young woman who was killed) filed suit. Yet, four years later, they appeared before me in a borrowed judge's chambers, still unable to resolve the matter. What was there to resolve? With the insurance policy offered, there were no other assets to speak of, as this defendant was very ill and owned little more than his modest home.

When the defendant's lawyers met with me, they first noted that they were unable to settle the case because the young woman's family was unreasonable. Their own lawyer said he was unable to get them to budge, and he had told them there was no more money to be awarded. I asked if I could meet privately with the family to see if I could uncover something below the surface we did not know about. Frankly, I suspected that there was something going on *at* the surface, but for some reason the lawyers could not see it.

The family came in and sat quietly in front of my desk. When I asked them to tell me their concerns, the young woman's father said, "All these lawyers want is for us to take this money and go away. Why don't they understand that we lost our daughter? We don't want to just go away. We want to know that this man will never do this again to another family. What happened here was wrong and we won't go away for a check. No amount of money is bringing our daughter back to us."

It was clear to me that this case was not about money; it was about an apology and a promise. An apology for wrong done and a promise to take steps to ensure it would not happen again.

I brought the lawyers back in and met with them. When I told them what the family wanted—which was all that they had wanted for the past four years, the lawyers were stunned. "You're kidding," said the defense lawyer. "That's all they want? We can do that." My response probably matches what you're thinking right now: "If you would have opened your minds to the possibility that there's more to life than money in some cases, you would have closed this case long ago."

I deliver many presentations to members of the insurance industry, and these individuals often talk about settling cases for something other than money. In one case, a woman was more concerned about who would shop for her groceries for the next six months during her recovery than the lump sum of money being offered by the insurance company. In the end, she accepted less money, but was offered a service that would shop for her and get her what she needed. So simple, yet so distant to minds not open to possibilities.

Help Us Listen, Please!

Mediation has been around for a long time, and some form of the process is routinely used in families and among friends. Mediation is finding an increasingly receptive audience among lawyers and the public at large. In essence, mediation involves using the skills of a neutral third party to help the parties in a dispute find their own resolution. Mediators do not make findings of fact or law, as judges and arbitrators do. Their job is to facilitate an open discussion between the parties about their own needs and interests. The process relies on active participation from the parties and their lawyers, which is why mediation only works when both parties are willing to engage in the process. For example, mediation is used in divorce and child-custody cases, but only when the "warring" individuals want to stop the combat. We would not use it, for example, in a divorce involving domestic violence because in that situation, one party broke a criminal law.

While alternative dispute-resolution tools are well-tried alternatives to arguing a case in court, attorneys still do not use them as often as they could. This may seem odd, but lawyer training emphasizes adversarial tactics over mutual resolution, and hence they tend to be inexperienced and their lack of familiarity breeds skepticism about the process. The adversarial attitude is tried and true, whereas mediation techniques may be viewed as the "softer" skill. However, as our courts become more crowded and we look for ways to cut legal costs, the role of mediation will continue to expand. Many contracts now require some form of alternative dispute resolution be tried before litigation is triggered.

Looking into a crystal ball, and assuming an ever-increasingly back-logged court system, we will likely see a clear majority of cases being resolved through these methods. The goal is to reach resolution early in the process as a means of reducing some of the tremendous amount of money spent on depositions, experts, and other discovery tools.

Saving Ourselves Some Headaches

It may seem odd that after discussing our court system, with all its adversarial processes and concepts, I now turn to a discussion of mediation. However, I am speculating about the future, and I believe its role will continue to grow because it offers many benefits and its use represents a positive development in our legal system. First, it is less time-consuming than litigation. Court backlog suggests that even people who can afford the high cost of litigation wait years for their day in court. A mediation session can be arranged quickly and produces resolution in hours, and most often in less than a day. Second, it is much less expensive than litigation.

Mediation includes exploring alternatives. Unlike a "fixed pie" distribution that litigation produces, mediation focuses on flexible solutions; it "expands the pie of opportunity." In addition, the process addresses the needs of all the parties. By definition, a consensual agreement reached through mediation will reflect the parties' needs. The same cannot be said for verdicts at trial. You might think that where money is the only issue, no room exists for compromise, but nothing is further from the case. Lawyers and mediators need to reach beneath the surface. When someone wants money, they seek it for a reason. Maybe it represents revenge, maybe it is compensation for incurred expenses, and maybe it is because the parties want to use an unfortunate situation as a way to buy a new home or start a new business. The latter has been known to happen. Once the mediator can find out what is motivating the client, that point becomes the means by which the sum of money can be negotiated.

I recall a case I mediated in which a woman sued her former boyfriend for a few thousand dollars, claiming that she paid for his clothes, rent, and other expenses. Now that they had broken up, she wanted her money back. He claimed that the clothes were a gift and so was almost everything else. The mediation session brought out the real issue. It turns out that she had become pregnant and he abandoned her, and did not agree to take on any responsibilities for the child. She was not happy. I felt like Maury Povich, Jerry Springer, and Jenny Jones rolled into one as we worked through the issues. Once he admitted his faults and fears, she was ready to negotiate the sum owed and the case settled after an hour of open discussion.

Also by definition, mediation improves communication between all the parties. Litigation fosters an adversarial environment that is not conducive to effective communication. In fact, communication is not only shut down, in some cases it is prohibited. Witnesses for one side may not be allowed to talk with witnesses for the other side, or even with witnesses on the same side. While necessary in the adversarial environment, ending all communication serves to drive the wedge between parties even deeper. But during a mediation process, a trained mediator interrupts this escalation and helps communication take place. Most importantly, disputes settled through mediation are more likely to result in compliance; that is, the parties do what they actually say they will do because they have taken part in crafting the agreement.

Where do trial consultants fit in during mediation proceedings? Usually they help lawyers prepare the settlement package, which might take the form of videotape or a folder of written documents. But our work is much the same as for trial. We want the lawyers to understand the likely consequences of trial and how jurors are likely to interpret the case. They use the information gathered during a focus group, for example, to help them determine what it will take to settle the case, or if they should settle at all. If mediation efforts fail, then as they prepare for trial, lawyers can use the body of work produced by the trial consultant for trial-strategy decisions.

In the multitude of Catholic Church cases, the goals of the litigation for many appear well beyond compensation of the victims. Many of these abused families demand systemic change and acknowledgment, not just by their own church, but by all bishops, that the abuse and wrongdoing occurred. This makes the private efforts of mediation more difficult, but for those who can achieve some sense of personal peace with specific steps being taken on a more personal level, there is a very good chance that mediation can resolve many of these cases. And this means that more of these victims can get on with their lives and focus on their personal growth, putting the difficult memories behind them, whenever possible.

When the participants take the process seriously, mediation has a good success rate. Some people may believe mediation is a "second best" solution, but in terms of time and expense—and attitude—it is actually the more sophisticated method to resolve conflicts.

Off to Arbitration

Arbitration is an additional alternative to a courtroom trial, and, like mediation, its use is likely to increase in the future. Whereas mediation is designed to eliminate the adversarial stance, arbitration brings the lawyers together to present their cases to an arbitrator or panel of arbitrators. I also serve as an arbitrator, which is much like serving as a judge. In that way, it is similar to a trial. This appears to contradict my point that juries are a better device in most cases than a single decision-maker. However, arbitration often is a more expedient alternative to trial. Lawyers can get their case to an arbitration hearing more quickly than they will get to a courtroom for a jury trial; in many cases, years earlier. So it is worth the effort.

As an arbitrator, I watch the behavior of the lawyers who argue and present before me and evaluate how effective and thorough I think they are being, and I am often dismayed to see how lightly the lawyers approach the process. They appear to believe they do not need to be as effective because they are appearing before a fellow lawyer—"one of their own." This is a big mistake. I still need plaintiffs to meet their burden of proof or I cannot make an award in their favor.

From time to time, the lawyers put it all on the line. "Don't settle the case for us, Mr. Arbitrator," they say. (Actually, they usually call me "judge," which everyone knows is not the proper title, but it's a "suck up" technique lawyers like to use in arbitrations). "We have been unable to do that ourselves and this is an all-or-nothing case. If you think the claimant has both made their case and proven liability, they get it all. If they have not, they get nothing." And I take that challenge. But in many cases, the claimant finds himself on the losing end.

It is tough to send a person away with no money when they have significant damages and injuries, but if this party's lawyer is unable to meet the burden of proof, then my decision must be to award no money. Although I am not working as a trial consultant in such instances, I cannot help but wonder how much research and home-work the lawyers have done to prepare their case. Do they take the time to prepare their witnesses to testify as effectively at arbitration as they will for trial? Usually, it appears they have not. In encouraging me to take an "all or nothing" approach, have they conducted their focus groups and other analysis to get a measure of the risk? Often, it appears not, at least in smaller matters. As in trial situations, it is likely difficult for lawyers to justify the expense of research if the ultimate arbitration award can't justify the spending.

My point is that whether lawyers are preparing for trial or for an alternative dispute-resolution forum, such as mediation and arbitra-tion, the issues remain the same. They need to make a thoughtful and thorough analysis of the case, the chances of winning and losing, and the impact of witnesses and demonstrative evidence. All this must be explored in every case and they may need trial consultants to help them. Clients have a right to expect this consideration.

Back to the Future

The next time you hear about a particular verdict rendered by a jury, (or you see it as "breaking news") you will have a better understanding of all that has been done to lead up to that moment. You will know that lawyers, and perhaps jury consultants, too, have been working for months, if not years. They have been developing case themes, drafting opening statements and closing arguments, preparing witnesses, gath-ering as much data as possible about the nature of the community, and creating juror profiles. Depending on the type of case we are dealing with, the lawyers and consultants may be working hard behind the scenes to help the parties settle the case; sometimes we may call on the skills of mediators and arbitrators using the jury consultant's research in this realm as well.

Along with news of verdicts and pending cases, you will also hear ongoing debates about our legal system. I am quite sure you will hear calls for reform of everything from mandatory-minimum sentencing to unanimous verdicts to questions about the relevance of juries in today's complex society. In the next few years, you will hear even more news about scientific methods that analyze evidence with even greater accuracy and in less time than we can imagine today. DNA testing alone is revolutionizing our system, and it will no doubt become simplified and less expensive. We may see fewer criminal cases go to trial because DNA exonerates suspects or makes the evidence against defendants so convincing that a plea agreement may be the best solution.

Perhaps jury consulting is a "damned if you do and damned if you don't" profession. That is, if we do not use them, then people complain that the system is too arbitrary and uncontrolled because we did not do an adequate job of keeping strong bias off the jury. And when we do use them, then a party is accused of "stacking the jury" and playing with the system. My bottom line is that human dynamics will always be a part of the jury system. Given this fact, lawyers have a duty to their clients to learn as much as they can about the jurors in order to know how to best present their case to the particular men and women sitting in the jury box.

The real problem is ensuring that these services are available to all parties who wish to use them, including those without adequate financial resources. Many jury consultants have long been in tune with these needs and take on many important cases without fees. In the criminal-justice world, each state system must work to ensure that defendants have such resources available to them. Death-penalty-case defense funds are in existence in many places to provide such guarantees.

Another remedy would be to require the prosecution to share any research it conducts with the defense team. This idea will not be popular among prosecutors, who will simply say: "Why should we share that trial-strategy information? We might as well not do it." Ultimately, the criminal system is about protecting the innocent as well as identifying and punishing the guilty. The strongest arguments will always be in support of disclosing anything the state has in its possession or knowledge base to the defense. After all, people are innocent until proven guilty, and defendants have the right to say, "Show me what you've got."

Mostly hidden from public view, jury consultants will continue to do their important work, but debates over the value of their work will probably continue as well. I believe we are in a period of great change, a time in which we are reevaluating our individual and collective attitudes and values.

September 11 moves further away in time, but the impact remains. How will future events affect us? Celebrity cases, and even non-celebrity cases that are transformed into celebrity cases (e.g., Laci Peterson and Chadra Levy) because news producers see the chance to capture America's attention and better ratings, will shape our views of the justice system.

Predictions about the future of our legal system may be risky, but I am willing to bet that decades from now, we will not only still celebrate our right to trial by jury, but the role of jury consultants will no longer even be notable, let alone controversial. This will happen because our society is well on the way to a sophisticated understanding that with all its flaws (including the reality of "fair but partial") our system remains the best any society has to offer.

CODE OF PROFESSIONAL STANDARDS

PREAMBLE

The purposes of the AMERICAN SOCIETY OF TRIAL CONSUL-TANTS are to foster communication among its members, provide a forum for development of trial practice methods, and promote knowledge of effective and ethical use of trial consulting techniques. One of the ways the AMERICAN SOCIETY OF TRIAL CONSULTANTS furthers these purposes is through a professional code of conduct to which its members subscribe.

SECTION I

Area of Practice

The trial consultant is dedicated to providing the litigant and the legal community with information on courtroom related behavior and communication. The member, when in the role of trial consultant, does not practice law, but seeks rather to enhance the practice of trial law by facilitating the skills of the litigant and legal practitioner.

SECTION II

Consultant–Client Relationship

The trial consultant is generally retained directly by the attorney, but may be employed by the litigant or insurer representing the litigant.

A. Attorney as Client:

The trial consultant who is retained by the attorney: (1) works under the direction and supervision of the attorney; (2) cooperates with the attorney to assure all consultant–attorney communication is subject, to the extent possible under the law of the jurisdiction, to attorney/client privilege and work-product doctrine.

B. Litigant as Client:

The trial consultant who is retained by the litigant informs the litigant, prior to retention, that the consultant's work will be treated as professionally confidential, but probably is not subject to legal protection from disclosure under any attorney/client privilege, work-product, or other doctrine.

C. Insurer as Client:

The trial consultant who is retained by the insurer: (1) informs the attorney that the trial consultant works under the authority of the insurer; (2) cooperates with the attorney to assure all consultant—attorney communication is subject, to the extent possible under the law of the jurisdiction, to attorney/client privilege and work-product doctrine.

SECTION III

Competency, Training, and Provision of Services

The trial consultant fully discloses academic qualifications and consulting experience to potential clients, specifies the services provided, and identifies the objectives of each consultation.

SECTION IV
Research Standards

The trial consultant who is retained to provide research services provides such services in accordance with the current practices, methodologies, and the professional standards of the field involved. The trial consultant provides data with interpretations and recommendations, and avoids material misrepresentation of data upon which an interpretation or recommendation is based. See Section IX, Guidelines for Professional Practice, for additional information.

SECTION V
Advertising and Publicity

The trial consultant may advertise services. Such advertisement avoids material misrepresentation of qualifications, experience, research, or trial outcomes. Client permission is obtained prior to the placement of any advertisement that identifies a client or case. The trial consultant does not publish a claim to a win-loss record.

SECTION VI
Conflicts of Interest

The trial consultant does not provide services for a client if those services appear to be in conflict with the interest of another client, unless the trial consultant informs each client of the nature of the conflict and both clients give their consent. The trial consultant remains alert throughout the consultant–client relationship for potential conflicts with present and past clients, and with present and past clients of trial consultants employed within the same trial consulting organization.

SECTION VII
Integrity of the Jury Pool

The trial consultant does not provide any services with the intent of jeopardizing the integrity of the jury pool.

SECTION VIII

Pro Bono Policy

The trial consultant endeavors to perform pro bono services annually to serve those in need, including the poor, or to improve the law, the legal system, the legal profession, or the trial consulting profession.

*Code of Professional Standards is reprinted with the permission and courtesy of the American Society of Trial Consultants.

Acknowledgments

The greatest pleasure of finishing a book is the opportunity it provides to extend appreciation to those without whom you would be reading something else, because this book would not have ever seen the light of day. First, my warmest thanks to Virginia McCullough, editor extraordinaire, who hung through every last word of this book. Virginia, on behalf of all the writers who have the pleasure of working with you, my deepest appreciation. While many of my ten or so books are written primarily for a legal audience, Virginia has ensured that my books written for the general public avoid legalese and aim for clarity. The success of this book is as much hers as mine.

My appreciation to Sourcebooks, and especially my editor, Hillel Black, who saw the promise of this book in its infancy and spent many hours working to keep me going in the right direction. He didn't let me give up, and I appreciate his faith in me.

Finding the time to write isn't easy, but it's a task made easier through the support of my work colleagues and team. To the whole Decision Analysis team in L.A., Chicago, and San Francisco, my thanks. Special thanks to colleague and friend Richard Gabriel for his insights and the fact that he has brought in some very important cases to the office, thereby giving me that much more to write about. On the local-office front, thanks to the tireless Richard Anton, Anne Brody

Elovic, Diana Briggs, Dina Douthitt, and Nancy and Bella D'Andrea. For making my work easier, thanks to Arlene Jurinek, Jean Primm, and to Bob Gittlin and the gang at JKG Group who meet my every request instantly and with top quality.

This book is about the field of jury and trial consulting. I owe much of my experience and professional development to the American Society of Trial Consultants. Honored to serve as its president and on its board of directors for years, I am so proud of the growth and fine reputation the association has earned through the years. Much of that success belongs to the association's long-time executive secretary and my dear friend, Dr. Ron Matlon. Other colleagues and pioneers like David Island, Joyce Tsongas, and Jo-Ellan Dimitrius were my early friends in the field, among the first to give me a professional break, and I acknowledge them as examples of professional excellence.

An amazing part of my career has been the honor to watch clients become friends. But among them all, a few stand out in my life and career. Special thanks to Randy and Becky Mathis, Robert and Jim Chapman, Bill (and Joyce) Hunt, Paul Alston, Cori Lau and David Nakashima, Louise Ing, and Howard Zlotnick. Thanks, too, to my agent Brian Palmer and everyone at National Speakers Bureau for keeping me busy on the national lecture circuit.

Television work is the most fun thing I do, both on the national and local levels. Thanks to the producers and talents of NBC, MSNBC, and Court TV. For my Chicago television family who produce my show, *Political Update*, my heartfelt thanks to Rick Buchli, Lynn Fotias, and Cameron Jenkins, and to Fernando Garron, Joe Tolitano, and Shawn Kowalski, and everyone behind the scenes who makes the show happen. I wouldn't look good enough to appear on television but for the magic of hair master Adel Madi who knows no end to kindness and giving, and to Evelyna, Lena, and Lee.

To my colleagues at BAR/BRI and the National Student Leadership Conference who support the education mission that drives so much of my career and life, it is an honor and pleasure to work with Rick Duffy (Duffster), Mike Zavvy Sims, Randal G. Mathews, Stephanie Kartofels, Rich Chip Douglas, Sandy Maldonado, John Yohan

Monahan, Ellen Sass, and to Nicole, Erien, Mike, Roger Meslar, Steve Levin, Betsy and the entire rest of the gang in Chicago and D.C. Deep appreciation to my dear and special friends Richard Conviser and Melanie Grabavoy Conviser (America's greatest lawyer/chef) whose frequent evenings of gourmet dinners and fine wine serve to enhance my writing, I am sure.

For me, family are friends and friends are family. Nothing gives me greater joy than the people who fill my life with love. To my parents, Seymour and Sandy Lisnek, for a lifetime of love and support. To Brian Lozell, Mertz, and Maude for being the spirit of my days, to my brother Rick and sister-in-law Judy for always seeing the positive side and to my nephews and nieces David, Michael, Danielle, and Jackie, who grow too quickly. To Ron and Ruth Lozell for your warmth and acceptance; for Janet, Alexandra, and Zachary who understand the power of love and family; to Al Menotti, Theresa Ehrhart and Dan Devening, Steve and Marla Cowan, Dottie, Jerry and Inca Fugiel-Smith, Michael Florenz Menefee and Charles Bundschuh, Michael, Wendy, and Charlie Marchant, Ron and Dorine Stefani, Alexandra Billings (Chicago's greatest star) and Chrisanne Blankenship, Cathy and Tony Parrilli, David Johnson and Terry Brady, Syma and Dallas Dodson, Michael Lonero and Joan Toland, Sheridan and Emma Turner, Ralph and Marty Gross, Pat Aylward, David Zak and Chris Kirbabas, Robert Bell and Tom Buchanan, Barry Arthur Litwin, Terry Noles (ya made it in), Bob Anderson, Arnie Pierson, Tim Lawson, Mike Mendelson, Angela Olsen and Ron Malachowski, Mark Buhrke and Lavon Lacey, Julie Eichorn and Joe Crosby, Dr. Ross Slotten, Linda Kenney and Dr. Michael Baden, Dr. Cyril Wecht, Dr. Henry Lee, Johnnie Cochran (The Master!) and Ambassador Carol Moseley Braun…dear friends, all. And always, to Angie (Granny) Sofiakis and Christina and John Hoidas for more than twenty years of the world's best banana pancakes and the sweetest of friendships. To Hollywood's best: Kaye Ballard and Myvomwe Jenn, Jim Nabors, Stan Livingston, and Kathy Garner.

To my dear Lucille Younger, poet, scholar, and friend, for being life's example of what it means to be a person of her word and to live the true meaning of friendship by example.

To the literally thousands of students I have had over the decades, the audiences kind enough to sit through my seminars and lectures and appearances, you are all the energy that propels me to take on the task of writing books.

Index

M

N

R

race, 10–12, 14, 37, 56–57, 122–25, 146
Ramsey, John, 225
Ramsey, JonBenet, 225
Ramsey, Patsy, 225
random selection, 18–19
reaction-measuring dials, 87, 88
Reading People, 170
reasonable doubt, 6, 256–58; creating, 69–70
reform, legal, 282
Reid, Richard, 227
remittitur, 14
reporting crimes, 218
Resnick, Faye, 134
right to die. *See* euthanasia
Rodriguez v. Bridgestone/Firestone, Inc., 273
Runnion, Samantha, 159–60
Runnion, Shannon, 159

S

Scheck, Barry, 112
Secret Garden, The, 164
Securities and Exchange Commission, 196
Seinfeld, 165
self-defense, 108–10
sentences, 270–72
September 11 attacks, 25, 54–60, 226, 280
settlements, 28, 35–36
Sherman, Mickey, 72, 200, 201
Sierra Club, 142
Simpson, O.J. *See People v. O.J. Simpson*
Simpsons, The, 165
Sixth Sense, The, 8
Skakel, Michael, 71–72, 200
Smith, Susan, 226, 271

About the Author

Paul M. Lisnek is one of the most sought-after and respected lecturers and keynote speakers on the continuing legal education and corporate circuits today. He is the cofounder of Decision Analysis, a leading trial-consulting firm that has worked in the Whitewater, O.J. Simpson, and Heidi Fleiss cases, among many other complex and multi-party litigation matters. He is past president, serving two terms, of the American Society of Trial Consultants. He has an extensive background as a communications expert, trial lawyer, educator, author, and trial consultant. Formerly the assistant dean of Loyola Law School in Chicago, Lisnek is executive director of BAR/BRI's Law School Prep Program and serves as a commissioner and inquiry-panel Chairperson of the Illinois Attorney Disciplinary Commission. He has authored twelve books, including *The Paul M. Lisnek Trial Communication* series for PESI, *Quality Mind, Quality Life,* and *Winning the Mind Game.* Lisnek has served as the jury expert for NBC News, appearing regularly on NBC, CNBC, MSNBC, and Court TV. He has been featured on numerous national television shows, including *The Today Show, Nightly News with Tom Brokaw, Rivera Live,* and Court TV's *Cochran and Company.* Lisnek was host and associate producer of an award-winning Chicago-area cable-television newsmagazine for more than a decade. He currently anchors *Political Update,* seen in the Chicagoland area. The author may be contacted through the publisher at info@sourcebooks.com.